FORGETTING

EXPLAINING MEMORY FAILURE

EDITED BY

MICHAEL W. EYSENCK

DAVID GROOME

SAGE

Los Angeles | London | New Delhi
Singapore | Washington DC | Melbourne

Los Angeles | London | New Delhi
Singapore | Washington DC | Melbourne

SAGE Publications Ltd
1 Oliver's Yard
55 City Road
London EC1Y 1SP

SAGE Publications Inc.
2455 Teller Road
Thousand Oaks, California 91320

SAGE Publications India Pvt Ltd
B 1/I 1 Mohan Cooperative Industrial Area
Mathura Road
New Delhi 110 044

SAGE Publications Asia-Pacific Pte Ltd
3 Church Street
#10-04 Samsung Hub
Singapore 049483

Editor: Donna Goddard
Editorial assistant: Marc Barnard
Production editor: Imogen Roome
Copyeditor: Aud Scriven
Proofreader: Leigh C. Smithson
Indexer: Alex Law
Marketing manager: Camille Richmond
Cover design: Wendy Scott
Typeset by: Cenveo Publisher Services
Printed in the UK

First published 2020

Library of Congress Control Number: 2019956919

British Library Cataloguing in Publication data

A catalogue record for this book is available from the British Library

ISBN 978-1-5264-6850-5
ISBN 978-1-5264-6849-9 (pbk)

At SAGE we take sustainability seriously. Most of our products are printed in the UK using responsibly sourced papers and boards. When we print overseas we ensure sustainable papers are used as measured by the PREPS grading system. We undertake an annual audit to monitor our sustainability.

CONTENTS

ABOUT THE EDITORS AND CONTRIBUTORS

Editors

Michael W. Eysenck is Professorial Fellow at Roehampton University and Emeritus Professor and Honorary Fellow at Royal Holloway University of London. He has published 62 books and approximately 160 articles and book chapters. He has written numerous textbooks on cognitive psychology and his main research area is concerned with the relationship between anxiety and cognition. His hobbies include bridge, croquet, travelling, and walking.

David Groome was Principal Lecturer in the Psychology Department at the University of Westminster, London. He retired in 2011, but he retains a research connection with the department. His research interests mainly involved cognition and memory, especially memory suppression and retrieval-induced forgetting, and he has also published papers on the effects of drugs and mood disorders on cognition. He is the author/co-author of nine cognitive psychology textbooks. In 2009 he received the BPS Award for Excellence in the Teaching of Psychology. His hobbies include tennis, dogs, travel, and music. In his spare time he is a keen guitarist, and he occasionally performs in public but without as yet achieving the stardom he feels he deserves. Despite the success of the singing detective and the singing postman, it seems that the world is not yet ready for a singing psychologist.

Contributors

Magdalena Abel is a cognitive psychologist and currently a post-doc in Prof. Karl-Heinz T. Bäuml's lab at Regensburg University. Her area of expertise is human memory. In her PhD work, Lena focused on the interplay of sleep-dependent memory consolidation and forgetting. Since then, she has worked on a number of topics, like voluntary forgetting of outdated information, retrieval practice effects, social influences on remembering, and collective memory.

Karl-Heinz T. Bäuml is Professor of Psychology at Regensburg University. He is a memory scientist working on the episodic memory of young adults, children, and older adults. He examines memory mostly by running behavioral experiments, but his research also includes electrophysiological measurements (EEG) and imaging methods (fMRI). His current research has a focus on retrieval practice effects, interference and context effects, as well as the voluntary forgetting of outdated memories.

Neal J. Cohen is Professor in the Department of Psychology, the Beckman Institute, the Neuroscience Program, and the Carle Illinois College of Medicine, and Director of the Interdisciplinary Health Sciences Institute, at the University of Illinois at Urbana-Champaign. He has published extensively on the cognitive neuroscience of memory, and particularly on the lessons about the nature and organization of normal memory to be learned from studies of memory disorders. He is an elected Fellow of the American Association for the Advancement of Science and of the Association for Psychological Science, cited for this pioneering work on memory and amnesia, laying the foundation for identifying and characterizing multiple memory systems of the brain.

Martin A. Conway is Professor of Cognitive Psychology, Director of the Centre for Memory and Law at City University London, and has been studying human memory for more than thirty years. He is known for his pioneering theoretical work on autobiographical memory, as well as for his studies of the neuropsychology of memory and memory's neurological basis. His research also includes memory impairment and enhancement, and he has recently explored the links between the ability of humans to remember past events and imagine future ones. He was awarded the British Psychology Society's Distinguished Contribution to Psychological Knowledge in 2018.

Coral Dando is Professor of Forensic Psychology at the University of Westminster, and a Consultant Forensic Psychologist. Previously a London police officer, her research is heavily influenced by the challenges of criminal investigation and is centered on developing psychologically informed techniques for supporting witnesses and victims of crime to remember and recount their experiences. Coral's research is funded by the UK and US governments, and she has worked extensively with police, and security organisations worldwide, including the US Dept. of Homeland Security and the International Criminal Court in The Hague. Coral has written in excess of 50 peer-reviewed international scientific journal articles and book chapters, and regularly writes for newspapers and social media outlets.

Melissa C. Duff is the director of the Communication and Memory Laboratory at Vanderbilt University Medical Center in Nashville USA. Her research focuses on the role of memory in language and social interaction, and the part played by the hippocampus in language use and cognitive processing. Her research team also investigates the effects of brain injury and the factors that influence long-term outcome. Melissa is the founder and director of the Brain Injury Registry, a repository of information and neuropsychological data from individuals with traumatic brain injury. She has an established record of research funding from NIH, and is the author of more than 100 research publications. In 2018, Melissa was named Fellow of the American Speech-Language-Hearing Association and received a Switzer Distinguished Research Fellowship from the National Institute on Disability, Independent Living and Rehabilitation Research.

Harlene Hayne is the Vice-Chancellor at the University of Otago in Dunedin, New Zealand. She also holds a personal chair in the Psychology Department. For more than 30 years, she and her students have conducted research on memory development in infants, children and adults. Their work has addressed questions of both theoretical and practical importance. Professor Hayne is a Fellow of the Royal Society of New Zealand and of the American Psychological Society.

Jane S. Herbert is an Associate Professor in the School of Psychology, University of Wollongong, Australia. She is a developmental psychologist who completed her PhD in 1999 at the University of Otago, New Zealand, examining age-related changes in memory during infancy. She previously held a faculty position at the University of Sheffield, UK, and served as Editor for *Infant and Child Development*. She is currently on the editorial board of three developmental journals. Now the director of the Wollongong Infant Learning Lab at Early Start, her research has been foundational in understanding when and how infants begin to use their memory in flexible ways, and the contribution of sleep to early memory processing.

John F. Kihlstrom is Professor Emeritus in the Department of Psychology, University of California, Berkeley; at the time of his retirement he was also the Richard and Rhoda Goldman Distinguished Professor in the Division of Undergraduate and Interdisciplinary Studies. A cognitive social psychologist with clinical training and interests, he graduated from Colgate University in 1970 and took his PhD in Personality and Experimental Psychopathology from the University of Pennsylvania in 1975, working with Martin Orne. Kihlstrom has also held faculty positions at Harvard, Wisconsin, Arizona, and Yale.

He has received a number of awards for his hypnosis research; his 1987 Science paper on 'The Cognitive Unconscious' is generally held to be a milestone in the revival of scientific interest in unconscious mental life.

Oliver Kliegl is a cognitive psychologist and currently a post-doc in Prof. Karl-Heinz T. Bäuml's lab at Regensburg University. He primarily conducts research on episodic memory. In his PhD work, Oliver focused on the study of voluntary memory updating as it occurs in directed forgetting. Since then, he has continued this work but also worked on a number of further topics, like retrieval-induced forgetting, the testing effect, and the development of episodic memory.

Seth Koslov is a doctoral candidate in the Cognitive Neuroscience area at the University of Texas at Austin. He is a past recipient of the Society for Neuroscience Trainee Professional Development Award and of the University of Texas Provost Graduate Excellence Fellowship. His work focuses on the interface between cognitive control and memory.

Robin Law is Senior Lecturer in Psychology at the University of Westminster. His teaching and research interests are psychophysiology and cognition, with a particular focus on circadian rhythms and memory. He has published a number of research papers on these topics, as well as co-authoring several textbook chapters. In his spare time, he enjoys travelling the world and playing for a (very) amateur football team on weekends.

Jarrod Lewis-Peacock is Assistant Professor of Psychology, Neuroscience, and Psychiatry at the University of Texas at Austin. He completed his PhD at the University of Wisconsin-Madison and a post-doctoral fellowship at Princeton University. Dr. Lewis-Peacock's research focuses on learning and memory in humans, exploring how voluntary and automatic processes in the brain contribute to goal-directed behaviors. His laboratory uses a combination of behavioral methods, functional neuroimaging, and computational approaches to study how we remember and why we forget. He currently lives in Austin with his wife, four children, and three dogs.

Michael K. Scullin is Assistant Professor of Psychology and Neuroscience at Baylor University. He completed his PhD at Washington University in St. Louis and a post-doctoral fellowship at Emory University School of Medicine. Scullin's work at the intersection of memory, sleep, and aging has been covered by news agencies including NPR, BBC Radio, Time, Fox, and Good Morning America. He has been awarded grant funding from the National Science Foundation, National Institutes of Health, and private foundations, and received several early career honors including the APA Brenda A. Milner award and the APS Rising Star award.

ACKNOWLEDGEMENTS

We would like to offer our sincere thanks to our chapter authors, who have all done a brilliant job in producing chapters that present the most up-to-date and comprehensive review of their field that is currently available anywhere. We would also like to thank the staff at Sage, especially Marc Barnard, Donna Goddard, Robert Patterson, Katie Rabot, Amy Jarrold, and Luke Block. Their expertise and professionalism (not to mention patience at an almost saintly level!) led to the creation of this book. Thanks are also due to Alex Law for help with proofreading, and the reviewers, Davide Bruno, Alexander Easton, Gerasimos Markopoulos, Ken Paller, Dan Clark and Kevin LaBar, who provided us with some valuable comments and suggestions.

David Groome & Michael Eysenck

1

INTRODUCTION

Memory failure and its causes

Michael W. Eysenck
and David Groome

INTRODUCTION

Forgetting is arguably the most important and obvious feature of human memory. If the human memory system were capable of retaining all of its stored memories perfectly and permanently, there would be little to find out about the memory process. The fact that our memories often fail us is the most significant (and annoying!) feature of memory, and it is the main reason why the forgetting process needs to be investigated.

Although this book is concerned primarily with memory failure, it must inevitably deal with both memory and memory failure because they are two aspects of the same thing. However, our emphasis will be mostly on memory failure, because it is from studying the failure of memory that we can best find out how memory works.

Forgetting is basically a failure of memory. However, we can only say something has been forgotten if we had actually stored it in our memory in the first place. Bearing this in mind, Endel Tulving (1974, p. 74) defined forgetting as 'The inability to recall something now that could be recalled on an earlier occasion'. We think that this is an acceptable definition, and it has the advantage of keeping things simple.

Memory is generally regarded as having three main stages (Kohler, 1947), which are as follows:

Input (Encoding) – **Storage** (Maintenance) – **Output** (Retrieval)

Forgetting occurs at the storage and output stages, but arguably not during input. If an item was not properly learned and encoded at the input stage, then the inability to retrieve it at some later point in time is not really caused by forgetting, but by a failure to learn it in the first place. Forgetting can therefore involve a failure of the storage process or a failure of retrieval. In practice, however, most forgetting in healthy people is probably caused by retrieval failure. This issue is discussed in more detail later in this chapter. The memory storage system seems to be fairly robust. However, it can fail when the brain suffers some kind of damage, as in the case of organic amnesia. (Forgetting resulting from organic amnesia is discussed by Melissa Duff and Neal Cohen in Chapter 7 of this book.)

People have long been aware that they tend to forget things as time goes by. Ebbinghaus (1885) carried out the first truly scientific studies of memory performance, and he confirmed that forgetting appears to be time dependent, as shown in his well-known forgetting curve (Figure 1.1).

The classic forgetting curve (as shown here) involves very rapid forgetting at first, but at longer retention intervals the rate of forgetting levels off. Ebbinghaus (1885) used meaningless nonsense syllables in his research, and he adopted the dubious approach of having only one participant (himself). However, subsequent studies involving more appropriate numbers of participants have confirmed the same general shape of forgetting curve for many other types of test material. In a review of more than one hundred years of research on forgetting, Rubin and Wenzel (1996) reviewed no fewer than 210 studies which confirmed the same basic forgetting curve for a wide range of different test materials.

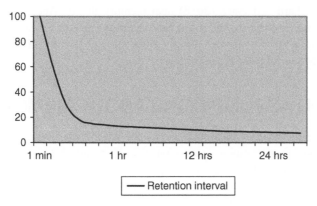

Figure 1.1   The forgetting curve (Ebbinghaus, 1885)

However, matters are not necessarily that simple. More recent studies have shown that repeated testing of the same material with the same participants sometimes shows no decline in memory performance over time (Erdelyi & Becker, 1974; Roediger & Karpicke, 2006). In some cases, memory actually improves with time if tested repeatedly. Some test items may be recalled in a later test session which could not be recalled earlier (a phenomenon known as 'reminiscence'), and in some cases there may actually be an overall improvement in memory performance over time (known as 'hypermnesia'). In these cases, it would appear that some of the memories that seemed to have been forgotten had not actually been lost from storage, but had just become temporarily inaccessible.

One possible explanation for the above findings is that there may be a limit on how much we can retrieve at one moment in time, thus causing a temporary bottleneck in the retrieval system which will subsequently pass. Alternatively, it is possible that some form of inhibitory mechanism may have suppressed the item for a short time, the effect of which will subsequently diminish.

Another possible explanation for forgetting is that the human brain lacks the ability to remember huge numbers of memories, and that is the main reason for forgetting. However, that claim is debatable. It has been estimated that the human brain has approximately 80–90 billion neurons (Azevedo et al., 2009). If only 10% of those neurons were used to store memories, then hypothetically we might be able to store one billion individual memories (Richards & Frankland, 2017).

Regardless of the explanation, the occurrence of reminiscence and hypermnesia is consistent with the view that memory loss is often caused by retrieval failure rather than the complete loss of the forgotten item from the memory store. These studies also demonstrate that memory is greatly enhanced by repeated testing and retrieval, the so-called 'testing effect' which was mentioned earlier. There are many explanations of why repeated testing benefits long-term memory. However, the most plausible explanation is probably the one provided by Rickard and Pan's (2018) dual memory theory. According to this theory, testing often leads to the creation of a second memory trace that is stored along with the first memory trace that was formed during initial study or learning. The original memory trace is thus improved by the act of testing it.

COMMON ASSUMPTIONS ABOUT MEMORY

Before considering the main theoretical explanations for forgetting, it is useful to discuss some of the popular or common assumptions about memory. Many of these assumptions are incorrect. We start with the work of Simons and Chabris (2011), who were interested in the general public's views on the nature of human memory, and in comparing those views against those of memory experts.

In response to the statement 'Human memory works like a video camera, accurately recording the events we see and hear so that we can review and inspect them later' (Simons & Chabris, 2011), 63% of the public agreed, compared to 0% of experts on memory. In response to the statement 'Once you have experienced an event and formed a memory of it, that memory does not change' (p. 3), 48% of the public agreed, compared to 0% of experts.

Similar findings were reported by Akhtar et al. (2018a), who considered the beliefs held about memory by members of the general public, police officers, and memory experts. Most members of the general public and the police officers believed that memories are like videos, and that accuracy of memory retrieval is determined by the number of details recalled and their vividness. In contrast, memory experts argued that memories are typically fragmentary rather than video-like and that the number of details recalled and their nature does not predict their accuracy.

ARE MEMORIES PERMANENT?

Another popular view about human memory is that information is stored permanently in long-term memory even if it cannot be retrieved. That view is consistent with the beliefs that memory is like a video camera and that memories do not change over time. Loftus and Loftus (1980, p. 410) asked psychologists and non-psychologists to decide which of two statements more accurately reflected their views:

1. Everything we learn is permanently stored in the mind, although sometimes particular details are not accessible. With hypnosis, or other special techniques, these inaccessible details could eventually be recovered.
2. Some details that we learn may be permanently lost from our memory. Such details would never be able to be recovered by hypnosis, or any other special technique, because these details are simply no longer there.

Loftus and Loftus found that 84% of psychologists and 69% of non-psychologists endorsed the first statement, thus indicating very clear majority support for the permanent memory hypothesis.

We can re-phrase the issue here by distinguishing between the availability and accessibility of memories (Tulving & Pearlstone, 1966). Memories are accessible if we are able to retrieve them, whereas they are inaccessible if we are unable to retrieve them. Memories are available if they are stored within the memory system, whereas they are unavailable if they are no longer stored. The notion of permanent memory implies that memories that are inaccessible are nevertheless available. According to this notion, no memories are both inaccessible and unavailable.

What does the evidence indicate? There is overwhelming evidence that many memories that appear inaccessible are nevertheless available within the memory system. For example, Tulving and Pearlstone (1966) used a condition where participants were presented with 48 words, with each word belonging to a different category. At the time of learning, each word was preceded by its category name (e.g. *Weapons – Cannon*). Some participants were given a test of non-cued or free recall: they were simply instructed to recall as many of the 48 words as possible. On average, they recalled 15 words, so that 33 of the list words were inaccessible.

Much of this inaccessibility occurred despite the relevant memory traces being available. Other participants were given a test of cued recall in which all of the category names were presented and their task was to recall the member of each category that had been presented initially. These participants recalled an average of 35 words. Thus, Tulving and Pearlstone (1966) showed that approximately 60% of words that were inaccessible on the non-cued recall test were nevertheless available in memory.

It has been claimed that the use of hypnosis lends credibility to the permanent memory notion by greatly increasing memory retrieval. However, the evidence is unconvincing. Hypnosis typically increases the amount of *correct* information recalled, but it also increases the amount of *incorrect* information recalled (Eisen et al., 2002). Thus, hypnosis merely increases rememberers' willingness to report information (correct and incorrect). When Whitehouse et al. (2005) restricted the amount of information rememberers were permitted to produce in response to each memory question, there was no beneficial effect of hypnosis on recall.

Penfield (1958) reported findings that have often been interpreted as providing strong evidence for the permanent memory hypothesis. He applied low-intensity electrical brain stimulation to the neocortex of epileptic patients while they were awake during neurosurgery. Such stimulation apparently produced amazingly detailed memories: 'Past experience, when it is recalled electrically, seems to be complete including all the things of which an individual was aware at the time' (Penfield & Perot, 1963: 689).

Subsequent research using low-intensity electrical brain stimulation has consistently failed to replicate Penfield's findings. Curot et al. (2017) reviewed eighty years of literature. Electrical brain stimulation produced reminiscences (involuntary recall of memories) on only approximately 0.5% of occasions, and vivid personal memories were recalled only very rarely.

What can we conclude? It is virtually impossible to rule out the permanent memory hypothesis because we cannot prove with certainty that an inaccessible memory has actually disappeared from the memory system. However, it is definitely the case that no convincing evidence supporting the hypothesis has been produced to date. It is important to note that there are many reasons why memory traces might be available but inaccessible. Several theories that address this issue are discussed briefly in this chapter and at more length in the other chapters of this book.

IS FORGETTING ALWAYS UNDESIRABLE?

Since the public's view is that our memories are accurate and unchanging over time, it is perhaps no surprise that most people agree that having a good memory is highly desirable. Is it true, however, that forgetting things is highly undesirable? It is clearly true sometimes. You have probably had the chastening experience of introducing people to each other when you realise with a sinking feeling that you have forgotten someone's name. Another distressing experience is to have arranged to meet up with a friend but you then forget all about it.

In spite of many negative consequences of forgetting, there can also be a negative side to remembering everything perfectly. Consider the famous Russian mnemonist Solomon Shereshevskii (often referred to as S.). He had exceptional memory powers (e.g. remembering lists of over 100 digits perfectly several years after learning). Ironically, his memory powers were so strong that they were very disruptive. For example, when hearing a prose passage, he complained, 'Each word calls up images, they collide with one another, and the result is chaos'. The adverse effects of his incredible memory precluded him from leading a normal life and he finished up in an asylum.

More evidence that an absence of forgetting can be disadvantageous comes from the study of individuals who can apparently recall almost everything they have ever experienced in vivid detail, a condition known as 'Highly Superior Autobiographical Memory' (HSAM). This condition may seem desirable if you are one of those individuals who sometimes finds it hard to recall clearly important events from your own life. However, consider the case of Jill Price, an American woman, who is one of the best-known individuals with HSAM. She regards her phenomenal autobiographical memory as a problem: 'I call it a burden. I run my entire life through my head every day and it drives me crazy!!!' (Parker et al., 2006).

Surprisingly, Jill Price (and most other individuals with HSAM) exhibit only average performance on standard laboratory memory tasks. The explanation of her HSAM is that she has many symptoms of obsessive-compulsive disorder and spends much of her time needlessly recalling events from her own life. Santangelo et al. (2018) reviewed research on individuals with HSAM, and reported that the great majority of them have similar obsessional characteristics to those of Jill Price.

The findings from S. and from individuals with HSAM support William James's (1890, p. 680) contention that 'If we remembered everything, we should on most occasions be as ill off as if we remembered nothing'. The implication is that forgetting can serve several useful functions. Nørby (2015) identified three such functions:

1. It can enhance an individual's psychological well-being by making them less able to retrieve painful memories from their past. (This function of forgetting is discussed at greater length by Groome, Eysenck and Law in Chapter 9.)
2. It can be very useful to forget outdated information so that it cannot interfere with current information. For example, remembering your current telephone number would be a serious challenge if all of your previous telephone numbers, and those of all of your friends, remained equally strong and retrievable memories.
3. When trying to remember information you have read or heard, it is usually optimal to forget the specific details and recall only the overall gist or message. If we focus on the details, our ability to think clearly will be impaired in the same way as S. In most laboratory-based research, people are typically encouraged to do their best to remember all the information that has been presented to them. In other words, the goal is to *maximise* their memory. In the real world, however, that is mostly *not* our goal. Instead, we use memory as a means to achieve other goals (e.g. feeling happy; having a successful career) rather than as an end in itself.

Intriguingly, much laboratory research on memory has probably contributed to the belief that forgetting is undesirable. In such research, the participants are generally given the goal of producing accurate recollection. In everyday life, in contrast, our social or communicative goals often conflict with the goal of accurate memory. Suppose you are describing your experiences at an event to a friend. Brown et al. (2015) found that 58% of students admitted to having 'borrowed' other people's memories while describing their experiences to another person. This often occurred because students had the goal of entertaining or impressing their audience.

If your description of an event in your life is deliberately distorted, does this produce forgetting of the original memory? Evidence that it can was reported by Dudokovic et al. (2004), who asked some people to recall a story as accurately as possible whereas others were instructed to recall the same story entertainingly. Entertaining recalls were more emotional but contained fewer details than accurate recalls. Subsequently, all the participants were instructed to recall the story accurately. Those who had previously provided entertaining recalls recalled fewer details and were less accurate than those who had previously been instructed to recall the story accurately. These findings illustrate the 'saying-is-believing' effect: tailoring what one says about an event to suit a given audience causes partial forgetting of that event.

How can we explain the saying-is-believing effect? Echterhoff and Higgins (2018) argued that humans are very social beings who prioritise the goal of constructing an agreed shared reality with others. This shared reality strengthens our social relationships.

Echterhoff and Higgins concluded that the saying-is-believing effect occurs to the extent that communicators have the goal of creating a shared reality with their audience, thereby making it a 'sharing-is-believing' effect (pp. iv–v). Thus, forgetting often occurs because we attach more importance to the goal of belonging than the goal of accurate remembering.

MEMORY AND DECISION MAKING

As William James (1890) pointed out, 'In the practical use of our intellect, forgetting is as important as remembering'. Richards and Frankland (2017) proposed an approach supporting that viewpoint and exemplifying some of the ideas discussed above. More specifically, they argued that 'the goal of memory is not the transmission of information through time, per se. Rather, the goal of memory is to optimise decision making. As such, transience [forgetting] is as important as persistence [remembering]' (p. 1071).

When does forgetting enhance decision making? According to Richards and Frankland (2017), effective decision making requires that we are not bombarded with multiple conflicting memories. However, this would be very likely in the absence of forgetting because we live in a world that changes rapidly and is 'noisy' (is highly variable). When the world changes rapidly, it is useful to forget information that is now outdated and misleading so that we can cope effectively with the changed environment.

When the environment is noisy, we would often make very poor decisions if we focused excessively on detailed memories for any given relatively rare occurrence. We are far more likely to produce effective decision making if we extract the gist from many occurrences so that we focus on what is true on average rather than exceptional specific events.

THEORIES OF FORGETTING

A number of theories have been put forward to explain why forgetting takes place. Most (but not all) of these theories are designed to account for forgetting where long-term memories are available but not accessible. The main theories of forgetting are briefly summarised below.

Spontaneous decay

The spontaneous decay theory (Ebbinghaus, 1885) proposes that memories simply fade away with the passage of time. This theory seems to offer a simple explanation for the time-dependent memory loss seen in the classic Ebbinghaus forgetting curve. However, most other theories of forgetting can also explain this finding. Research over the last century has failed to provide any clear evidence for the occurrence of spontaneous decay in long-term memory, and indeed there is evidence that memories do not seem to decay during periods of low brain activity, for example when we are asleep. Consequently many researchers have concluded that there is no clear evidence for the spontaneous decay theory (McGeoch, 1932; Brown & Lewandowsky, 2010). However, decay theory cannot be totally ruled out as a possible cause of memory loss, and some recent studies have provided possible evidence for its existence (Altmann & Schun, 2012; Hardt et al., 2013).

Decay with disuse

Thorndyke (1914) put forward a rather different version of the decay theory, in which it is argued that memories will only decay if they remain unused for a long period of time. A more recent version of this theory, known as the 'New Theory of Disuse' (Bjork & Bjork, 1992), proposes that access to a memory trace is strengthened whenever it is retrieved. A memory that is never retrieved will therefore eventually become inaccessible. However, this may be a result of an inhibitory process removing unused and unwanted memories, rather than being the result of spontaneous decay. The New Theory of Disuse receives support from the finding that access to a memory becomes stronger when it is frequently retrieved (the testing effect).

Interference

The interference theory (Ebbinghaus, 1885) proposes that access to a memory can be impeded or blocked by the input or presence of other items in the memory store. There is a considerable amount of evidence confirming that interference can impede access to a memory (Ebbinghaus, 1885; Underwood & Postman, 1960; Wixted, 2010). Interference can arise from previously learned items ('pro-active interference') or from items learned subsequent to input ('retro-active interference'). One possible explanation of interference is based on the principle of response competition, where a number of different memories are competing for retrieval, thus raising the possibility that the wrong one may be retrieved. Whilst earlier studies mostly focused on the interfering effect caused by the input of other new material, interference has also been found to arise from the retrieval of rival items. This is known as 'output interference', and it has been shown to have a significant effect on memory performance (Tulving & Arbuckle, 1963; Anderson, 2003).

Ineffective retrieval cues

Retrieval cues can help to activate a memory, but for a cue to be effective it must match up in some way with the content of the memory trace which was originally placed in storage. In other words there must be some similarity or 'feature overlap' between the retrieval cue and the stored memory trace, a hypothesis known as the 'Encoding Specificity Principle'

(Tulving & Thomson, 1973). This theory receives support from many different findings, notably the occurrence of 'Transfer-Appropriate Processing' (Morris et al., 1977), which is the finding that memories are more retrievable when the type of retrieval processing at the output stage resembles the processing that was carried out at the input stage. The Encoding Specificity Principle (ESP) also provides a possible explanation for the finding that retrieval is improved when the initial learning context and surroundings are reinstated at the retrieval stage (Greenspoon & Ranyard, 1957; Godden & Baddeley, 1975), a phenomenon known as 'Context-Dependent Memory'.

Cue overload

Another kind of retrieval-failure theory proposes that memory failure may be caused by cue overload (Earhard, 1967; Wixted, 2010), whereby a retrieval cue becomes associated with a number of different memory traces, thereby reducing the chance of retrieving the correct one. Cue overload theory resembles some aspects of interference theory, as memory failure is assumed to be caused by the presence of competing memory traces.

Repression

Freud (1914/1957) suggested that memories we find unpleasant or distressing may sometimes be repressed, which means that they are forced into the unconscious part of the mind so that we are no longer able to retrieve them consciously. However, Freud believed that repressed memories could still exert an influence over our conscious thoughts and behaviour, and in fact the uncovering and release of such repressed memories was an important part of Freud's psychoanalytic therapy. Repression is an example of motivated forgetting, since it involves the purposeful suppression of unwanted memories. However, the existence of repression as a cause of forgetting remains controversial. Repression is discussed fully later in this book (see Chapter 9).

Consolidation

Consolidation is the process by which temporary memories held in the conscious working memory (WM) are converted into more permanent memory traces stored in the long-term storage memory (SM). In typical cases of organic amnesia there is severe impairment of the SM but a relatively intact WM, which suggests that in such cases amnesia is caused by a failure of the consolidation process (Milner, 1966). Consolidation failure occurs in normal non-amnesic individuals too, especially if they are distracted or overloaded by other perceptual input, or simply failing to pay full attention to the target input. It could be argued that the failure to consolidate a memory is a disorder of learning and encoding rather than memory failure as such. However, there is some evidence for the occurrence of a more gradual form of consolidation which may take months or even years to be completed (Squire, 1992b; Steinvorth et al., 2005), which can affect the strength of a memory long after its initial acquisition. In practice, memory loss due to consolidation failure is most evident in amnesic individuals, but it may possibly occur in non-amnesic individuals too.

Reconsolidation

Some recent studies have shown that the retrieval of an item from memory may bring about further consolidation of that memory (Nader et al., 2000). This is known as 'reconsolidation', and it causes changes in the memory trace which can make its accessibility either stronger or weaker. Most studies of reconsolidation involve the use of psychoactive drugs to alter the trace during retrieval, but it has been found that psychological interventions such as emotional arousal can also produce reconsolidation effects (Finn & Roediger, 2011). These reconsolidation effects are therefore likely to occur naturally in everyday life, and they may be involved in some types of forgetting.

Inhibition

There is some evidence that inhibitory systems may be at work in the brain, whose purpose is to remove or weaken unwanted memories. Indeed such an inhibitory system could be the mechanism underlying the kind of adaptive forgetting described in the previous section. There is some evidence for the existence of such inhibitory systems. For example, it has been shown that the retrieval of one item from memory can make other similar items harder to retrieve (Anderson et al., 1994), a phenomenon known as Retrieval-Induced Forgetting (RIF). Anderson (2003) argues that the act of retrieving an item activates an inhibitory mechanism whose purpose is to suppress the retrieval of rival items, in order to facilitate selective retrieval. However, not all researchers accept this explanation of RIF, and some have proposed alternative explanations which do not involve an inhibitory mechanism (Jonker et al., 2015). At the present time inhibitory theories of memory remain hypothetical, but they do offer a possible explanation for some aspects of memory function. (Research and theory on retrieval inhibition are discussed fully by Karl-Heinz Bäuml and colleagues in Chapter 8 of this book.)

The theories of forgetting listed above are not totally separate and independent of one another, and in fact some of them may overlap considerably. For example, it is possible that memory inhibition could be the mechanism underlying the occurrence of decay with disuse, or possibly interference. However, until we have clear evidence for the relationship between the various theories, we prefer to keep each theory under consideration as many of them will be revisited in the chapters that make up the rest of this book.

THE CHAPTERS OF THIS BOOK

The early chapters in this book focus on the forgetting of particular types of information, usually relating to a real-world setting, such as autobiographical memories or eyewitness memories. These chapters on normal forgetting are then followed by two chapters on amnesia, and finally there are two chapters that consider the possible underlying mechanisms and processes which may be involved in memory function and forgetting.

In Chapter 2 of this book Harlene Hayne and Jane Herbert consider what is known about the forgetting of *childhood memories*, which involve autobiographical memory (memories we have for our personal experiences and the events of our lives), but for an early period of life that is especially susceptible to forgetting.

In Chapter 3 Martin Conway also discusses forgetting in *autobiographical memory*, but focusing on fictitious memories, which are things we think we can remember which did not actually take place.

In Chapter 4 Coral Dando reviews the research on *eyewitness memory*, and the reasons why eyewitnesses forget information relating to crimes they have observed. It is very important for judges and jurors to be aware of the fallibility of eyewitness testimony, as there is evidence that the memories of eyewitnesses are more prone to forgetting and systematic distortion than is generally recognised.

In Chapter 5 Michael Scullin, Seth Koslov and Jarrod Lewis-Peacock review the research on *prospective memory*, which involves remembering to carry out some task in the future, at the appropriate time or in the appropriate situation. Prospective memory was strangely neglected by memory researchers until comparatively recently, despite its obvious importance in everyday life.

In Chapter 6 John Kihlstrom investigates the phenomenon of *posthypnotic amnesia*, which involves the use of hypnosis and hypnotic suggestion to suppress memories. This is an interesting area of research, as it sheds some light on the processes possibly underlying retrieval failure and psychogenic amnesia.

In Chapter 7 Melissa Duff and Neal Cohen discuss the processes associated with forgetting in individuals with *organic amnesia*, a form of memory impairment which is caused by a brain injury of some kind. Organic amnesia can be a severely disabling condition, which clearly justifies extensive research.

In Chapter 8 research on *memory inhibition* is reviewed by Karl-Heinz Bäuml, Magdalena Abel and Oliver Kliegl. Memory inhibition is usually studied in laboratory experiments, but it is thought to be the mechanism underlying some types of forgetting in real life, such as retrieval-induced forgetting and motivated forgetting.

In Chapter 9, David Groome, Mike Eysenck and Robin Law discuss *motivated forgetting*, in which forgetting takes place for some purpose, such as the avoidance of memories of unpleasant or distressing experiences. In some cases this may involve a deliberate effort to forget certain events.

Each of the nine chapters of this book offers a different perspective on forgetting and memory failure, and it is our hope and intention that each chapter provides its own unique insights into the memory process and the reasons why we forget.

Further Reading

Baddeley, A. D., Eysenck, M. W., & Anderson, M. C. (2020). *Memory* (3rd edn). Abingdon: Psychology Press.

Eysenck, M. W., & Keane, M. T. (2020). *Cognitive Psychology: A student's handbook* (8th edn). Abingdon: Psychology Press.

Groome, D. H. (2020). *An Introduction to Cognitive Psychology: Processes and disorders* (4th edn). Hove: Psychology Press.

2

CHILDHOOD FORGETTING

What childhood amnesia tells us about memory development

Harlene Hayne
and Jane Herbert

'When I try to remember, I forget.'

A. A. Milne

One of A. A. Milne's most beloved characters, Winnie-the-Pooh, was notorious for his forgetting. Pooh was bothered not only by his own forgetting, but also by his fear that others, including Christopher Robin, would forget about him. Many of us can empathise with Pooh's predicament. Sadly, our memory does not work like a tape recorder, logging our experience with complete fidelity and then storing that information indefinitely until we need to use it again. Instead, memory is a much more reconstructive process and forgetting is an often annoying, yet normal, part of everyday life. We are constantly forgetting things – a friend's birthday, where we left our keys and our phone, or where we parked our car at the airport. In addition to these everyday episodes, forgetting can also be pathological, leading to disorienting and frightening consequences. Both ageing and brain damage can render individuals completely amnestic for important people and events in their lives. Following a severe head trauma, for example, it may be difficult for the victim to remember the events that immediately preceded their injury (retrograde amnesia), and in the wake of more severe brain damage, it might become impossible to create new memories at all (anterograde amnesia). In one now-famous case, the patient HM underwent a bilateral medial temporal lobectomy in an attempt to cure his intractable epilepsy; although the surgery reduced his seizures, it also rendered it impossible for him to form new memories, leaving him forever trapped in the present (Scoville & Milner, 1957; Milner et al., 1968; Scoville, 1968).

Ironically perhaps, much of what we know about memory in adults, particularly autobiographical memory, we have learned from studying instances in which memory fails in the course of forgetting and amnesia. Extensive testing of patients like HM, for example, has led researchers to differentiate between the memory skills that were damaged and those that were preserved following his surgery; this database has allowed us to infer the importance of the medial temporal lobe for some kinds of memory (Corkin, 2002; Milner & Klein, 2016). From a developmental perspective, studying forgetting by infants, children, and adolescents can also shed light on memory development. Across development we experience typical everyday forgetting, but we also experience a unique forgetting phenomenon – infantile or childhood amnesia, which refers to the inability to recall events that took place during infancy and early childhood.[1] In contrast to the kind

---

[1] Freud (1920/1935) originally coined the terms 'infantile amnesia' and 'childhood amnesia' to refer to adults' inability to recall the experiences of their infancy and early childhood. Researchers working with nonhuman animals have subsequently used the term 'infantile amnesia' to refer to more rapid forgetting by younger members of a particular species. Although researchers working with human participants often use the terms 'infantile amnesia' and 'childhood amnesia' interchangeably, for ease of exposition, we will use the term 'childhood amnesia' here to refer specifically to the lack of autobiographical memory for early experiences by children, adolescents and adults.

of amnesia that results from disease or brain damage, however, childhood amnesia is a normal part of human development. In fact, some researchers have argued that this kind of forgetting is highly adaptive (Richardson & Hayne, 2007; Rovee-Collier & Cuevas, 2009; Howe, 2011). According to this view, early memories are of limited value and may actually interfere with the developing organism's ability to adapt to their rapidly changing niche. As such, these early memories are easily lost or overwritten, making way for new memories (and the behaviours they support) to take their place. Given the pervasive nature of this phenomenon, understanding when and why childhood amnesia occurs may yield new insights into the encoding, storage and retrieval of our early memories. In the present chapter, we will review what we know about the phenomena of childhood amnesia and what these data tell us about memory and forgetting.

WHY IS AUTOBIOGRAPHICAL MEMORY IMPORTANT?

Memory comes in all shapes and sizes. We use our memory to ride a bicycle or play the bagpipes. Memory is also critical for formal education: we use our memory when we learn a new language, calculus or history. In addition to supporting these skills and achievements, memory also forms a fundamental part of who we are. In many ways, we are the sum of our memories. Our recollection of the events in our lives is more than a mere repository of the past. These recollections shape our sense of self (Klein, 2001; Prebble et al., 2013; Steiner et al., 2017), connect us to our families, our communities and our cultures (Fivush et al., 2011), influence our fears, phobias and general mental health (e.g. Halligan et al., 2003; LaBar & Cabeza, 2006; Dunsmoor et al., 2012), and provide a springboard for us to plan for the future (Pillemer, 1998, 2003; Bluck et al., 2005; Tulving, 2005).

Over the years, researchers and theoreticians have drawn a sharp distinction between different kinds of memory. The two most common dichotomies are declarative versus nondeclarative memory and explicit versus implicit memory (Squire & Zola-Morgan, 1996; Tulving & Markowitsch, 1998; Tulving, 2002; Squire, 2004). Although these two dichotomies are not identical, they share the fundamental assumption that one system supports higher-order processes and conscious recollection (declarative memory and explicit memory), while the other system supports lower forms of learning like habit formation and skill learning (nondeclarative memory and implicit memory). According to these theoretical distinctions, riding a bike or playing the bagpipes relies on nondeclarative or implicit memory, while learning complex concepts in language, calculus or history requires declarative or explicit memory. Moreover, autobiographical memory, like that involved in childhood amnesia (and other forms of retrograde and anterograde amnesia), relies on a special subset of explicit (or declarative) memory that involves conscious recollection that the memory is about something that happened to 'me', which Tulving (2002) has called 'autonoesis'. In this chapter, our primary focus will be on the development of autobiographical memory and the loss of our early autobiographical memories to childhood amnesia, but many of the issues we will traverse are consistent with what we know about other forms of episodic memory in infants and young children and we will also draw on that literature (for a review see Hayne, 2004; Hayne & Herbert, in press).

HOW DO WE STUDY CHILDHOOD AMNESIA?

The phenomenon of childhood amnesia provides a unique opportunity to study the mechanisms required for autobiographical memory. Freud originally coined the term 'childhood amnesia'. In the course of his clinical practice, he noted that most of his patients had little or no recollection of events in their lives that took place prior to the age of 6 or 8 years (Freud, 1920/1935). Freud believed that this lack of memory was due to repression – or the active forgetting of early memories that were characterised by overly sexual and aggressive content. Although Freud is often credited with discovering the phenomenon of childhood amnesia, Miles (1895) and Henri and Henri (1895) were the first researchers to document the widespread finding that adults typically experience virtually complete amnesia for events that occurred during their infancy and early childhood.

In much of the work that followed the publications by Miles and Henri and Henri, researchers studied childhood amnesia by asking adults to recall their earliest personal memories, a specific event that took place when they were very young (e.g. the birth of a younger sibling), or the first memory they could identify that was associated with a particular word (for a review, see Jack & Hayne, 2007). On the basis of these retrospective accounts by adults, researchers have reported a number of consistent findings. Overall, in contrast to Freud's view, the average age of adults' first memories is not 6–8 years, but typically closer to 3–4 years (Dudycha & Dudycha, 1933a, 1933b; Kihlstrom & Harackiewicz, 1982; Mullen, 1994; West & Bauer, 1999; MacDonald et al., 2000), and women tend to report earlier first memories than do men (Mullen, 1994, but see also MacDonald et al., 2000). The age of earliest memories is also influenced by the individual's cultural background; Asian adults tend to report later and leaner early memories than do adults from European backgrounds (Mullen, 1994; MacDonald et al., 2000; Wang, 2006a), and adults from cultures with a strong emphasis on the importance of the past, such as the Maori in New Zealand, tend to report the earliest memories of all (MacDonald et al., 2000).

For over 100 years, studies conducted with adults dominated research on childhood amnesia; these studies have both advantages and pitfalls. On the one hand, working with adults is straightforward – they are easy to recruit and they genuinely try to answer the questions you pose them. On the other hand, adults' superior linguistic skill and their extensive experience and well-developed knowledge base mean that what we learn by asking them to report their earliest memory undoubtedly reflects not only what they encoded at the time the event took place, but also all the other bits and pieces of information that they have added to that memory each time it was retrieved. In a number of studies, for example, adults' retrospective reports of their early experiences have been shown to be more comprehensive and contain more details than we might expect on the basis of interviews with children of the corresponding age (cf. Davis et al., 2008; Gross et al. 2013; Strange & Hayne, 2013; Tustin & Hayne, 2019). For example, in our research we have interviewed both children (Gross et al., 2013) and adults (Davis et al., 2008) about the birth of a younger sibling. When participants were matched for age at the time of the birth, adults reported significantly more information than did children, despite the fact that the retention interval between the birth and the interview was substantially longer for adults relative to children.

In another study of this kind, Tustin and Hayne (2019) interviewed adults about events that took place during their childhood and they also interviewed children about an event that had happened within the last month. When matched for age at the time of encoding (i.e. 5 years old), adults reported significantly more information than did children, despite the fact that the retention interval for the adults was more than a decade and the retention interval for the children was less than a month. Furthermore, additional research has shown that children do not report the kinds of details (e.g. clothing, weather, emotion, verbatim conversation) that adults often include in their narratives about their early experiences (Strange & Hayne, 2013). Thus, what all these studies tell us is that when we elicit early memories from adults, any conclusions we might draw about the content of those early memories must be tempered by the fact that we are always studying memories that have been recycled and changed over days, weeks, months, years, and even decades. Clearly, the impact of this repeated opportunity for memory strengthening and modification increases over the course of development.

Prior research with adults has also shown that the 'earliest memory' that people report is highly malleable and can vary over time and as a function of testing conditions (Kingo et al., 2013; Wang & Peterson, 2014; Ece et al., 2019; Wessel et al., 2019). Adults have also been shown to postdate their earliest childhood memories, potentially overestimating the duration of the childhood amnesia period (Wang et al., 2019). Thus, what was originally conceived of as a 'childhood amnesia barrier' is probably more akin to a 'childhood amnesia sieve' containing holes of different sizes that allow more or different memories to leak through, depending on the nature of the original memories and the nature of the testing conditions.

A DEVELOPMENTAL APPROACH TO CHILDHOOD AMNESIA

Although retrospective studies in adults have made important contributions to our understanding of childhood amnesia, more recently researchers have taken a prospective approach to the phenomenon by asking children and adolescents to report their earliest personal memories or by tracking the fate of particular memories during childhood. In one study designed to examine childhood amnesia during childhood, Tustin and Hayne (2010) asked 5-year-olds, 8- to 9-year-olds, 12- to 13-year-olds and adults to recall their earliest personal memory. Consistent with prior research, the average age of earliest memory reported by the adults was between 3 and 4 years of age. In contrast, the average age of earliest memory reported by children and young adolescents was significantly younger. Although adults reported more total information about their earliest memories than did the children or young adolescents, the accounts provided by all participants included a high proportion of episodic and autonoetic content and these proportions did not differ as a function of the age of the participant. Using slightly different age bands from those used by Tustin and Hayne (2010), Peterson et al. (2005) also found that 6- to 9-year-olds reported earlier first memories than those reported by adults. Furthermore, across age, participants' reports of their earliest memories were similar in structure, social orientation, and the nature of the event recalled.

Taken together, the findings reported by Tustin and Hayne (2010), Peterson et al. (2005), and others (Reese et al., 2010) illustrate that the age range for childhood amnesia during childhood and early adolescence is significantly lower than that typically seen in adults. The finding that children can recall events from very early in development leads us to conclude that the lack of memory for this period of life by adults is not due exclusively to a failure to encode the memories in the first place. Our conclusion is bolstered by a large body of work showing that very young children can provide coherent accounts of prior mundane or exceptional experiences when interviewed days, weeks, months, and sometimes years after the fact (for reviews, see Nelson & Fivush, 2004; Howe, 2011; Bauer, 2015). Given this clear evidence for the encoding of at least some early experiences, what happens to these memories? Why can't we retrieve them later in development?

A number of explanations for childhood amnesia have been offered in the past (Howe & Courage, 1993; Nelson & Fivush, 2004; Newcombe et al., 2007; Hayne & Jack, 2011; Bauer, 2015). Some initial attempts to explain childhood amnesia focused on a single mechanism, but most researchers now agree that childhood amnesia is the result of a complex series of mechanisms including neurological, cognitive, social, emotional, and linguistic developments. Here, we have applied an approach to understanding childhood amnesia that is analogous to that which we have used in our research with preverbal infants, attempting to explain this phenomenon in the context of what we know about age-related differences in basic memory processes (Hayne, 2004; Jones & Herbert, 2006; Hayne & Herbert, in press).

In the simplest terms, we can conceptualise 'remembering' as a three-stage process: something happens to us that we encode in memory and we store that information until we need to use it again (see Figure 2.1). At some point in the future, when presented with the appropriate cues, we can retrieve that memory and talk about it or use it to guide our subsequent thinking or behaviour. Each time a particular memory is retrieved, new details can be added to the representation. Over time, if the representation is not retrieved and expressed, what is stored eventually decays due to forgetting – this forgetting makes retrieval of the original memory more difficult, if not impossible.

If we consider Freud's repression account of childhood amnesia through the lens of the schematic in Figure 2.1, Freud believed that our early memories were encoded in

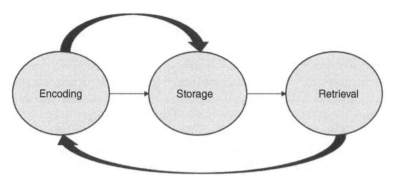

Figure 2.1   Three stages of memory processing

virtually pristine condition and that they remained in storage throughout our lifetime. The reason we can no longer recall these memories, according to Freud, is that they have been actively repressed or blocked from conscious retrieval because their aggressive and sexual content is too threatening to the individual as an adult. To date, there is virtually no empirical evidence whatsoever for repression as described by Freud (Hayne et al., 2006; Loftus et al., 2008; Otgaar et al., 2019). Instead, using the schematic in Figure 2.1 as a guide, we will review what we know about age-related changes in encoding, forgetting, and retrieval and map these findings on what we know about childhood amnesia in both children and adults.

ENCODING

Over the last three decades a large number of researchers have examined age-related differences in the nature and content of children's memories, and without exception these researchers have shown that older children encode richer memories than do younger children. In one experiment for example, Gross et al. (2013) interviewed 2- to 5-year-old children within 2 months of the birth of a younger sibling. During the interview, children were asked to provide a free-recall account of the sibling's birth and to answer a series of 17 questions that are typically asked of adults in work of this kind (Sheingold & Tenney, 1982; Usher & Neisser, 1993; Davis et al., 2008). The amount of information reported and the number of questions answered increased as a function of age. When compared to retrospective reports provided by adults who were also interviewed about the birth of a younger sibling when they were 1 to 5 years old, the findings were exactly the same (Davis et al., 2008). That is, the older the adult was at the time of the birth, the more information they reported during free recall and the more universal questions they answered.

  In a related series of studies, Peterson and her colleagues have interviewed children of different ages about medical events that required a trip to the emergency room. In their first study of this kind, Peterson and Bell (1996) interviewed 2- to 13-year-old participants about a traumatic injury. When interviewed within a few days of the injury, all of the participants reported considerable detail about the event, but the amount of information reported increased as a function of age. When these same participants were re-interviewed 6 months later, although some forgetting had occurred, the older participants continued to report more information than did the younger participants. This same pattern continued to occur when the children were re-interviewed after even longer delays of up to five years (Peterson & Rideout, 1998; Peterson, 1999; Peterson & Whalen, 2001). Importantly perhaps, the biggest age-related difference in memory performance occurred between the ages of 2 and 3 years (see also, Simcock & Hayne, 2003) – a period that corresponds to the typical lower boundary of childhood amnesia in adults.

In additional research, Peterson and her colleagues have shown that not only the amount of information encoded, but also the narrative coherence of that information, changes as a function of age during childhood. Narrative coherence is defined as how well a particular memory is structured, organised and elaborated (e.g. Fivush, 2007; Morris et al., 2010; Reese et al., 2011) and provides a proxy for the quality of encoding of the memory for a particular event. Peterson et al. (2018) have shown that age-related changes in narrative coherence may be a key factor in childhood amnesia. In their study, they repeatedly interviewed 4- to 9-year-olds about their earliest personal memories over a period of eight years. Although there was little overlap in the memories that these children nominated as their earliest memory across subsequent interviews, when they were cued about memories that they had previously reported, older children were more likely to recall the events than were younger children. One of the best predictors of whether a particular memory would be recalled following cuing was the narrative coherence of the child's account at the time the memory was initially reported. This finding provides some of the best evidence to date that age-related changes in initial encoding play an important role in childhood amnesia.

The role of narrative coherence in the longevity of our early memories may also help to explain some other childhood amnesia-related phenomena, including the role of parental narrative style. A large body of research has clearly shown that parents differ in the way in which they recount the past with their children (for a review, see Fivush et al., 2006). Parents who exhibit an elaborative narrative style ask their children a range of questions and provide richly detailed information about the event in question. In contrast, parents who exhibit a repetitive narrative style tend to focus on more limited aspects of the event, repeat the same questions over and over again, and provide little additional detail themselves. Not only do children whose parents exhibit an elaborative narrative style report more information about the target event (e.g. Leichtman et al., 2019), as adolescents they also report more and earlier first memories (Jack et al., 2009; Reese et al., 2010; Reese & Robertson, 2019). Similarly, Asian parents are more likely to exhibit a repetitive narrative style when discussing the past with their children (Wang, 2006b; Wang et al., 2000), and Asian adults report later first memories than do European adults (Mullen, 1994; MacDonald et al., 2000). Moreover, when discussing the child's own birth, Maori mothers use a more elaborative narrative style than do European mothers (Reese et al., 2008) and Maori adults report earlier first memories than do European adults (MacDonald et al., 2000).

STORAGE

In addition to age-related differences in original encoding, age-related differences in the rate of loss from storage (i.e. forgetting) may also contribute to the phenomenon of childhood amnesia. That is, even once a memory is encoded, it may decay more rapidly for younger relative to older children. If a particular memory is completely forgotten during childhood, it is hardly surprising that it would be unavailable during adulthood. From an experimental perspective, age-related differences in forgetting are often difficult to disentangle from age-related differences in original encoding. In order to study differences in forgetting per se, it is important that the level of encoding is initially equivalent among age groups – a requirement that is often difficult to achieve in studies with verbal children.

Much of what we currently know about age-related differences in forgetting, per se, has come from studies conducted with preverbal and early-verbal participants. For example, in the mobile conjugate reinforcement paradigm, 2- to 6-month-old infants learn to kick their feet to produce movement in an overhead crib mobile (for a review, see Rovee-Collier et al., 2001). In a procedurally similar operant train task 6- to 8-month-olds learn to push a lever to produce movement in a miniature train (Hartshorn et al., 1998). Because the participants in these studies are trained to a specific criterion, it is possible to match the level of encoding across age and examine age-related differences in forgetting by manipulating the age of the infants and the length of the delay. Taking this approach has shown that, when the results of these two paradigms are combined, there is a clear linear decrease in the rate of forgetting between 2 and 18 months of age (Hartshorn et al., 1998).

Similarly, in the deferred imitation paradigm, another memory paradigm used to study memory in preverbal and early-verbal participants, an experimenter performs a series of actions with objects and the infant or toddler is given the opportunity to reproduce those actions following a delay. In one study designed to test age-related differences in forgetting, Herbert and Hayne (2000) tested independent groups of 18- to 24-month-olds either immediately or after a delay of 1, 14, 28 or 56 days. Although both age groups exhibited the same level of imitation when tested immediately, there were age-related differences when tested after longer delays. That is, 18-month-olds exhibited forgetting when tested after retention intervals of longer than 14 days, but 24-month-olds continued to exhibit retention when tested after 56 days (Herbert & Hayne, 2000).

Finally, in the visual recognition memory (VRM) paradigm, infants and children (as well as adults) are familiarised with a visual stimulus; following a delay, they are presented with that stimulus and a novel one and their looking to each is compared. Longer looking to the novel stimulus (novelty preference) is typically interpreted as evidence of retention. In one study, for example, Morgan and Hayne (2011) familiarised 1-, 2-, 3-, and 4-year-olds with the same visual stimulus and then tested independent groups within each age either immediately or after delays ranging from 24 hours to 6 months. Despite equivalent performance when tested immediately, there were clear age-related differences in retention following a delay. The 1-year-olds exhibited retention when tested immediately, but not after a delay. The 2-year-olds exhibited retention when tested after 1 day, but not after 1 week. The 3-year-olds exhibited retention after 1 week, but not after 1 month. Finally, the 4-year-olds continued to exhibit retention when tested as long as 6 months later. The Morgan and Hayne data clearly show dramatic age-related changes in forgetting during early childhood, underscoring the importance of forgetting for childhood amnesia. Moreover, the most abrupt age-related change in the slope of the forgetting function occurred between the ages of 3 and 4 years, the ages typically associated with the lower ledge of childhood amnesia. Although the VRM paradigm does not rely on children's receptive or productive language skills, data collected using this paradigm are completely consistent with predictions we would make on the basis of what we know about autobiographical memory. This consistency adds further ballast to the argument that we cannot discount the role of age-related changes in fundamental memory processes in any comprehensive model of childhood amnesia.

RETRIEVAL

Most memory theorists agree that memory retrieval by adults depends upon a match between the cues present at the time of the test and the attributes that have been stored as part of the memory representation; this match was described by Tulving and Thomson as the encoding specificity hypothesis (Tulving & Thomson, 1973). According to this hypothesis, if the cues present at the time of the test do not match those present at the time of encoding, then retrieval fails. Ironically, perhaps, the best evidence for the encoding specificity hypothesis has actually come from studies of infants and young children (for a review, see Hayne, 2006). For example, for infants tested in the mobile conjugate reinforcement paradigm, the deferred imitation paradigm, or the visual recognition paradigm, changes in the stimuli or in the environmental context disrupt retrieval. Only as a function of age and experience do older infants and children begin to break the shackles of encoding specificity, retrieving and expressing their memories when tested with novel stimuli or in novel contexts. Hence, at least one reason why we cannot remember the experiences of our infancy and early childhood is undoubtedly due to the fact that the nature of our environment changes so dramatically between our early life and adulthood. That is, given that memory retrieval is disrupted by changes in context within the period of childhood, it is hardly surprising that the even larger changes that take place over more significant periods of development also make our early memories difficult (if not impossible) to access. Over the course of development, however, the nature of the match becomes less specific, such that the kind of sledgehammer effects we see in infants and young children no longer occur. This increase in representational flexibility increases the probability that memories encoded later in development will remain accessible to retrieval. In turn, whether these memories are retrieved or not will also influence their ongoing accessibility over time (e.g. Rovee-Collier & Hayne, 2000; Hayne, 2004, 2006).

In addition to overcoming the constraints of encoding specificity, there are other reasons for suspecting that memory retrieval becomes easier as a function of development. For older children and adults, for example, verbal retrieval cues often serve as powerful reminders. In the course of daily conversation, we use verbal retrieval cues hundreds of times of day (e.g. 'Do you remember where you left your gym bag?'; 'Do you remember our trip to Detroit?'; 'Do you remember when my chapter is due?'). In our past research with infants and young children, we have traced the development of children's ability to use verbal retrieval cues. In a series of studies using the visual recognition paradigm, for example, 2-, 3-, and 4-year-olds were familiarised with a novel stimulus and were then tested after a long delay (Morgan & Hayne, 2007; Imuta et al., 2013). Prior to the test, half of the children at each age were presented with a general, nonspecific verbal retrieval cue (e.g. 'Do you remember coming here before?'). The remaining half of the children at each age were tested without the verbal reminder. At all ages, children who were tested with the reminder exhibited excellent retention, while children who were tested without the reminder did not. That is, for children as young as 2, a verbal retrieval cue alleviated forgetting that occurred over the passage of time, but that same cue was also effective over a longer period of time for older children.

In another series of experiments, Hayne and Herbert (2004) used the deferred imitation paradigm to examine the effect of verbal cues on memory retrieval by 18-month-olds. In their study, the experimenter demonstrated a series of actions with novel objects and the infants were tested after a 4-week delay. Some infants were given a verbal cue prior to the test (e.g. 'We can use these things to make a rabbit. Can you show me how to make a rabbit?'). Other infants were not. In the absence of verbal cues, infants exhibited no evidence of retention during the delay. In contrast, when they were verbally reminded, they exhibited outstanding retention. In additional experiments, we also found that the provision of a verbal cue helped infants to overcome the negative effects of novel retrieval cues during the test (Herbert & Hayne, 2000; Herbert, 2011; Taylor et al., 2016). Thus, consistent with findings obtained with the visual recognition paradigm, infants were able to successfully exploit verbal retrieval cues long before they were proficient speakers themselves.

Although the effectiveness of verbal retrieval cues undoubtedly unlocks a multitude of opportunities for retrieval to occur, the transition to language also creates problems of its own. For example, in the studies described above, the provision of a verbal retrieval cue alleviated forgetting of a nonverbal memory. What these findings demonstrate is that, beginning very early in development, *verbal* cues are effective in initiating the retrieval of a *nonverbal* memory. In contrast, the kind of autobiographical memory that is lost in childhood amnesia is typically measured using verbal recall, raising an important question, that is, given that the experiences of our infancy and very early childhood are undoubtedly encoded without the benefit of significant amounts of language, how effective are verbal (and nonverbal cues) when we try to access and express a preverbal memory using language?

In the first experiment designed to address this question, Simcock and Hayne (2002) tested 2- to 4-year-olds with a special apparatus that they referred to as the Magic Shrinking Machine. In that study, children were given the opportunity to play with an apparatus that appeared to make objects smaller. The children's productive and expressive language skills were assessed both at the time of the original event and at the time of the test that was scheduled 6 to 12 months later. Not surprisingly, children's language skill and their nonverbal and verbal memory for the Magic Shrinking Machine increased as a function of the age at the time of originally encoding. By the time of the test, in fact, children of all ages had acquired most of the vocabulary that was required in order to describe the event. Despite this increase in language skill, in no instance did a child use a word to describe the Magic Shrinking Machine that had not been part of their productive vocabulary at the time of the event. That is, children did not appear to map their emerging language skills onto their preverbal representation. Consistent with this laboratory-based experiment, Peterson and Rideout (1998) also found that children could not provide a verbal report of a trip to the emergency room if that trip took place when they were 18 months old or younger.

In other experiments, however, some researchers have reported that, under some circumstances, children might be able to map their fledgling language skills onto a preverbal memory. In one study, for example, Morris and Baker-Ward (2007) taught 2-year-old children to play with a special bubble machine that produced bubbles when a specific colour of soap was added to the machine. Children's verbal and nonverbal recall was tested 2 months later. For some of the children, the target colour was not part of their productive language skill at the time of the original event. During the retention interval, these children were explicitly taught the name of the target colour. Of the 31 children who learned the name of the colour during the retention interval, 9 used the colour label during the test 2 months later. In another study, Jack et al. (2012) tested 46 children who had originally interacted with the Magic Shrinking Machine when they were between the ages of 27 and 51 months old. These children were tested 6 years later when they were between 8 and 10 years old. Of these children, 9 were able to provide some verbal recall of the event. Of these 9, 2 children used a word during the 6-year test that had not been part of their productive vocabulary at the time of the event (see also Dahl et al., 2015).

When considered against the backdrop of Simcock and Hayne (2002), subsequent work by Morris and Baker-Ward (2007), Jack et al. (2012), and Dahl et al. (2015) demonstrated that it is not impossible for children to report a preverbal aspect of their memory after they have acquired the relevant vocabulary. At the same time, however, it also important to acknowledge that in none of these studies (including Simcock & Hayne, 2002) were the children truly preverbal. All of the participants had at least minimal comprehension and production of their native language. Furthermore, in each of the studies in which researchers observed evidence of translation, that evidence was rare within each sample and was more likely to occur when relevant physical cues were present. Most importantly perhaps, what children translated was so lean that their ability to do so does not challenge the basic premise that much of what we encode in a preverbal format is lost to us as we acquire language. We would strongly argue that the transition to language is a very important rate-limiting step in determining the first entry in our autobiography. Not only does language provide a greater opportunity to retrieve and express our memories, but also those memories encoded without language are largely left behind.

The role of language acquisition in childhood amnesia has been recognised for a long time. For example, Waldfogel (1948) found that if you plot the number of early childhood memories that adults report as a function of the age at the time those events occurred, the slope of the function is identical to that obtained by plotting the number of new words that are incorporated into a child's vocabulary as a function of age. Furthermore, the most rapid increase in vocabulary development occurs between the ages of 2.5 and 4.5 years, which roughly corresponds to the age of most adults' earliest memories. In fact, when Morrison and Conway (2010) asked adults to identify the earliest memory they could recall in response to specific cue words, there was a consistent lag between the age at which those words are typically acquired and the age of the memory. In other words, the ability to use a particular word in the service of memory lagged behind the ability to use that word in the here and now. Thus, although there is some evidence for limited translation of preverbal aspects of a memory into language, studies with both adults and children have shown that most of the time, language is not simply superimposed on a pre-existing preverbal representation. For the most part, verbally accessible memories must be established anew after the language has been learned. In fact, many of the other factors that we know influence the age of earliest memory (e.g. sense of self, parent–child conversations about the past, narrative coherence, culture) have their roots in language.

GONE BUT NOT FORGOTTEN?

The biggest paradox of childhood amnesia is that it flies in the face of the fact that we know that early experiences play an important role in subsequent development (Fraley et al., 2013; Struber et al., 2014). How is it possible for these events to leave their mark if, for the most part, we have little or no recollection of them? Partial resolution of this paradox is beginning to emerge through new research with nonhuman animals. In an elegant series of experiments, Richardson and his colleagues have recently shown that even after behavioural evidence for memory has disappeared, there is some evidence that a lingering neural trace continues to exist (for a review, see Li et al., 2014). Behavioural studies with children have also shown that even in the absence of overt recollection, children respond differentially to new and familiar people when tested over long delays (Newcombe & Fox, 1994; Kingo et al., 2014). Although on the basis of our traditional definition these memories would be considered lost to childhood amnesia, the experiences that underpin them continue to impact both brain and behaviour. These findings raise exciting questions for future research.

SUMMARY

Returning to Figure 2.1, how do age-related changes in basic memory mechanisms like encoding, storage and retrieval contribute to the decline in childhood amnesia? As a function of both age and experience, infants and young children encode more information, they retain that information over longer delays, and they exploit a wider range of effective retrieval cues allowing them access to a wider range of available representations. As we have argued here, language development is also inextricably tied to many of these changes and is reflected in many of the factors that have been linked to the emergence of autobiographical memory and the decline of childhood amnesia. The neural mechanisms that support these changes are undoubtedly many and varied (Newcombe et al., 2007; Olson & Newcombe, 2014; Travaglia et al., 2016), but much of the evidence for the relation between specific aspects of brain maturation and memory development in humans remains largely circumstantial (Josselyn & Frankland, 2012; Bauer, 2015; Canada et al., 2019).

PRACTICAL IMPLICATIONS

Since 1895, the study of childhood amnesia has allowed researchers the opportunity to learn more about memory and forgetting during development. The vast amount of knowledge that we have now accumulated has implications beyond our academic community. The maturity of our science is such that we are now in the position to bring at least some of what we have learned to bear on practical issues in parenting, education and the courtroom.

There are many events from a child's early years that a parent might hope will be maintained over the long term – a once-in-a-lifetime family holiday to Lapland to visit Santa Claus, or a precious interaction with an ageing relative. In contrast, other events, like becoming separated from family during a shopping trip or a terrifying experience with a neighbour's dog, might be considered best lost to childhood amnesia. Although the ability to identify which specific memories will survive to form our early autobiography remains limited, our review highlights the important role that adults play in laying the groundwork for long-term recall of particular events. During encoding, for example, a parent can help their child to create a coherent narrative of the target event by asking and answering questions to support encoding, by facilitating the child's understanding of the emotional content of the event, and by relating the event to the other experiences in the child's world (e.g. Tessler & Nelson, 1994; Salmon et al., 2007; Peterson et al., 2014). Beyond the encoding stage, long-term retention of these specific memories can be supported by the parent and child engaging in joint reminiscing (see Wu & Jobson, 2019, for meta-analysis) or the provision of rich event reminders such as videos and photographs (e.g. Sheffield & Hudson, 2006; Barr et al., 2013). Although the memory that results from these repeated retrievals and elaborations is best considered as a co-construction, rather than as a verbatim memory of veridical experience, the gist of the experience and its importance to the child's emerging autobiography can nonetheless be preserved and treasured in this way.

The findings from research on memory development also speak directly to questions about how to best equip the early childhood education and care (ECEC) sector to support children's learning and cognitive development. For children in the two years prior to school entry (an age that aligns with the end of childhood amnesia), the long-term benefits of developmentally appropriate education are unequivocal (Sylva et al., 2010). According to Melhuish (2011), 'the benefit arriving from 18 months of pre-school is similar to that gained from 6 years of primary school'. Prior to 3 years of age, the evidence base for long-term benefits of ECEC has been less clear, likely reflecting the considerable differences in the quality of learning experiences provided across the sector (Bassok et al., 2016). Although the effects of early experiences in sculpting the infant's brain and cognitive capabilities are well recognised in the field of developmental cognitive neuroscience (Nelson, 2000), early cognitive needs are inconsistently recognised within the ECEC sector. We argue here that we can now begin to draw on systematic research on memory development to establish high-quality learning environments for very young children.

From an educational perspective, the retention of early childhood memories may appear relatively fleeting – typically surviving only days, weeks or months before forgetting takes hold. However, the role of ECECs in preparing children for formal schooling is to provide foundations for knowledge, rather than to deliver a catalogue of precise pieces of knowledge. We know that when infants and young children have the opportunity to interact physically with objects and hear appropriate language cues during a focused learning experience, their ability to retrieve that information and apply it to new, related, problems increases. That is, they become more capable learners, better able to flexibly retrieve past knowledge in new situations (Hayne, 2006; Hayne & Gross, 2015, 2017). Furthermore, even at 6 months of age, prior learning facilitates new learning (e.g. Barr et al., 2011, 2014). Well before memories can be encoded and retrieved over the long term through language, they are being stored in an associative network such that cueing retrieval of one item in the network cues retrieval of other, related items. Through the provision of rich, varied and well-supported experiences, early educators (and parents) can set the scene for developing children's later academic success.

Finally, the research on remembering and forgetting during childhood that we have reviewed here has important practical implications for the courtroom, where decision makers must often rely on children's accounts of their prior experiences in cases of custody, access, or physical and sexual abuse. A large body of both laboratory-based and naturalistic research has now shown that young children can provide an accurate account of their prior experiences even when questioned after a long delay (e.g. Gross & Hayne, 1999; Peterson, 1999). Despite this finding, there are also important ways in which children's accounts of real events can be altered, or in which they can come to report entirely false events that never took place. For example, we now know that the way in which a child is questioned about an event will influence both the content and the accuracy of their accounts. Although veridical accuracy is typically not paramount in the course of much of daily life, in the courtroom, mistakes can have significant consequences. By and large, children report more accurate information in response to general, open-ended questions, relative to more specific, yes/no, option-posing or leading or misleading questions (for recent reviews, see Brown et al., 2013; Righarts et al., 2015; Lamb et al., 2018).

Moreover, once children have been exposed to more specific or misleading questioning, the errors that they make often become incorporated into their subsequent accounts of the same event and will be repeated even in response to general open-ended questions (Bruck et al., 2000; Gross et al., 2006). The process by which this occurs is illustrated in Figure 2.1. Thus, even under ideal questioning conditions, children who have previously been interviewed inappropriately will make mistakes. Given this, the adults tasked with obtaining a child's account in forensic contexts must understand current best practice guidelines for interviewing children, and juries and judges must be briefed on how deviations from this best practice might influence the veracity of the child's account.

In addition to the way in which children are questioned, their memory of a prior event can also be tainted or created from scratch following exposure to additional sources of information. For example, researchers have now shown that children can create entirely false memories on the basis of suggestions provided by adults, through exposure to books or other media, or by simply overhearing adults or their classmates discussing a false event (Poole & Lindsay, 2001, 2002; Strange et al., 2008; Principe & Schindewolf, 2012; Lawson et al., 2018). Again, these false memories are often repeated in response to general, open-ended questions, and continue to endure even when children are told specifically to report only what they have experienced rather than what they may have learned from others. This kind of memory contamination is not unique to children – adults who are exposed to other sources of information will also incorporate this information into their own accounts (Meade & Roediger, 2002; Zajac & Henderson, 2009; Zhu et al., 2012). In fact, when recounting potentially traumatic but entirely false memories, adults who believe the false events took place experience physiological symptoms that are similar to those following actual traumatic experiences (McNally et al., 2004). Thus, once again, it is critical for fact finders to understand the potential impact of other sources of information on children's accounts and to test alternative explanations for aspects of the child's report as required, particularly when it contains bizarre, implausible, or impossible information. In addition, given that most members of the public hold a number of fundamental misconceptions about memory and forgetting (Akhtar et al., 2018a), it is also important that juries are adequately briefed about basic memory principles as part of the judicial process in cases that rely primarily on memory.

Finally, over the past few years, there has been an increase in the number of cases in which complainants bring charges of abuse that allegedly occurred decades earlier when they were very young. The research reviewed here casts new light on adults' ability to retrieve and report memories from their infancy and early childhood with a high degree of fidelity. Although it is possible for people to recall genuine memories of abuse over a lifetime, the research that we reviewed here also demonstrates that through repeated retrieval and discussion, what is reported as a memory sometimes includes not only kernels of true memory, but also information from other sources. In some instances, that additional information may lead to the construction of a new but entirely false memory. When these memories are reported in court, we know that juries are persuaded by a high degree of detail in the complainant's account (Bell & Loftus, 1989; Howe, 2013). On the basis of the extant literature on memory and forgetting in children, if the alleged events took place when the person was very young, it is highly unlikely that their accounts would contain complex descriptions of people and places, verbatim conversation, or clothing (Gross et al., 2013; Strange & Hayne, 2013). In fact, on the basis of what we know about memory in children, the presence of these details in reports provided by adults of childhood experiences should lead us to question its veracity rather than to accept it. Sadly, by the same token, misconceptions about the process of memory and forgetting of childhood memories can also lead us to reject genuine accounts of abuse based on more sketchy or patchwork accounts.

In conclusion, the overarching goal of this chapter was to review what we know about how memories are made and forgotten during childhood. On the basis of that review, we conclude that age-related changes in encoding, storage and retrieval play a vital role in determining which memories are lost over time and which memories become part of our stable autobiography. We also note that our autobiography, like all historical records, is influenced by a range of different sources including our own opportunities for retrieval, re-processing and reflection. Given our facility with language, our accounts of the past are also easily altered by what we hear from others around us. These additional sources of information can either augment or detract from the accuracy of our memories. We have highlighted the important practical implications of memory and forgetting in childhood for parenting, education and the court.

We want to end by acknowledging that childhood is not all about making memories of specific experiences. As adults we can look back with fondness on memories of summers spent on the beach or playing in the park, without remembering the details. Our first autobiographical memory may be a significant life event, or simply the image of looking down from a once-visited bridge and seeing light sparkling on a stream. In our view the memorable opportunities in childhood will be diluted if adults spend too much time planning structured events to create the 'best' childhood memory, without recognising the value of endless hours spent in unstructured play and self-discovery. The events we remember, the events we forget, and the events we paid little attention to during childhood but later come to recognise as important, all weave together to form our personal identity and forge our connections with others who shared those experiences. What makes an event memorable to one person may differ from that of another, even within the same family, which is why there is a still a long way to go before the complexity of childhood amnesia is fully unravelled.

Further Reading

Eysenck, M. W. (2020). Memory in childhood. In A. D. Baddeley, M. W. Eysenck, and M. C. Anderson (eds), *Memory* (3rd edn). Hove: Psychology Press.

3

AUTOBIOGRAPHICAL FORGETTING

Fictional autobiographical memories

Martin A.Conway

The starting point for this chapter is the following statement: *All memories are false*. But what does this mean? False in what respects? Before providing a brief account of what autobiographical memories are, let's consider some general ways in which memories are false. Perhaps one of the most obvious, originally noted by the great French neuropsychologist Théodule Ribot (1882), is that memories are *time compressed*. This simply means that remembering an event's duration that was in fact hours, takes place in memory in seconds and minutes. Of course, a rememberer could ruminate on a memory of an event but that still would not lead to a memory that covered the full duration of the original event. Indeed, if one could in fact *fully recall* any event that would be highly dysfunctional and would take up as much time as the original event. Thus, memory has been shaped by adaptive pressures to create a *representation* of past experience, and a representation of something is not the thing in itself. As the historian Svetlana Alexievich comments, 'memories are neither history nor literature. They're simply life, full of rubbish and not tidied up by the hand of an artist' (1985/2017, p. 6). So how does time compression work? How is it done? The answer simply is that we do not know. Of course, there are some suggestions: perhaps we only remember those details we attended to during an experience, or only those that triggered some emotion in us, or only those that are relevant to personal goals and concerns. Possibly there is some truth to all of these, yet on the other hand some or all of them might be wrong. Indeed it is particularly difficult to explain why we recall certain details (Alexievich's 'rubbish'). Indeed it is not uncommon to recall a memory, sometimes a long-'forgotten' memory, and have no idea why or what it means.

Memories, however, are not false simply because they are time compressed. Memories are also full of details that the brain infers unconsciously and these are not 'remembered'. For example, in recalling attending an important interview, say several years ago, remembering what socks one was wearing, the colour of each of the interviewing panel's tops, the type of light in the interview, the weather that day, and so on, these are all details that are only very rarely remembered (Wells et al., 2013). Nonetheless, in our memories such details are non-consciously inferred. And, of course, some details are consciously inferred, dates being the prime example. Importantly, beliefs (see Akhatar et al., 2018a) may have a central role to play not only in inferring memory details but also even in inferring whole memories. Memories then are in no sense a literal representation of a past experience; they may to a degree faithfully represent some details, although many details will be inferred and embellished (Akhatar, et al., 2018b), some consciously and some non-consciously.

We are not, however, mainly concerned with memory errors here – there is a lengthy more mainstream literature on memory errors and false memories for everyday events, and recent comprehensive reviews can be found in, for example, Brainerd and Reyna (2005), the papers in Perfect and Lindsay (2014) and work by Howe et al. (2018). Our main concern here is with what many would consider 'impossible' memories, memories rarely if ever considered by memory researchers. Fantastic memories such as pre-birth memories, memories of other lives, memories of conception, memories of near-death experiences, and so forth. One important point about fantastic memories is that they are strongly believed by many people, indeed thousands and probably millions of people. There are entire cultures that believe in reincarnation and associated memories of past lives (e.g. in many Asian countries). Moreover, the literature on fantastic memories is prolific – books such as *Children's Past Lives* (Bowman, 1997), *Life Before Life* (Tucker, 2005), *Proof of Heaven* (Alexander, 2012), to mention only a limited few, sell many hundreds of thousands of copies. Similarly, websites on the same topics have thousands of hits and even some scientifically high-quality work on such 'memories' has received wide acclaim (see for instance *Consciousness Beyond Life*, van Lommel, 2010). We will see later that many of these so-called memories are the product of beliefs, particularly strongly held beliefs about the self. Before coming to the fantastic, let us first consider a current model of autobiographical memory that is well supported by neurological and behavioural research: we will need this model once we get into the realm of the fictional and fantastic, if only as a sort of touchstone to reality.

THE SELF-MEMORY SYSTEM

In the *Self-Memory System* (SMS) model of autobiographical memory, memory and goals are intricately and reciprocally linked (Conway, 1996, 2005, 2009; Conway & Pleydell-Pearce, 2000; Conway et al., 2004). Goals, at different levels of specificity, autobiographical knowledge of one's life, and episodic memories for experienced (or even imagined) events form the main content of self. There are three key processes central to the SMS.

The first is that memories are mental representations that are *constructed* out of autobiographical knowledge and episodic memories. Knowledge and episodic memories are organised in autobiographical memory knowledge structures in our long-term memory (see Figure 3.1), and transitory patterns of activation constantly arise and dissipate in these knowledge structures. These patterns of activation can coalesce into memories or the patterns of activation can themselves be channelled, by control processes, into specific memories.

The second key process is that all patterns of activation in autobiographical memory knowledge structures are caused by *cues*. Cues can be anything from a sound, to a taste, to a smell, to a visual feature, to a feeling or a thought, even the conceptual structure of a problem (Schank, 1982), etc. The key point is that a cue maps onto specific items of knowledge in autobiographical memory knowledge structures and in so doing causes a rise in activation that then spreads, and dissipates as it spreads, to associated items of knowledge (Collins & Loftus, 1975).

Thirdly, *central control processes* (it is at this stage that goals enter into the memory construction process) can access the activation caused by cues, evaluate the activated knowledge, elaborate it, and then use the elaborated cue to cause further activation in an iterative cycle of knowledge access, cue elaboration, and further knowledge activation as sought-for knowledge is eventually activated (Williams & Hollan, 1981). This iterative

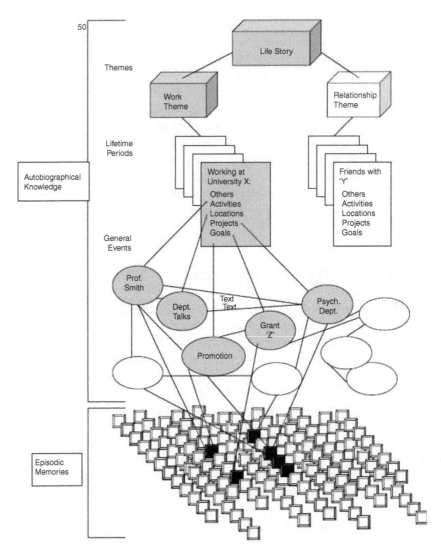

Figure 3.1

process creates a *complex cue*, or what Norman and Bobrow (1979) termed a *memory description*.

Finally, it should be noted that all of this can happen non-consciously and also without any conscious intention (what Schank, 1982, originally termed *remindings*, and what later researchers have called *involuntary memories*, e.g. Berntsen, 2012). Indeed, in the SMS model it is only possible to become consciously aware of the *outputs* or *effects* of non-conscious processes (e.g. highly activated knowledge); it is not possible to become consciously aware of the (retrieval) processes themselves. Similarly, it is not possible for control processes to modulate the search process directly; this can only be achieved by elaborating cues, although the central control process may be able to inhibit activated knowledge or at least prevent it entering conscious awareness (Barnier et al., 2004, 2007).

Figure 3.1 (adapted from Conway, 2005) depicts how autobiographical knowledge and episodic memories may be represented in our long-term memory (see Conway, 1996, and Conway & Pleydell-Pearce, 2000, for earlier versions). There are several points to note about Figure 3.1, perhaps the most important being that the lines that connect knowledge representations (e.g. lifetime periods to general events) illustrate the action of cues. This action is transitory and occurs only when a cue is activated. Also the lower portion of Figure 3.1 depicts episodic memories not as knowledge representations but rather as episodic representations. That is, as representations that contain details derived from single experiences, they are *experience-near* (Conway, 2005). Episodic memories are accessed by cues, however, and they may also have an additional form of organisation, and that is that they are represented contiguously, in groups (see Conway, 2009), and so are additionally organised along a temporal dimension. One implication of this is that when an episodic memory is accessed the accessibility of other temporally related episodic memories is raised. Nonetheless, when indexed by higher order autobiographical knowledge structures their organisation is primarily thematic and goal orientated (see, for example, Anderson & Conway, 1993).

The nature of the representation of autobiographical memories as envisioned in the SMS model is based on findings from a very wide range of areas, including experimental psychology, neuropsychology, clinical psychology, and neuroscience (reviewed in Conway & Pleydell-Pearce, 2000, and Conway, 2005, 2009). We will not go over this evidence again here, but see Conway et al. (2019) for a recent review. Another reason for this conception of the representation of autobiographical memory in the SMS is to preserve an important distinction in memory theory, that is, the distinction between *stored* and *transitory* representations. Knowledge representation in the SMS allows the inferential and creative use of autobiographical memory – critically important in simulating future events, reconceiving the past, imagination, and insight (Conway & Loveday, 2015; Conway et al., 2016).

Consider a simple example. Suppose you are a participant in an autobiographical memory experiment and you are asked to recall memories that centrally feature *items of furniture*. Of course you and other participants in the experiment can do this, and indeed you probably can do so for a very wide range of ad hoc categories (Barsalou, 1983) from memories of buying clothes to great meals you have had, but it does not follow that this is how the underlying knowledge structures are organised. According to the SMS model it reflects your ability to use a cue to construct a wide range of specific memories. This is the creative use of memory, which Moscovitch (1992) memorably termed *working with memory*. From an evolutionary perspective this ability to use individual cues to construct a diverse range of autobiographical memories confers a considerable survival advantage because we can be reminded of diverse cue-relevant events that help guide us in the present in dealing with environmental challenges. Interestingly, most of those challenges may relate to the social world and social interactions. And, as we shall see, these memory constructions can also be used to support various (erroneous) beliefs about memory.

From the perspective of the memory researcher interested in how knowledge is represented in the mind, it does, however, pose a major difficulty and that is how to distinguish between what is stored and what is transitory or computed. The organisation shown in Figure 3.1 is based on a wide range of findings that converge to support it. Because these findings use many different techniques to probe the underlying knowledge, taken together they probably do, with at least some degree of accuracy, reflect the nature of the organisation of autobiographical knowledge and episodic memories. Thus the SMS model identifies to some extent what is stored, and because of its constructive nature supports the creative use of autobiographical memory.

The SMS is conceived as domains of knowledge representation at different levels of specificity. At the most abstract level is what Conway et al. (2004) termed the *conceptual self* (not shown in Figure 3.1), which is a repository of personal beliefs, traits, and other self-referring attributes (see also Klein & Gangi, 2010). Knowledge represented in the conceptual self may consist of what we termed *self-images*. Such images may access beliefs about past selves, the current self, the future self, wanted selves, and feared selves. Taken together we termed them, after Markus and Nurius (1986), the *universe of possible selves* that form a central part of the conceptual self. Such representations might also be organised around a visual image or set of visual images forming knowledge structures that can be used as cues, or their details used as cues, to access other knowledge in more specific knowledge structures. For example, an image of oneself as a student, stored in the conceptual self, might access a lifetime period representation of 'When I was at university'. Note that this specific knowledge also instantiates the corresponding image in the conceptual self. Thus, it constrains the contents of the conceptual self. In a normally functioning autobiographical memory, knowledge at different levels constrains what knowledge there can be at other levels. In other words, the universe of possible selves is limited by the specific knowledge its cues can access. However, it may be the case that when beliefs drive memory construction new and creative memory-based representations can be constructed. Usually though, it is only in certain types of brain damage and psychological illness that this constraining function may malfunction or stop functioning altogether, giving rise to delusion, confabulation, and false beliefs.

Figure 3.1 illustrates the autobiographical knowledge structures with which the conceptual self interacts. The *life story* schema (Bluck & Habermas, 2000; McAdams, 2001; see too Kris, 1952/1975) contains conceptual knowledge about the self over the lifespan, providing an overall representation of a person's entire life. At a more specific level, knowledge in *lifetime periods* is generally of goals, people, places, activities, emotions, thoughts, etc., that were characteristic of the period. Note that lifetime periods, although having marked beginnings and endings, are not chronologically exclusive. For example, the lifetime period 'When I was at university' might overlap or even be chronologically completely parallel with the lifetime period 'When I lived with X'. What distinguishes them is that they contain different knowledge, sometimes wholly so, and sometimes there is much overlap, the main difference being in knowledge they represent about the goals of that particular lifetime period. Lifetime period knowledge can be used as cues to access knowledge in *general events*. General events are also of extended periods of time but shorter than lifetime periods, for example work projects, holidays, repeated events, etc. (see Conway & Bekerian, 1987; Barsalou, 1988). They too contain information about people, locations, activities, emotions, and so on, that define the period they represent. Knowledge represented in general events can be used as cues to access *episodic memories* (see lower part of Figure 3.1). Episodic memories contain knowledge that derives from experience and also some conceptual knowledge (see Conway, 2009). For example, a specific episodic memory will contain episodic details, frequently in the form of visual images with some unifying conceptual knowledge, for example images of a cinema experience unified by the conceptual knowledge 'When we went to see XXX'.

This whole system of knowledge representation (Figure 3.1) can be viewed as sets of hierarchical partonomic autobiographical knowledge structures, in which groups of episodic memories are parts of general events that are parts of lifetime periods which themselves are parts of the life story. However, although some of this may be stored as knowledge structures in long-term memory, the SMS model views such structures as being largely transitory. By this view patterns of activation caused by the effects of cues spreading between different levels of knowledge create transitory knowledge structures. Specific autobiographical memories are then transitory patterns of activation in the SMS, and when they are specific they always feature activated episodic memories. It is important to recognise that patterns of activation are constantly arising and dissipating in the SMS and this occurs non-consciously outside awareness. These patterns of activation may sometimes form specific memories and occasionally they may enter consciousness, giving an experience of spontaneous memory retrieval. Nonetheless the construction of specific autobiographical memories, particularly the intentional rather than incidental construction, is frequently mediated by control processes prior to any conscious experience of a memory.

Although the process of memory construction is always the same (i.e. driven by the activating effects of cues), conscious awareness of the retrieval process is variable. According to the SMS model we cannot be aware of the construction/retrieval process itself, which is always non-conscious, but we may be intermittently aware of inputs to and outputs from the process. Within the SMS, when a rememberer is aware of inputs and outputs of the construction process, then they undergo what is termed *generative retrieval* (Gilboa et al., 2006, termed this *strategic* retrieval; see below). The main idea of generative/strategic retrieval is that the rememberer can consciously evaluate outputs from the construction process and elaborate them into a more effective cue (Williams & Hollan, 1981, were the first to make a similar proposal based on protocol data collected during retrieval; see also Norman & Bobrow, 1979, and Haque & Conway, 2001).

In contrast to generative retrieval is so-called *direct retrieval*, which simply refers to the situation in which a memory 'pops into mind' without the rememberer being aware of any output from the construction process. This can occur in intentional remembering when a person consciously attempts to recall a memory and is aware of the initial cue, but unaware of any other aspects of the construction process until a specific autobiographical memory comes to mind. Direct retrieval is sometimes thought to be more rapid than generative retrieval, and in the main this may be the case, although there are instances where a memory cannot be intentionally recalled, only to 'pop into mind' hours or even days later. Whatever the case, within the SMS model all acts of memory construction are considered to terminate in a moment of direct retrieval – it is not possible to be aware of what will come to mind before it comes to mind. That is to say, one cannot be aware of what a cue will activate prior to the effects of the activation.

The SMS is, then, a cue-driven model of the construction of autobiographical memories. Cues cause activation in the autobiographical knowledge base and that activation spreads and dissipates. This process takes place non-consciously, is continuous, and at any one time there are probably multiple sources of activation, some intersecting. This can give rise to *remindings* (Schank, 1982), when a memory spontaneously and incidentally comes to mind: a process within the SMS termed *direct retrieval*. In contrast, memory construction may be intentional, rather than incidental, and in this case executive/control processes elaborate cues and accessed knowledge into increasingly more effective cues. The outputs of the repeated search-and-elaborate cycles may become conscious or partly conscious – a process in the SMS model termed *generative retrieval*.

The whole process of memory construction is thought to take place in a complex set of temporary interlocked widely distributed neural networks termed the *default network* (see, for example, Buckner et al., 2008). The default network is activated when people are remembering, planning, imaging future events, anticipating upcoming events, thinking about past events, imaging more generally, thinking about others, etc. Importantly, mental representations that arise from imaging (the creative use of long-term memory) may themselves come to be represented in long-term memory, especially if they are repeatedly imagined. One consequence of this is that when such representations enter into a mental construction, formed in the default network, they may be experienced *as* memories. In other words, the source of the knowledge that forms the 'memory' is not accessed and a *source monitoring error* occurs (see Johnson et al., 1993). Indeed, the person might have *recollective experience* (Gardiner and Richardson-Klavehn, 2000) for what they take to be a memory rather than recognising the source as imagination. The overlap between remembering and imaging is so extensive that such source monitoring errors may be relatively frequent in the SMS. With the SMS model in mind let's now consider some realms of increasingly fantastic memories.

FICTIONAL MEMORIES

In a recent analysis of a database of over 6,641 accounts of first memories, Akhtar et al. (2018b) found about 40% of such memories dated to when the rememberer was 3 years of age, or younger. Of these, 893 dated to when the rememberer was younger than 1 year. The general view, derived from many studies of earliest memories (memories normally supplied by people in their 20s, i.e. university students), is that the average timing of the first memory dates to the third year of life. There are often individuals who date their earliest memory to somewhere in the second year of life, but memories dating to younger ages than this are extremely rare. There are several potential reasons for this: the brain is undergoing considerable post-natal neuronal development and so cannot represent at this stage knowledge structures such as those that feature in the SMS; language is still developing and this may be important for memory (e.g. to generate and evaluate cues); and most importantly the very young child and infant have yet to develop a conceptual understanding of the world. Thus, the finding of Akhtar et al. (2018b) of a substantial number of earliest memories in a broad sample of the population is unusual. Even more unusual was the content of these memories, which in the main featured details that an adult would know but an infant would not. By way of illustration here are some accounts from the database:

> A television being delivered for the coronation of the queen in 1953. I was approximately 9 months old at the time, interestingly enough the memory is in black and white.

> Having been born on 6th July 1946, my earliest memory is being held in my father's arms and being shown a number of large icicles descending from an iron grate outside the basement. I believe this was during the severe winter of 1946/7. In this case I would have been little over 6 months old!

> I can remember being at the bottom of the stairs looking up and calling my grandmother who was staying with us at the time. I used to call her 'Dan' as I couldn't manage 'gran'. She died when I was 15 months old.

> I remember a view from a low viewpoint, of a five-barred gate, with tall beech hedges either side and a field beyond. This picture often came back to me; as an adult I asked my father about it, he readily identified it as a gateway opposite where we lived when I was an infant. I was born on 20 April 1939, and we left this house in December 1940, so the memory [beech in full leaf] must have been acquired between June and September 1939, aged 16 to 19 months. I will add that Dad said we never returned to the house [poor plus wartime privations].

> I was born on 1st May 1936. I distinctly remember my father picking me up and saying "Look at those flames, that is Crystal Palace burning." I have checked the date of that and it was 30th November 1936. I can't believe I could remember something when I was only 7 months old. But it was something we did not speak of

subsequently, so I have not been constantly reminded of it. My husband says I said to him several times over the years that this was my earliest memory. I am amazed.

Do infants know what a television is? What icicles are? What stairs are? What a five-bar gate is? Or even what Crystal Palace was? Almost certainly not, and much the same was true of the content of many of the memories dating to below the age of 3 years. How then have these memories come about? Note too that the people we sampled indicated that they had a strong recollection for their earliest memories – they were adamant that they remembered them and that they did not arise from some other sources (a family story for example). Akhtar et al. (2018b) argue that these 'memories' ultimately derive from imagination; that some knowledge about their early childhood has come to the individual via some source, the family maybe, or even simply by imagining it. In all cases it is suggested that such *fictional* memories arise through a process of repeatedly imagining (literally bringing visual images to mind), and embellishing what is, to begin with, simply a hazy single indistinct detail into a mental representation that when conscious is experienced as a memory, but the source of the memory has been forgotten.

We termed these 'fictional memories' to bring out the point that they are an important part of the life story. They anchor the life story in the very earliest years of life, and in doing so allow the self to reach back into a time that is not well-remembered but one which is perhaps of great importance to the individual. They depict caring parents, loved but now departed grandparents, cherished locations and objects, and so on. Thus, although fictional they are also true: true to the self. And this is a critical aspect of autobiographical memory, that is, that the knowledge and memories it contains and constructs should be coherent in themselves and with other self-beliefs.

FANTASTIC MEMORIES

In the sections that follow I examine some of the research into memories from near-death experiences (NDEs) (van Lommel, 2010, provides the best current review and attempted explanation). What is important from our memory perspective is that memories of NDEs are from brief periods when the brain metabolism was not functioning, that is, memories from periods when the brain was in effect dead, so no neurological mechanism of encoding into long-term memory could have been operative. We will also consider memories supposedly originating from other lives, namely reincarnation. The leading work on this is by Stevenson (1990, 1997), and see also Shroder (1999) for an excellent journalistic account of Stevenson's work, and others who have followed on from Stevenson (e.g. Woolger, 1994; Tucker, 2005). As we will see, the memory evidence is not as instantly dismissible as one might have thought, but also note that other than invoking the endurance of the soul, fantasies of heaven, and other unknown worlds, there is no mechanism that could possibly or plausibly account for such memories, which almost certainly are best thought of as fictional. However, we start this section with a special case of reincarnation memories in very young children.

Remarkably, it might just be the case that there is a mechanism that (with a stretch of the imagination) could tentatively begin to explain such memories. We consider this and other explanations in a closing section. But as we shall see, what is most striking about the work of all these authors is their almost complete lack of understanding of human memory. That, of course, is quite helpful when placing one's faith in what in the main must be fictional accounts of impossible memories.

OTHER-LIFE MEMORIES

Stevenson has documented phobias related to previous lives in young children (1990), birthmarks and birth deficits related to previous lives (1997), and children who claim to remember previous lives. Children who give accounts of previous lives typically recall factual information from their previous lives such as the names of friends, relatives, floor plans of houses, clothing, streets in their town, and various other objects. These are things that within the SMS would be termed *autobiographical knowledge*. They rarely recall any specific episodes with the exception of their death, especially if this was a violent one, and even then the account of the memory tends to be more factual than episodic. There are sometimes also recollections of what happened after death, and how they returned to their new body. We will come to those shortly. The point of Stevenson's work is that he is meticulous in at least trying to establish that the child could not have obtained the other life information they recall in any other way than by reincarnation. Thus the child must not have heard anything of the person they claim they once were, been told anything about them, or visited where they were claiming they once lived. Stevenson (1997) presents a few cases from the many he has studied that meet these criteria. Nonetheless, even in these rare and special cases there is always a possibility that the child has been informed and shaped, consciously or non-consciously, into believing and 'remembering' their previous life. Given the curious nature of their recall (i.e. little in the way of episodic detail but plenty in the form of factual knowledge), the possibility of 'contamination' (the child being supplied with the information in some way, somehow, by someone else) remains high. Obviously, in cultures and/or religions where there is a strong belief in reincarnation (e.g. the Indian subcontinent and Buddhism) the possibility of a persuasive indoctrination is no doubt increased. Given the constructive nature of autobiographical memory, and the raised suggestibility of young children, a social indoctrination account of memories of other lives, one that does not require postulating ethereal concepts such as reincarnation, appears more plausible. However, it should be noted that Stevenson was not unaware of this possibility and in fact reports cases of knowledge from other lives across a range of cultures, including North America and Europe, where notions of reincarnation are not dominant. Nonetheless the social indoctrination accounts remain the most likely explanation of autobiographical knowledge and memories from other lives by children. From our perspective they are interesting examples of memory and imagination working together and, importantly, show how widespread, and indeed how extreme, this can be.

Other types of other-life 'memories' – such as being a crusader, or a courtier in the middle ages, or a leper dying alone in a desert, or a soldier dying on a First World War battlefield, and so forth – are generally regarded as pure fantasy. A work that has been influential in promoting such fictional memories is Woolger's *Other Lives, Other Selves* (1987), revealingly subtitled *A Jungian psychotherapist discovers past lives*. Woolger's discovery of his own past lives (in the form of memories) and those of his patients was through hypnotic regression. Memories from the past lives are usually traced from some psychological symptom in the present life, and by recalling the past-life troubles (often memories of violent death), the present symptoms are alleviated. There is, of course, no known mechanism for the recall of such memories, and revealingly they are rarely of the more mundane of life's experiences, such as meeting an old friend, a pleasant walk by the sea, playing in a snow storm, a productive day at work, a romantic encounter, etc. Indeed, just the sort of memories that are widely recalled when we study autobiographical memory. It seems that, as with the social indoctrination account of reincarnation memories of a recent past life, other-life memories emerging in hypnotic regression are atypical of autobiographical memory as a whole. They are most likely a product of a belief system – held, it must be noted, by mostly vulnerable people – that facilitates a supernatural account of the present created by memory and imagination, which explains troublesome aspects of the present. To the extent this is helpful, then these fictional components of the life story are of value to the individual, although we suspect they come with a cost.

Lastly in this section, consider recent work by one of the main proponents of other-life memories, Bowman (1997, 2001). The memories collected here are from children, however, and they have an interesting feature: they are memories from the life of a dead relative (recently deceased) who the child claims to have been. Bowman in her (1979) book *Return from Heaven*, subtitled *Beloved relatives reincarnated within your family*, gives a number of examples of children recalling memories from past lives, details of which are, reportedly, independently verified. Here's one example:

> Around the same time that the night terrors began, during the day when Peter [Bowman's 3-year-old son] was awake, he began telling me stories about his "friend" Gary and how had he died. He talked about Gary all the time and especially about the night Gary's family were awakened by the barking of their dog to find the house on fire. He described the house, always calling it the "yellow house". He said it had a big pine tree next to it that burned too, and a driveway that made a circle in front of the house, not like our driveway. He added that Gary's grandparents, who lived across the road, ran over and stood outside in the cold with members of the family who had escaped the burning building watching helplessly as the house burned down. He described the three fire trucks that came with their lights flashing and one big fireman with a brown beard. (Bowman, 1997, pp. 14–15)

In fact Gary's family were Bowman's family, and although she could not remember the fire (she was 2 years old at the time) she was able to check the details with her mother, who was one of the grandparents who came out and helplessly watched the fire. Bowman checked the details with her mother, who confirmed them all. The claim is that Gary (Bowman's 3-year-old brother at the time of the fire) who died in the fire was subsequently reincarnated as Peter (Bowman's 3-year-old son, who reported the 'memory') and this is why Peter had this memory of a fire he could have had no knowledge of. One major problem is that Gary could not have had this memory in the first place, as he had been sheltering under a mattress in the house (where his body was found) and so could not have seen the tree, the fireman, or indeed the grandparents. Further, the grandmother's confirmation that one of the burly firemen had a beard is just the sort of detail that is not remembered and/or misremembered in autobiographical memories (Wells et al., 2013). It seems then that Peter's other-life memory is questionable. Possibly he had acquired the information from a more normal rather than supernatural source.

Bowman's books are replete with memories and sources of memories that originate from spiritual/supernatural experiences – in particular being in heaven after death, being invited by God or often an old man (interestingly never an old woman) to choose their new parents (apparently they remember viewing various couples and being given a choice), subsequent memories of being (often suddenly) in the womb, and even memories of conception are reported. A typical example is as follows: a mother hears her young daughters, infants, laughing and talking in bed, and when she approaches the bedroom door overhears the following:

> I heard Molly ask Caroline if she still remembered what it was like before she was born. "Yes," replied Caroline. "I remember picking Mommy, Daddy, Liana and you! I could see you from up there! And I saw Grandma and Grandpa, too. They were smiling, I see'd everything". "Oh yeah" said Molly slowly. "Caroline, I'm starting to forget …" (Dyer & Garnes, 2015, pp. 7–8)

These internationally best-selling books, of which there are many, are replete with such 'memories', sometimes supposedly spontaneously recounted by children or retrieved by adults in hypnotic regression. Bowman comments that during regression when a person is instructed to 'go back to a past life', the suggestion acts like a 'key to unlock experiences held in the subconscious, the storage vault of memories. If the key fits, the door to memory will open' (1997, p. 76). For even more extreme other-life memories see Weiss's (1988) book, *Many Lives, Many Masters*, which sold over 1.5 million copies. The alternative view we put here is that such memories are fictional; they are a product of memory and imagination interacting in a belief system that incorporates ideas of heaven, the soul, and reincarnation. They are mental constructions derived from imagined events rather than experienced events.

MEMORIES FROM MOMENTS OF DEATH

Memories of NDEs were first documented by cardiologists. Sabom (1982), in his book *Recollections of Death*, presents a survey of 116 cardiac patients who recalled memories of what occurred when they, in effect, died and were later resuscitated. Resuscitation is usually by restarting the heart by defibrillation (electric shock). There have since been several other such studies and the whole field is reviewed in van Lommel's (2010) book, *Consciousness Beyond Life: The science of near-death experience*. One of the main differences between the NDE researchers and the rejuvenation group is that the former by-and-large have strong science backgrounds, good training in scientific methods, and do not draw on spiritual/religious concepts to account for the NDE memories. On the other hand, they are or have become dualists (rather than physicalists) who believe in the existence of something other than this life, and it is that 'something' which, at the point of death, is interacted with and subsequently gives rise to memories of NDEs. As Sartori (2006, pp. 23–25), comments:

> The phenomenon remains unexplained when considered from the current scientific perspective of consciousness being ... a product of neurological processes ... The fact that clear, lucid experiences were reported during a time when the brain was devoid of activity ... does not sit easily with current scientific belief.

It is important to understand that NDEs vary in their nature. In virtually all NDEs the patient is unconscious, but there are, however, degrees of unconsciousness. This somewhat contentious subject will not be gone into here, but we will simply note that in cardiac arrest blood flow to the brain is reduced and in some cases ceases altogether, at least for a while. In these later more extreme cases brain metabolism may cease altogether too – indexed by flat EEG readings – and, therefore, there is no *physical* way in which new memories could be formed (see van Lommel, 2010, ch. 8, for an extended discussion of what occurs when the heart suddenly stops). Nevertheless, it transpires that memories of NDEs during cardiac arrest have some common features.

Moody (1975) described 12 possible elements of an NDE and emphasised that not all of these elements are experienced in every NDE; people usually only experience a few of them. Moreover, the NDE memory account is of a coherent episode rather than fragmented details, making them immediately unlike the vast majority of autobiographical memories. Moody's 12 elements or characteristics (as listed in van Lommel, 2010, pp. 11–12) are as follows:

1. The ineffability of the experience – its indescribable nature.
2. A feeling of peace and quiet; pain is gone
3. An awareness of being dead, sometimes followed by a noise.

4. An out-of-body experience (OBE); from a position outside and above their bodies, people witness their own resuscitation and/or operation.
5. A dark space, experienced by very few people as frightening; the person is drawn toward a small pinpoint of light in this dark space, which they describe as:
   - a tunnel experience; they are drawn rapidly toward the light;
   - a frightening NDE; only reported by a few people in which they linger in the dark space (aka as a hell experience).
6. The perception of an unearthly environment, a dazzling landscape with beautiful colours, gorgeous flowers, and sometimes music too.
7. Meeting and communicating with deceased persons, mainly relatives.
8. Seeing a brilliant light, or a being of light; experiencing complete acceptance and unconditional love and gaining access to deep knowledge and wisdom.
9. A panoramic view of life, or review of life from birth: people see their entire life flash before them, there appears to be no time or distance, everything happens at once, and people subsequently can talk for days about a life review that lasted a few minutes or less.
10. The preview or flash forward: people have the impression that they are witness to a part of life that is yet to come, and again there is no time or distance.
11. The perception of a border: people are aware that if they cross this border or limit they will never be able to return to their body.
12. The conscious return to the body, accompanied by great disappointment at having something so beautiful taken away.

These characteristic features of memories of NDEs can be placed in subgroups (see Sabom, 1982; Greyson, 1983); here we simply list Moody's original elements and comment on some of them. First, however, it will be useful to consider a couple of accounts of NDE memories.

This first account, taken from van Lommel (2010, pp. 1–2), is from a woman who was about to give birth when major complications set in:

> The delivery room becomes extremely quiet. People are rushing around and talking to one another in soft yet urgent voices. When I ask what is happening neither I nor my husband receives a reply. The contractions stop, but I'm feeling fine. Meanwhile the gynecologist has joined us, along with some more nurses. We have no idea what's happening. I'm told to start pushing. "But I have no contractions!" This doesn't seem to matter. There's a rattling of tongs, scissors, trays, and tissues. My husband passes out and is pulled out of the delivery room and left in the corridor.
>
> Suddenly I realise that I'm looking down at a woman lying on a bed with her legs in supports. I see nurses and doctors panicking, I see a lot of blood on the bed and on the floor, I see large hands pressing down on the woman's belly, and then

> I see the woman giving birth to a child. The child is immediately taken to another room. The nurses look dejected. Everybody is waiting. My head is knocked back hard when the pillow is suddenly away. Once again I witness a great commotion. Swift as an arrow, I fly through a dark tunnel. I'm engulfed by an overwhelming feeling of peace and bliss. I feel intensely satisfied, happy, calm and peaceful. I hear wonderful music. I see beautiful colours and gorgeous flowers in all colours of the rainbow in a large meadow. At the far end is a beautiful, clear, warm light. This is where I must go. I see a figure in a light garment. This figure is waiting for me and reaches out a hand. It feels like a warm loving welcome. Hand in hand we move toward the beautiful warm light. Then she lets go of my hand and turns around. I feel something pulling me back. I notice a nurse slapping me hard on my cheeks and calling my name.

The whole medical episode was caused by blood loss during the birth that went undetected. When it was detected her head was forced back and an emergency blood transfusion started. It was at this point in the NDE she remembers she returned from the 'heavenly paradise'.

In a similar case Sabom (1982, pp. 78–80) recounts, among many other cases, the recollection of a man undergoing cardiac surgery whose heart stopped and was then defibrillated and who subsequently recalled a vivid NDE. In this NDE he was at first floating above the operating table, then he was in darkness, and then moving towards a bright light. As the light became brighter he was aware of angels around him and then the angels all turned out to be his children. He then recalled various emotionally important memories of activities he had undertaken with each of his children, when they were children. Eventually he recalled hearing a voice saying 'Go back', and he questioned why, and then heard a voice saying his work here on earth was not over yet. The final part of his memory was waking up in intensive care 2 days later.

These accounts typify memories of NDEs in that they contain two common components: (a) the patient has an out-of-the-body experience and sees themself being operated upon; and (b) there is a journey in the dark, often down a tunnel, towards a bright light where they eventually meet angels and a being that might be God, and eventually they are instructed to return to their body or reach a border that they know that if they cross they can never return. There are other features that can occur too, as listed by Moody (1975; see above). From the perspective of the SMS the characteristics of (b) above are most probably produced by the interaction of memory and imagination operating through a particularly western cultural lens. In other words, they are fictional memories. We suggest they are formed post-operatively once blood flow is returned to the brain. However, the characteristics of (a) are more difficult to account for, and this is because when the details of what occurred in the operating room/theatre are factually checked (and presuming that check is correct) it is very often the case that the patient's memories of who was there, who did what, even what was said, the surgical instruments used (of which the patient can have had no prior knowledge), and so forth, are often correct (Sabom, 1982). Such detailed memories are rare in the first case and usually not especially accurate, but to be formed while blood flow to the brain is either non-existent or severely attenuated requires an explanation that is beyond our current understanding of human memory.

EXPLANATIONS OF FICTIONAL AND FANTASTIC MEMORIES

Scientific explanations of fictional and fantastic memories are virtually non-existent; however, we consider three here. The first is that all the memories considered above are products of memory and imagination operating within a belief system. The belief system, at least for the memories considered above (it would be different for other belief systems), is largely a Christian one in which there is a god, heaven, and angels, in another world that can be travelled to. Memories of other lives and near-death experiences are imaginations that arise from this belief system. How this might in practice work is not known. Moreover, the NDEs that include out-of-the-body perspectives, with accurate details that the patient could not have known, clearly require something more than a memory–imagination–belief explanation. What that might be is also not known. Possibly notions of what it means to be non-conscious will have to be developed and elaborated. As will our understanding of the encoding of information into long-term memory, especially under conditions in which brain metabolism has been compromised or has ceased altogether.

In the case of other-life memories within a family, for instance a child recalling memories attributed to a dead relative, or – as in Bowman (1997) – a child claiming to be a reincarnation of her deceased maternal grandmother, there might be at least a very tentative physical explanation. This explanation draws on recent thinking about genetic inheritance and, specifically, epigenetics (for an accessible introduction see Ennis & Pugh, 2017; for a more advanced introduction see Carey, 2012, or Ward, 2018). The famous double helix of deoxyribonucleic acid (DNA) constitutes the genetic information that is inherited and it is our genes that instruct our cells to generate the proteins of which we are made. Less commonly known, however, is that there is an extensive network of molecular control of gene expression and of histone activity (the proteins that DNA is wound around). One of the main mechanisms here is that of methylation, in which a small molecule from the methyl group becomes attached to DNA and in so doing silences gene expression from that location on DNA. The process of methylation is then a means of molecular control of gene expression that occurs only after the genome is initially formed and is thus epigenetic. Epigenetic control of gene expression occurs throughout life and can be triggered by the processing of external events. To take just one example, Dias and Ressler (2014) conditioned a fear response in mice to the smell of cherry blossom. They then studied the descendants of the fear-conditioned mice and found that they too showed a negative reaction to the smell of cherry blossom, as did their grandchildren. The process of methylation when first discovered was almost immediately perceived as a potential memory mechanism (see Holliday, 2006, for an historical overview), but could this mechanism possibly function in the claimed reincarnation of recently deceased relatives? It has to be the case that memories are represented in the brain in some way. Simple (synaptic) strengthening of connections between neurons in the brain may be one way in which certain types of *procedural* memory come to be represented (e.g. riding a bicycle), but it is difficult to envisage how such a simple mechanism could represent autobiographical knowledge and episodic memories. It would seem more likely that gene expression and the proteins that it creates form some sort of code that represents aspects of this more complex knowledge. That in itself would be shaped by control mechanisms such as methylation, and the pattern of methyl attachments to the DNA might then be inherited, at least to some extent. This pattern would be changed and gradually overwritten by the epigenetic effects of experience on the developing child's brain, and so it would be slowly erased. Our assumption here is that the pattern of methylation in the adult controls gene expression and the production of proteins that either code for memory and knowledge or somehow influence patterns of neuronal firing, and it is these neural patterns of activation that encode knowledge and memories and which, because of the methylation, can be reinstated to some extent during remembering. If the methylation is inherited to some degree then so might knowledge and memories. This is, of course, pure speculation on my part.

Finally, consider one even more speculative account of NDEs and certain features of them. Prominent features of Moody's original list, and ones noted frequently since, are that time and distance (space) are absent. Moreover, when a patient experiences life review as part of their NDE, that life review appears to take place all at once. The patient experiences, or even sees, the events of their life simultaneously. Van Lommel (2010) noticed that these features of the NDE are rather similar to aspects of quantum physics in which interactions between entities can have a non-local aspect – that is to say an effect on each other that is outside time and place and one that takes places simultaneously, referred to as 'entanglement'. Entanglement takes place in non-local space. Van Lommel's suggestion is that there is another realm (universe maybe) paralleling our own that exists in a non-local space. In NDEs the individual somehow makes some sort of contact with this non-local realm and hence the experiences of entanglement. (In fact van Lommel goes further, arguing that the brain is a receiving device for information from the non-local realm.) Nonetheless the problem still remains of how memories can be formed when the brain is physically non-functioning.

We have been on a strange journey! One reason for taking this journey was to help develop an appreciation of just how extensive (and how wild) fictional and fantastic memories are. Literally millions of people have such memories. Books about them sell hundreds of thousands of copies, and websites experience very large numbers of hits. We suggest that this shows us that the relationship between memory and imagination is far stronger than perhaps previously thought. Mistaken memories about early childhood are to some extent scientifically understandable, but other-life memories and transcendent NDE memories are beyond the science of memory. Similarly, other fantastic memories, such as those of alien abduction, meeting beings not of this universe, experiencing heaven, and so forth, are outside our current understandings of memory. However, taken together, they collectively illustrate the malleability of memory and how that which is imagined can eventually come to be experienced as a memory. False memories, given the imaginative nature of memory as revealed by the above review, are hardly surprising. In fact they are probably the norm.

Further Reading

Baddeley, A. D. (2020). Autobiographical memory. In A. D. Baddeley, M. W. Eysenck, and M. C. Anderson (eds), *Memory* (3rd edn). Hove: Psychology Press.

Howe, M. L., Knott, L. M., & Conway, M. A. (2018). *Memory and Miscarriages of Justice*. Abingdon: Routledge.

4

EYEWITNESS FORGETTING

Eyewitness retrieval and police questioning techniques

Coral Dando

Worldwide, criminal justice systems rely heavily on witnesses and victims[1] of crime. From the outset, the information witnesses provide is fundamental to the investigative process, and should criminal proceedings follow, witness testimony can be the most compelling and straightforward evidence presented to judges and juries (see Fisher et al., 2017; Dando & Milne, 2018). Typically witnesses provide information about a crime during a formal face-to-face interview conducted by a police officer (although see the section on mitigating the misinformation effect). During the interview, not only do they explain what they have personally experienced (e.g. seen, heard and smelt), but also they often indicate the presence of other witnesses and offer contextual and environmental information which can alert investigators to additional potential lines of enquiry. As the criminal investigation process progresses, witnesses can be asked to undertake numerous recognition tasks, such as identifying suspected perpetrators from photographic, live or video line-ups and identifying various objects such as clothing and weapons. Here, witnesses are asked to make a familiarity decision and indicate whether the person, object or environment was involved in the crime event in question (see Albright, 2017; also Wixted et al., 2015, for brief overviews of the eyewitness identification literature). Finally, witnesses may be called to testify in a court of law during a prosecution or an appeal hearing.

Witness information is important, and witness testimony is extremely powerful. Contrary to popular belief (e.g. Simons & Chabris, 2011), an extensive body of scientific literature reveals that eyewitness memories are not objective 'recordings' that can be replayed like a video recording. Rather, they are reconstructed records of personal experiences which can be likened to other trace evidence such as fingerprints and DNA (Wells, 1995) in that what a witness experiences leaves a memory trace. Like physical trace evidence, memory traces can deteriorate, become inaccessible and inaccurate. Erroneous memories can be created anew, which can then become seamlessly subsumed as part of the original memory, and completely false memories can be created about personal experiences that have never happened.

Unfortunately, the consequences of eyewitness errors, false memories and forgetting can be serious. At best, when witnesses cannot recall events or are unable to provide much detail about what has happened, a criminal investigation process may struggle to progress. At worst, when eyewitnesses make errors or report false memories, innocent people may be convicted of crimes while the perpetrators escape justice (see Bull, 2019; Loftus, 2019). Of particular note are findings from the era of post-conviction DNA profiling. To date, in the USA over 360 people have been exonerated because their DNA was discovered to be incompatible with evidence collected from the crime scene (the Innocence Project). In approximately 70% of cases, erroneous eyewitness identification was a significant contributory factor in the prosecution and subsequent conviction.

Eyewitnesses are asked to recount personally experienced crime events, the people involved, their actions and the environment etc., which necessarily include information

---

[1] From hereon we use the term 'witness' to refer to both witnesses and victims of crime.

specific to the time and place of acquisition. This is a type of declarative memory generally referred to as episodic memory (Tulving, 1984, 2005). Episodic memory is associated with autonoetic consciousness, a subjective sense of time and of the self as the one who experienced the episode and possesses the memory. In order to provide episodic information, be this during an interview or when giving testimony at court, witnesses have to initiate the recollection process to relive or re-experience the event. This process is akin to mental time travel and is contingent on the establishment of episodic retrieval mode whereby witnesses consciously search their long-term memory for the relevant 'what, where and when' information. Once located, they then reconstruct their experiences and verbalise the reconstructed recollection (see Tulving & Craik, 2005).

For witnesses, the inherent demands of recalling and reconstructing an experienced event are further compounded, not only by having to repeatedly recount what they have seen (e.g. initial witness interview, follow-up interviews, giving testimony at court, and being questioned repeatedly at court), but also by numerous individual, contextual, crime event and post-event factors that are typically absent from the demands of everyday remembering. The psychological literature on eyewitness memory, and on the impact of individual, crime event, post-event experiences and criminal justice procedures on the quality and quantity of information witnesses are able to remember, is extensive. In addition, there is an extant theoretical literature on the architecture of memory and the numerous cognitive processes involved in everyday remembering and forgetting, which are also relevant to eyewitness memory performance. Many of these topics fall outside of the scope of this chapter, although some are covered elsewhere in the book (e.g. retrieval-induced forgetting in Chapter 8). Rather, this chapter concerns typically developed adult eyewitness recall memory, and introduces two key areas of eyewitness errors and forgetting, namely post-event misinformation and false memories arising from experiences immediately post event and during the process of retrieving information in the course of a witness interview. Each area is introduced and discussed with reference to the contemporary psychological literature, and where relevant, how advances in empirical knowledge might be, or are being, applied towards reducing errors and mitigating eyewitness forgetting at the point of retrieval.

POST-EVENT INFORMATION AND MISINFORMATION

In the immediate aftermath of an event, that is, in the minutes and hours immediately following a crime, witnesses are often exposed to multiple sources of information that can introduce additional event details they themselves have not experienced (post-event information) and which may be incorrect (post-event misinformation). The impact of post-event misinformation, termed the 'misinformation effect', is one type of eyewitness error that has been widely researched in the laboratory since the mid-70s. There exists a plethora of research that has demonstrated that post-event misinformation can change reported details, or cause individuals to report details that were never experienced, and even more so when that post-event misinformation is repeatedly presented, or is introduced by a credible source (e.g. Frenda et al., 2011; Davis & Loftus, 2017).

The typical misinformation research paradigm can be deconstructed into three stages. First, participants witness an event, typically a mock crime via a video, slides or a narrative. Second, participants are presented with incorrect information embedded in reports of other witnesses, in photographs, in a questionnaire, or in the form of misleading questions asked during a post-event interview. Finally, participants are asked to report what they recall about the original mock crime and to discriminate between the original event and the latterly introduced misinformation. Irrespective of how the misinformation is presented (i.e. presentation mode), the misinformation has been found to affect participants' memories of the event whereby memory for details appears altered in accordance with the deliberately presented misinformation, which typically becomes integrated into their verbal or written reports. There also exist several real-world examples where a witness's memory appears to have been altered following exposure to post-event misinformation presented in the media, for example. One well-cited instance was the Trans World Airlines Flight 800 that crashed into the sea on 17th July, 1996. It was reported in the print media, and verbally by some commentators, that a missile may have caused the crash. This theory quickly spread among witnesses, some of whom went on to provide testimony that they had seen a missile, despite the existence of physical evidence suggesting this was not the case.

Witnesses can also incorporate misinformation into their testimony without any indication that post-event misinformation has been explicitly provided (Gross et al., 2005). For example, script-based interpretation of events can be a source of misinformation, particularly where the unfolding events are unclear, or an event is only partially experienced. Here, witnesses can try to make sense of what they have just experienced, and in doing so can unconsciously fill in gaps, culminating in erroneous post-event information becoming part of their memory of an event (see Koriat et al., 2000; Mirandola et al., 2014; Davis & Loftus, 2017).

Conversations between co-witnesses is another source of post-event misinformation. Many crimes involve co-witnesses, sometimes hundreds (e.g. terrorist incidents), other times there may be just one or two (e.g. robbery or assault), and often the witnesses talk to each other. One survey has indicated that 86% of real eyewitnesses have discussed their memory with other witnesses (Paterson & Kemp, 2006). Indeed, media coverage of major crime events such as mass shootings or terrorist incidents often shows co-witnesses talking, huddling together, comforting each other and discussing what has occurred. In today's digitalised, trans-national and convergent media landscape, witnesses are able to very quickly and easily communicate remotely with others who were physically present, and with those who may have seen the event unfold via CCTV or live streaming platforms.

In such circumstances remembering does not unfold in social isolation, rather remembering occurs in the presence and with the active participation of others (e.g. Rajaram & Pereria-Pasarin, 2010; Hirst & Echterhoff, 2012; Nash & Ost, 2016), and memory can be shaped and reshaped by others, as demonstrated by the social memory and collective memory literature (see Hirst & Manier, 2008; Blank, 2009). Because memory is a reconstructive process, co-witnesses can easily incorporate misinformation into their own memory that has not been explicitly provided but gleaned from each other after the event and without the realisation that they have done so (e.g. Frenda et al., 2011). Co-witnesses may share the same experience, but their individual recall of the event is likely to differ for many reasons, including naturally occurring differences in attention paid to various details of an incident, positioning and distance from aspects of the incident, and individual differences associated with age, eyesight or hearing, which means that not all details of an event will have been committed to memory (e.g. Cui et al., 2007; Nori et al., 2018; Otgaar et al., 2018; Pajón & Walsh, 2017; Loftus, 2019). Furthermore, as with everyday remembering, co-witnesses make errors simply because memory is not infallible per se.

It is clear that people also adapt their memories to those of others. Laboratory research has consistently demonstrated that when co-witnesses discuss their memories their accounts become more similar, typically resulting in memory conformity (Gabbert et al., 2003; Jack et al., 2014; Zawadzka et al., 2016). Memory conformity arises when witnesses incorporate post-event information verbalised by other witnesses into their own reports, which can be conscious or unconscious. There appear to be a number of reasons why memory conformity may occur. One key distinction is between informational and normative conformity (Deutsch & Gerard, 1955), which differ in terms of the motivation and processes involved. In the case of informational conformity, if eyewitnesses are uncertain about exactly what they have seen or are less confident in their ability to remember what has occurred, they may rely on others as a source of information to reduce uncertainty. Research reveals that where two witnesses are shown slightly different versions of the same event and come together to discuss their recall of events, following the joint recall session the least confident participant typically conforms with the more confident participant, agreeing with their recollection of events (e.g. Wright et al., 2000; Gabbert et al., 2003). Memory conformity can also occur when witnesses move through the criminal justice process. Where police interviewers or prosecutors reveal or suggest event information, or if witnesses come into contact with other witnesses at a later stage in criminal proceedings, they may mistakenly believe that newly presented information originated from the event itself, a phenomenon known as source misattribution (Zaragoza & Lane, 1994). Here the memory trace becomes distorted because witnesses incorrectly identify the source of the experience and the newly encountered misinformation/information becomes integrated into a witness's memory for an event (Mitchell & Johnson, 2000; Lindsay et al., 2004).

Normative conformity, on the other hand, is where witnesses appear to choose to alter their reports to include information learned from others to avoid the perceived social impact of not being able to remember as much as they would like, or disagreeing with other witnesses (e.g. Cialdini & Goldstein, 2004). In such instances, it would appear that the memory trace is not necessarily altered (Blank, 2009; Blank et al., 2017). This can be seen in research where confederate co-witnesses seek to directly influence other witnesses. One example is where confederate co-witnesses are very confident in their claims to have witnessed non-existent footage of a highly charged public event. Participants completed a questionnaire in the presence of a confederate concerning their memory for closed-circuit television (CCTV) footage of an explosion, although in reality no such footage existed. About 40% of participants reported having seen the non-existent footage, and increased or suppressed their reports in line with confirmative or disconfirmative social influence exhibited by their confederate (Ost et al., 2006).

The misinformation effect is not necessarily limited to eyewitnesses. Research has also investigated whether the misinformation effect could filter through the criminal justice system to cause errors in jurors' decision making, with the potential to bring about wrongful convictions (Foster et al., 2012). Here, bait questions – where an interviewer questions a suspected offender about the existence of hypothetical evidence – were found to be a potential vehicle for misinformation. In an adaptation of the misinformation effect paradigm, mock jurors were asked to read a police report describing several pieces of evidence. They then watched a police interview including bait questions that provided misinformation about the evidence. Mock jurors came to believe that the hypothetical evidence in the bait questions actually existed, and despite warnings about the possibility of misleading information in bait questions, the misinformation effect was clear because they misremembered the evidence (also see Davis & Loftus, 2017).

More recently it has been found that misinformation emanating from gestures has the potential to influence eyewitness memory (see Gurney et al., 2016). Hand gestures that accompany speech, often referred to as illustrators, are a fundamental part of language and communication, and illustrators typically occur with little conscious thought or effort (McNeill, 1992; Krauss & Chiu, 1998). In a series of experiments, Gurney and colleagues reported significant gestural misinformation effects. The type of gestures used (e.g. punching or stabbing) influenced mock eyewitnesses' responses and their interpretation of the crime. Furthermore, participants appeared not to identify the misleading gestures nor report feeling misled by them, which led the authors to suggest that gestural influence was comparable to verbal influence.

Misleading claims are thought by some to be more credible when made by multiple sources, while others argue that repetition is more impactful because simply repeating misinformation makes it more accessible and encourages a reliance on automatic processes, which can change people's judgements (Mitchell & Zaragoza, 1996; Harris & Hahn, 2009). Using the traditional misinformation paradigm, mock witnesses first watched a video of a crime and later read eyewitness reports attributed to one or three different eyewitnesses. Misleading claims were made in one report, or the same misleading claims were repeated in all three. Mock witnesses were more misled by claims that were repeated, regardless of how many eyewitnesses made the claims. They were also more confident, appearing to interpret the familiarity of repeated claims as an indicator of accuracy, demonstrating how repeating information and repeated exposure can make misinformation seem more credible (Foster et al., 2012; see also Unkelbach, 2007). The task used by Foster and colleagues was a recognition task, but the effect of repetition has also been found to impact on recall performance (e.g. Unkelbach & Stahl, 2009). In the real world, multiple co-witnesses are likely to repeat their experiences, and so the impact of repeated and multiple misleading information may well be additive.

Most of the research introduced on the misinformation effect in this chapter concerns typically developed adult participants. However, it is important to briefly note that children can be more susceptible than adults (e.g. Holliday et al., 2002) and older adults are often more susceptible than younger adults to the misinformation effect (Polczyk et al., 2004; Roediger & Geraci, 2007). One of the primary reasons these groups may be more likely to incorporate the misleading post-event information into their subsequent verbal accounts stems from developing cognition in children, which can lead to confusion regarding what they have actually seen and source monitoring errors (see Otgaar et al., 2018). For older adults the impacts of natural ageing on cognitive processes associated with the frontal cortex and the hippocampus can impair source monitoring, and episodic memory in particular (e.g. Roediger & Geraci, 2007; Dando, 2013; Otgaar et al., 2018; Dando et al., 2020).

However, social factors associated with the retrieval environment are also important for children and older adults. When children provide testimony or are being interviewed as witnesses, a real or perceived imbalance of power can increase susceptibility to post-event misinformation (see Toglia et al., 2017). Likewise, older adults are known to be less confident in their memory abilities in general, and stereotypical perceptions of older adults' memory performance can affect memory performance, including accepting post-event misinformation more readily than might otherwise be the case (see Wylie et al., 2014, for a meta-analysis). Misinformation presented to older adults in a social environment has been found to be more impactful than when presented in a written narrative (Gabbert et al., 2004).

MITIGATING THE MISINFORMATION EFFECT

Post-event co-witness discussions are an established source of post-event information and misinformation that can bring about memory conformity, alter memory for an event, increase errors, and reduce the reporting of correct event information (e.g. Dalton & Daneman, 2006; French et al., 2008; Hope et al., 2008). Accordingly, co-witness discussions are an example of an estimator variable (see Wells, 1978) that has repercussions for both the quantity and quality of witness testimony to follow (e.g. Davis & Loftus, 2017). In real life co-witness discussions are almost impossible to prevent in the immediate aftermath of an event. Likewise, access to digital news media cannot be controlled, and so the impact of co-witness discussions and media can only be estimated, usually on a case-by-case basis. Similarly, the illustrators that accompany verbal interactions that have been found to be a source of misinformation are natural behaviours that accompany speech.

Separating eyewitnesses as quickly as possible at the scene of an event, or later when collecting formal eyewitness accounts, is one straightforward and obvious way of reducing the impact of co-witness discussions. The empirical literature also highlights a number of techniques and procedures that offer promise for practice towards reducing the post-event misinformation effect. The passage of time appears to increase the misinformation effect because the memory trace becomes weaker with time, so the discrepancy between the misinformation and the original event appears to go more unnoticed. Furthermore, this effect can further magnify over time with witnesses becoming more confident after a longer delay, despite being incorrect (e.g. Mudd & Govern, 2004; Wang et al., 2014; Huff, Weinsheimer, & Bodner, 2016). Many studies have found that an immediate recall, or a recall as quickly as possible, can sometimes protect eyewitnesses against the misinformation effect. As a consequence, a significant amount of research has been conducted on how to collect eyewitness information quickly and in a manner that protects the integrity of the information should there be criminal proceedings in the future.

One promising area is the use of immediate-recall questionnaires, which are completed individually. These have been found to inoculate participants against post-event misinformation, and mock witnesses tend to report more correct information one week later and are more accurate following an immediate post-event recall (Wang et al., 2014). Tools such as the Self Administered Interview (SAI), a paper-based questionnaire completed as soon as possible after an event, not only improve memory for that event (e.g. Gabbert et al., 2009; Hope et al., 2011; Dando et al., 2019) but can also make eyewitnesses more resistant to post-event misinformation (e.g. Gabbert et al., 2012).

The SAI was developed to harvest eyewitness information quickly and efficiently, and takes the form of a standardised protocol of instructions and questions that enable witnesses to provide their own statements, without the need for a professional to conduct a formal interview. The SAI structure and questioning approach is guided by the Cognitive Interview technique (Fisher & Geiselman, 1992), which is the prevalent empirically informed method for retrieving information from witnesses. The SAI comprises a series of open-ended and probing questions for quickly consolidating a memory trace and reducing interference that can occur in the post-acquisition period. The SAI is currently advocated by the UK College of Policing (the professional body for policing in England and Wales) for collecting initial accounts from multiple eyewitnesses, and the evidence indicates that the sooner the SAI is completed the better, with research indicating it appears to be most effective when administered within 24 hours of the event (e.g. Paterson et al., 2015).

Eliciting a free-recall narrative immediately post event can also inoculate against misinformation (King et al., 1998; Sutherland & Hayne, 2001; Wang et al., 2014). In dynamic time-critical situations where an SAI may be impossible, a simple free narrative account could be sought. Currently, the SAI is a pen-and-paper method, which may be inappropriate for many eyewitnesses, such as children and those with visual and/or physical impairments. Equally, because the SAI is paper based, it relies on professionals to deliver and collect it. Accordingly, the SAI in its current form does not lend itself to remote, immediate, 'real-time' harvesting of eyewitness information, and the available empirical evidence currently only supports a paper-based SAI, although that is not to say that the procedure would not easily lend itself to being modified for collecting witness information remotely.

Warning about the possibility of misinformation may also help witnesses to resist the influence of post-event misinformation. Although the findings of empirical research have been mixed, it is typically believed that a warning is best given prior to the misinformation being presented and processed (Wright, 1993; Echterhoff, Hurst & Hussy, 2005), and that warnings are most effective only where the post-event misinformation is in a low state of accessibility (Eakin Schreiber, & Sergent-Marshall, 2003). Decades of memory research have demonstrated a need for effective methods of correcting misinformation, particularly once it has been encoded. Unfortunately, much of the empirical literature has used a paradigm where participants are exposed to an event, following which the misinformation is introduced and encoded, and then corrected using indirect memory questions during a formal interview or when completing an SAI. Here, participants are asked to provide a global account of their experiences, rather than asked directly about the post-event misinformation items. Where participants are directly questioned about the misinformation items alone and then immediately corrected, the misinformation effect can be reduced (Calvillo & Parong, 2016; Jones et al., 2018), although warnings have not been found to eliminate the misinformation effect altogether.

A recent meta-analysis (Blank & Launay, 2014) has found that warnings following the presentation of misinformation might be more effective than initially believed for the misinformation effect. However, it depends on the type of warning given, as some types of warning appear more effective than others, or when compared with no warning at all. Warnings may also be less effective for misinformation that has been read rather than heard or seen, and where the correction has been presented in a written form (Ecker et al., 2010; Crozier & Strange, 2019). Nonetheless, providing an explicit warning prior to harvesting an eyewitness account (be this face-to-face or when collecting a free narrative, or an SAI, for example) may prove an efficient way to encourage eyewitnesses to focus on the source of their memory, particularly where warnings emphasise the need for *good* quality information rather than encouraging vast quantities of information.

Finally, it has recently been reported that detecting and remembering changes can enhance retention of encoded information, thereby mitigating the misinformation effect. Putnam et al. (2017) exposed participants to visual information and then presented them with a narrative that introduced misinformation. Where the misinformation in the narrative was detected and remembered, recognition of the visual information was improved and the misinformation effect reduced. As advocated by the Cognitive Interview (Fisher & Geiselman, 1992), encouraging eyewitnesses to mentally reinstate the physical and psychological context of the to-be-remembered event might be an effective technique for highlighting misinformation, helping witnesses to detect and remember post-event information. Indeed the Cognitive Interview, which includes the mental reinstatement of context technique (Tulving & Thomson, 1973), not only increases the quality and quantity of information provided by eyewitnesses during retrieval interviews, but has also been found to mitigate the misinformation effect (e.g. Roebers & McConkey, 2003; Holliday et al., 2012; Dodson et al., 2015).

While the relative contribution of the Mental Reinstatement of Context technique to reducing the misinformation effect is unclear, encouraging eyewitnesses to focus on the details of the actual event using contextual cues supports an in-depth and detailed search for event information. A likely by-product of this technique is that they are better able to discriminate the sources of their memories (see Johnson et al., 1993). The sketch reinstatement of context is an effective alternative to the mental reinstatement of context technique that may also be beneficial for reducing the misinformation effect. Designed for eyewitnesses who may struggle with the complex cognitive operations required to mentally reinstatement the context (e.g. children, older adults, and individuals with intellectual disabilities), sketching is at least as effective for improving eyewitness performance but has yet to be investigated for reducing the misinformation effect. However, since the method draws on the same theoretical framework there is reason to expect it may be effective (Dando et al., 2009a, 2011; Dando, 2013; Mattison et al., 2015, 2018).

Enhancing self-confidence and reinforced self-affirmation (RSA) also has the potential to reduce the misinformation effect (Szpitalak & Polczyk, 2014). RSA, which occurred either before the post-event misinformation or before the final recall test, consisted of self-affirmation (recalling the greatest achievements in life) and external positive feedback (simulated 'good' results in a memory test or fake favourable personality test). Irrespective of when RSA took place, it significantly diluted the misinformation effect across a series of five experiments. RSA in a real-world environment may be challenging to implement, and as yet it appears that the empirical literature in support of this technique is limited. However, this is an interesting avenue for future research.

FALSE MEMORY

The term *false memory* broadly refers to memory accounts of experiences that did not actually occur, and accounts of experiences that are markedly different from those that did occur. In the case of the latter, a false memory is embedded in the memory of an event that has occurred. Most people have memories that are inaccurate or false, which – while annoying – are usually inconsequential. However, for the criminal justice system false memories are dangerous. In the previous section the post-event misinformation effect was introduced and discussed, and clearly the literature on false memory is not entirely distinct from the misinformation effect, particularly where false memories are embedded in true memories. However, here a distinction is made between false memory and the misinformation effect. The misinformation effect involves impairment or alteration of memory, or reports of experiences after exposure to post-event misinformation. False memories occur as a result of suggestion or pressure at retrieval, and in the absence of post-event misinformation (Loftus, 2005; Zaragoza et al., 2007).

The field of false memory research developed rapidly in the late 1980s in response to a number of well-publicised law suits in the USA and elsewhere where children accused their parents of historic sexual abuse, which had apparently continued for years but which the alleged victims had not remembered until they had entered into therapy as adults. Typically, therapists had assisted their clients to 'recover' apparently repressed memories of abuse in an effort to cure them of their current illnesses, using guided imagery techniques, hypnosis, repeated questioning, dream interpretation, and group therapy sessions (Loftus, 1993; Lindsay & Read, 1994). Sometimes also referred to as 'repressed' memories, there is no reliable empirical evidence that individuals 'repress' or 'dissociate' memories of traumatic events, albeit they may choose not to report such events (McNally, 2003; see also Chapter 9 of this volume for a more detailed discussion of repression). There is, however, much evidence to indicate that individuals do report vivid and detailed 'memories' of occurrences that did not happen (see Schacter, 1995, for a review).

Cognitive psychologists have used the typical misinformation effect paradigm (described above) and the 'crashing memory', 'forced fabrication' and 'parental misinformation' paradigms to investigate whether false memories could be created in the laboratory, and to establish the circumstances under which people come to report events or details about events that they did not experience. The parental misinformation method (Hyman et al., 1995; Loftus & Pickrell, 1995) typically entails the collection of information about events that had actually happened during a participant's childhood from family members (parents and siblings), which are presented to the participant alongside accounts of events that had not happened. Participants are repeatedly interviewed about each of the events, during which they are prompted to recount the fictitious event in detail. Usually, participants begin by stating they did not recall the fictitious event, but as the interviews progress participants begin to apparently 'recover' memories of the false event. This technique has been used to implant a variety of false childhood memories, for example being lost in a shopping centre, where 25% of participants erroneously reported recalling all or part of the event (Loftus & Pickrell, 1995; see also Hyman & Loftus, 2001), being attacked by an animal (Porter et al., 1999), and riding in a hot air balloon (Hessen-Kayfitz & Scoboria, 2012).

Using the forced fabrication paradigm, it has also been found that when participants are exposed to a suggestive manipulation after experiencing an event, the suggestive manipulation can be seen to contaminate their memory for the originally witnessed event. The forced fabrication paradigm differs from the misinformation paradigm in that rather than being told a falsehood participants simply engage in face-to-face mock interviews during which they answer questions about events they did not actually witness. They are also asked questions about the false objects or events and are pressed to provide answers to these unanswerable questions. Participants are not allowed to evade answering false-event questions. Although they initially resist answering false-event questions, the interviewer *forces* them to comply by repeatedly encouraging and insisting that they should just 'give a best guess' until participants simply acquiesce and provide a relevant response (Pezdeck et al., 2007, 2009; Compo & Parker, 2010).

These studies indicate that repeated verbal instructions that prompt and encourage people to remember events have the potential to bring about false memories or false reports. However, the extent to which false childhood memories are influenced by the context and manner in which the verbal instructions are delivered is less than clear. Ost et al. (2005) used the parental misinformation method to investigate the impact of interviewer style. Interviewers were trained to conduct non-pressure interviews during which participants were asked questions about positive and negative events, as in previous studies (e.g. an accident and a birthday party). Despite participants reporting low social pressure, over 20% of participants reported remembering full or partial information about childhood events that did not occur, indicating that repeated interviewing may be sufficient to bring about false memories, even where there is little or no social pressure for retrieval. Indeed, Loftus and Pickrell (1995) reported that their interviewers were all pleasant and friendly, likewise Erdmann et al. (2004), and both report similar findings with children.

The 'crashing memories' method asks participants to remember seeing some significant event such as film of a plane crash (Crombag et al., 1996), a video of the car crash in which Diana Princess of Wales was killed (Ost et al., 2002), or a film of the sinking of the *Estonia* ferryboat (Granhag et al., 2003). Between 44% and 66% of participants in the aforementioned studies reported seeing the non-existent or non-released footage of the events in question. In the case of the latter study, participants completed the recall questionnaire in the presence of a confederate who claimed to have either seen the footage or not. Participants displayed either decreased or increased levels of reporting in line with the confederate's position, indicating the impact of social pressure on the reporting of false information (also see Ost et al., 2006).

The creation of false memories in the laboratory is a reliable effect, and the natural cognitive changes associated with ageing increases older adults' vulnerability to false memories still further (see Devitt & Schacter, 2016). Nonetheless, this is a controversial area of research. The validity of the results and methodology outside of the laboratory has been questioned, and clearly methodological limitations do limit the generalisability of results. Some argue that in the real world very few people create completely false memories as occurs in the laboratory, and that the experimental literature reveals that many participants expressed some doubt about their false memories, which calls into question the robustness and utility of findings (Brewin & Andrews, 2017). Others have counter-argued that the research on creating false memories has never been concerned with assessing the numbers or percentages of people likely to develop false memories (albeit that these metrics are always reported), but rather with investigating whether and how false memories could be created. Irrespective of these criticisms, the findings are consistent. People *do* create and report false memories, and under certain circumstances it is relatively simple to create false memories in a laboratory context (Lindsay & Hyman, 2017; Nash et al., 2017; Otgaar et al., 2017). What is less clear is whether researchers are actually 'implanting' false memories, and whether participants continue to believe false memories once the experiments are complete.

MITIGATING EYEWITNESS FALSE MEMORY

Despite the challenges and controversy associated with the false memory literature, given the significant body of psychological research on false memories, those tasked with gathering eyewitness accounts should be cautious and sensitive to the findings of laboratory investigations. One important goal of research into false memories is to understand how to distinguish between memories for events that did actually happen and are later remembered and memory for events that did not happen at all. This is challenging, maybe even impossible in real life. However, consideration as to how eyewitness memory was retrieved, and how memories for events were probed, is a useful indicator for alerting forensic professionals to the possibility of false memory, particularly where they are reading or evaluating recent or historic eyewitness accounts that they themselves have not been involved in retrieving.

Qualitative eyewitness confidence judgements have recently been used to evaluate report accuracy in a laboratory study. Mock eyewitness participants watched a mock robbery video and were interviewed 48 hours later. Participants' recall was coded as 'recalled with very high confidence' (certainties), 'recalled with low-confidence utterances' (uncertainties), or 'recalled with no confidence markers' (regular recall). Certainties were far more accurate than uncertainties and regular recall, but uncertainties were less accurate than regular recall, indicating that eyewitnesses may be capable of qualitatively distinguishing between highly reliable information, fairly reliable information, and less reliable information, a distinction which can be important for investigative professionals who want to estimate which information is more likely to be correct (Paulo et al., 2019).

The literature also provides much guidance on how to retrieve eyewitness information to reduce the risk of false memories emanating, for example, from social pressure by an interviewer or inappropriate questioning techniques. False memories often appear to evolve following a suggestion that something may have occurred, or when witnesses are repeatedly questioned using inappropriate or suggestable techniques. Indeed, the false/recovered memory debate is centred on whether suggestions by therapists and others regarding the possibility of forgotten childhood experiences had been central in implanting apparently false memories (see Patihis et al., 2014). With this in mind, researchers have considered the possibility that eyewitnesses could develop false memories as a result of being questioned about an event during a witness interview, or while giving testimony at court. During forensic interviews, police and other legal professionals are tasked with assisting witnesses to recall as much detail about an event as possible (see St-Yves, 2014; Paulo et al., 2019). In doing so they have to tread a fine line between supporting the retrieval process by encouraging an effortful search of long-term memory and fully exploring verbalised accounts, and 'pushing' witnesses to report more event information than is comfortable for them.

Psychological scientists have long recognised that expectations for eyewitness memory performance can exceed witness memory capability, and that intrusions from the techniques used by police and others to collect information from witnesses can alter witness memory in subtle ways, often unrecognised by investigators and witnesses themselves. One of the most researched and generally accepted methods for 'safely' collecting eyewitness information is the Cognitive Interview (Fisher & Geiselman, 1992; Köhnken et al., 1999; Memon et al., 2010). Comprising a series of mnemonic techniques that draw on the experimental cognition literature, such as imaging and mentally reinstating the context, the Cognitive Interview also offers a framework for conducting an eyewitness interview and includes strategies for optimising the social and communication aspects of the interview without pressuring eyewitnesses. The findings are consistent. When applied appropriately, correctly and in accordance with training and guidance, a timely Cognitive Interview can minimise the development of false memories associated with suggestive misleading questions during repeated retrieval attempts. It can also reduce the reporting of errors, and substantially increase the reporting of correct event information. While some researchers have reported small increases in errors, this has not had an impact on the overall percentage accuracy of recall performance (see Memon et al., 2010; Köhnken et al., 1999, for meta-analyses).

Unfortunately, research has consistently revealed that forensic interviews are not always conducted in accordance with best practice, both in the UK and elsewhere. For example, the Cognitive Interview mnemonic techniques are often used inappropriately and incorrectly, which can result in confusion (e.g. Dando et al., 2008, 2009b, 2011; Clarke et al., 2011). Further, interviewers sometimes persist in robustly questioning eyewitnesses even after they have said they cannot remember, cannot recall all of the event, or did not see the person in question (see Milne & Powell, 2010). In such circumstances it is possible that interviewees may speculate, fabricate or be persuaded to report false memories in a similar manner as can occur when seeking confessions from suspected perpetrators (see Lassiter & Meissner, 2010; Kassin, 2014).

The false fabrication literature offers considerable evidence that following fairly short delays between being interviewed and being asked to report information about events, participants can develop false memories for incidental information they have knowingly been forced to fabricate or guess (e.g. Chroback & Zaragoza, 2008; Memon et al., 2010). In some cases, mock eyewitnesses have been found to fabricate entire events, even when warned that they may have previously been asked questions about fabricated events. Some months later when asked to freely recall the events in question, nearly 50% freely reported the forced fabrications and performed similarly to those mock witnesses who had not been warned. This is concerning because participants were not questioned about the fabricated events, rather they were simply asked to provide an uninterrupted freely narrative account. Typically, freely recalled information is the most accurate, albeit least detailed information provided by eyewitnesses because they are able to exercise strategic control over what to report and what to withhold, usually only reporting information they are confident is absolutely correct (Koriat & Goldsmith, 1996; Weber & Brewer, 2018; Chrobak & Zaragoza, 2013).

To mitigate false memories associated with the method of retrieving eyewitness information, forensic professionals should take the time to consider the types of questions they ask and their content in face-to-face witness interviews and when questioning or cross-examining eyewitnesses in court. Suggestive questioning, whereby eyewitnesses are exposed to false or misleading information in the course of a criminal investigation, can induce false memories. Where an eyewitness to a robbery 'learns' or 'hears' a piece of misinformation from a professional source (a police officer, for example) – for instance that the robber was carrying a knife, when the robber had no weapon at all – the eyewitness may subsume this information into their mental representation of the robbery. Later, when asked for details about the robber, the eyewitness may then go on to construct specific and detailed information about the non-existent knife. There is a significant body of evidence indicating that detailed probing of suggested information can increase false memory (Drivdahl & Zaragoza, 2001; Shaw & Porter, 2015; Bernstein et al., 2018), so suggestive or leading questions, be they accidental or otherwise, must be avoided.

CONCLUSION

The vast literature on eyewitness memory and forgetting means that providing an overview in a book chapter is almost impossible. However, the literature makes it clear that there are numerous ways in which an eyewitness might come to believe and report misinformation or a false memory, and in doing so forget what they have actually seen or choose not to report that information. Further, a highly confident eyewitness can go on to provide details that are completely false. It may be that the eyewitness did not ever notice or encode the original detail, it may have simply been forgotten, or the memory trace may have weakened over time so that the eyewitness becomes unsure, which may make him/ her susceptible to post-event misinformation and/or false memory. Or, despite having a solid and fresh memory for the event in question, having interacted with co-witnesses and read or seen media reports, the eyewitness can be exposed to post-event information and misinformation that serves to undermine confidence in their own memory, or interfere with the original memory trace so that this new information becomes part of the original memory.

There is now a significant knowledge base for understanding how to support eyewitnesses to give their best testimony, some of which has been introduced in this chapter. What is abundantly clear is that the manner in which eyewitnesses are treated in the immediate aftermath of a crime is key. The speed at which a first eyewitness account is retrieved, the methods and techniques used to gather eyewitness information, face to face or otherwise, and the questions asked when eyewitnesses are recounting their personal experiences have the potential to reduce false memories and limit the impact of post-event misinformation. It is, however, important to highlight that our knowledge base is largely underpinned by laboratory-based research, where variables are controlled and ethical constraints limit the extent to which the encoding and retrieval environments can be manipulated to mimic the experiences of real witnesses and victims. That said, the Innocence Project and other instances of miscarriages where eyewitness testimony has been found to be erroneous serve to indicate the utility of laboratory research, because memory errors in the real world are akin to those found in a laboratory environment.

The malleability of eyewitness confidence has also been reported in numerous real-world cases, for example where eyewitnesses have identified the person they believe to be the perpetrator from a line-up. Initially, some eyewitnesses have reported not being very confident that their choice was correct. After having received positive feedback they have then moved to report being extremely confident despite their choices sometimes turning out to be incorrect (see Garret, 2011; but also see Wixted et al., 2015). While the limitations of laboratory base research are obvious, it must also be noted that laboratory research has been fundamental in bringing about significant reforms to the manner in which witnesses are interviewed, and to how eyewitness identification procedures are carried out in the UK, the USA and elsewhere (see Dando & Milne, 2018; Wells, 2018; Milne, Griffiths, Clarke & Dando, 2019).

Further Reading

Eysenck, M. W. (2020). Eyewitness testimony. In A. D. Baddeley, M. W. Eysenck, and M. C. Anderson (eds), *Memory* (3rd edn). Hove: Psychology Press.

Milne, R., & Bull, R. (2016). Witness interviews and crime investigation. In D. Groome and M. W. Eysenck (eds), *An Introduction to Applied Cognitive Psychology* (2nd edn). Abingdon: Routledge.

Milne, B., Griffiths, A., Clarke, C., & Dando, C. (2019). The cognitive interview: A tiered approach in the real world. In J. J. Dickinson, N. Schreiber Compo., R. N. Carol., B. L. Schwartz, & M. R. McCauley (eds), *Evidence-based Investigative Interviewing: Applying Cognitive Principles* (pp. 56–73). Abingdon: Routledge.

5

PROSPECTIVE MEMORY FORGETTING

Forgetting to do something

Michael K. Scullin, Seth Koslov,
and Jarrod Lewis-Peacock

When people think about forgetting, they may think of the time they forgot someone's name, forgot an answer to a test, or forgot the location of a friend's house. Such examples are common errors of *retrospective memory* (memory for past events), and the causes and consequences of retrospective memory errors are detailed in other chapters of this book. By contrast, when some people think about forgetting, they may lament their 'to-do list' items that went unchecked, such as forgetting to buy a card for a family member's birthday, forgetting to order a medication refill, or forgetting an approaching deadline for a writing assignment. When someone fails to remember to perform such intended actions in the future, they are experiencing an error of *prospective memory*.

Prospective memory is typically conceptualised as any intended action that must be completed in the future, so long as there is not an agent that prompts retrieval (as is the case for experimenter-prompted recall tests; see Meacham, 1982). In the typical laboratory paradigm (Einstein & McDaniel, 1990), participants are not only engaged in an 'ongoing' task such as lexical decision making (responding to whether a string of letters forms a word), they are also instructed to perform a target action (e.g. press the F1 key) if they ever see a target cue (e.g. the word 'table'). If this were a test of *retrospective* memory, then an experimenter would ask participants to free recall or recognise the target cue or action; what makes this a test of *prospective* memory is that participants have to 'remember to remember' to make the F1 key response when they see the word 'table' rather than simply make the ongoing task response that 'table' is a word. While this laboratory paradigm is somewhat artificial, it allows researchers to isolate the basic mechanisms supporting prospective memory.

The field of prospective memory was ahead of its time in conceiving of memory as a future-focused ability (Szpunar et al., 2014). However, in the 1990s the prospective memory field incited substantial debate amongst cognitive psychologists. The primary issue was whether prospective memory was a new type of memory, distinguishable from retrospective memory, planning, and attention. Such claims led Crowder (1996) to dismiss the concept of prospective memory as 'misleading if not downright careless' (p. 143), Rabbitt (1996) to rebuke the term 'prospective memory' as a 'generic label' (p. 239), and Roediger (1996) to caution the prospective memory field against confusing itself with 'hopes and wishes and dreams' (p. 153). Their critical commentaries were an important reminder that prospective memory was not a new or unique cognitive process. What was important – and continues to be important – is that the study of prospective memory provides a platform for investigating how a diversity of memory, planning, attention, and other processes interact to support a complex behaviour.

THEORETICAL VIEWPOINTS

Prospective remembering is a complex ability that involves the encoding of an intention, maintenance of that intention over a variable amount of time (from minutes to weeks), and the retrieval and execution of that intention. Deactivation of the completed intention – essentially 'checking off the intention from your mental to-do list' – is the final step in the process.

Prospective memory intentions differ in being event-based or time-based. In event-based prospective memory, retrieval must occur in a particular context or in response to some external event. In time-based prospective memory, retrieval must occur after a specific elapsed time (e.g. in 10 minutes) or at an absolute time (e.g. at 2 p.m.). In general, time-based prospective memory tasks are more difficult than event-based prospective memory tasks because they lack strong retrieval cues and are reliant on an individual's meta-awareness of elapsed time (Jäger & Kliegel, 2008). Yet the line between event- and time-based tasks can become blurred, for example when one uses a clock (external event) to help them remember a 'time-based' task at 2 p.m.

Most prospective memory theories contend that remembering to execute an intention requires the interplay of attention and memory processes. However, theoretical views differ in their emphasis on top-down versus bottom-up processes, such as whether attention must be engaged proactively or can be engaged reactively (Shelton & Scullin, 2017). One general theoretical view is that people must proactively monitor their environment for the opportunity to perform their intention (e.g. Harris & Wilkins, 1982; Guynn, 2003; Burgess et al., 2007). According to the monitoring perspective, bakers who forget to remove the cookies from the oven after 10 minutes do so because they stop monitoring the clock (which is exactly why this author always sets a timer). The most influential view of monitoring has been Smith's (2003) preparatory attention and memory processes (PAM) theory. The PAM theory contends that attention-consuming processes such as rehearsing the intention and trial-by-trial checking for target cues (i.e. monitoring) must be engaged immediately *prior to* processing the target cue. If such preparatory processes are engaged, then processing the target cue leads to a retrospective memory check, for example one might ask themself '*Is this stimulus my target cue?*' and '*Is this the correct time to perform my intention?*' Because both the preparatory attention and the retrospective memory check are theorised to require working memory capacity, engaging these processes leads to a cost in performance of the ongoing task, such as slower or less accurate responding on non-target trials.

Another prominent prospective memory theory is the multiprocess theory (McDaniel & Einstein, 2007). By this view, monitoring or other preparatory processes are engaged when the prospective memory task is difficult, when prospective memory cues are presented frequently, and when the importance of the prospective memory task is emphasised. However, a core assumption of the multiprocess view is that, in general, people are biased against effortful monitoring, and biased towards relatively effortless spontaneous retrieval processes (McDaniel & Einstein, 2007). Spontaneous retrieval is characterised as a bottom-up, cue-triggered process that is introspectively experienced as a memory 'popping' into mind. For example, after putting the cookies in the oven and walking into the backyard, one might glance through the window and see the mixer on the counter. To the extent that the mixer is associated with baking cookies (in long-term memory), seeing the mixer may trigger the associated intention to return inside to check on the progress of the cookies. A growing body of behavioural and neural data support the dissociation between monitoring and spontaneous retrieval for prospective remembering (Cona et al., 2015; McDaniel et al., 2015). In general, effortful processes are characterised by ongoing task costs and sustained neural activity in regions implicated in working memory, especially the dorsal attention network. Spontaneous retrieval is characterised by no or transient ongoing task costs, as well as transient activity in the ventral attention network and medial temporal lobe when target cues occur.

According to the multiprocess theory, spontaneous retrieval is most likely when there is a strong cue–intention association and the target cue is focally processed. Focal processing occurs when the features of the target cue overlap with the processing requirements of the ongoing task, such as if the target cue is a green font colour during an ongoing colour-naming Stroop task (note that a non-focal cue would be a word cue in an incongruent Stroop task; see Bugg et al., 2011). In contrast to the PAM theory, the multiprocess theory predicts that prospective remembering *can* occur without the engagement of preparatory processes, specifically when there are no ongoing task costs immediately prior to target cues.

Recently, the multiprocess theory has evolved into the dynamic multiprocess view (DMPV; see Scullin et al., 2013; Shelton et al., 2019). According to the DMPV, participants are biased towards monitoring when target cues are expected (e.g. when the intention can soon be performed), and biased towards spontaneous retrieval when target cues are not expected (i.e. unexpected cues can still trigger a retrieval without needing to engage preparatory attention). Furthermore, these top-down and bottom-up processes are theorised to interact dynamically. For example, when one spontaneously retrieves an intention, that retrieval will often lead the person to monitor, with the duration of monitoring determined by metacognitive processes (e.g. one's determination of how soon the intention can be performed). The more that a person then engages monitoring/rehearsal processes, the more likely the individual is to generate new retrieval cues or strengthen existing cue-intention associations, thereby increasing the later probability of spontaneous retrieval. Thus, the DMPV states that prospective remembering is not accomplished by *either* top-down processes *or* bottom-up processes; prospective remembering is accomplished via the flexible interplay of *both* top-down processes *and* bottom-up processes. Throughout this chapter, we take the perspective that both types of processes operate at intention formation (encoding stage), intention testing (retrieval stage), and post-intention testing (deactivation stage).

ENCODING ERRORS

Imagine you are a parent and are preparing to go on a family road trip. You know that the entire trip will be derailed if you forget to pack specific pacifiers, preferred snacks, favourite stuffed animals, and an assortment of 'correct' entertainment items (any given week there is a *right* firetruck and a *wrong* firetruck). But how do parents avoid such errors that are seemingly small, yet of high consequence? Generating a list of reminders is a reasonable solution, but many people forgo making to-do lists due to overconfidence in their ability to remember prospective memory intentions (Cauvin et al., 2019). Behavioural studies have found substantial individual differences in prospective memory encoding, with individuals who have greater working memory capacity tending to make more detailed and effective plans (Kliegel et al., 2000). Neuroimaging evidence also supports the notion of individual differences in encoding. Greater activity during encoding in the rostral prefrontal cortex (PFC) and motor regions predicts greater prospective remembering during test blocks (Eschen et al., 2007; Momennejad & Haynes, 2013).

The most common encoding error is to encode a prospective memory intention too broadly (Gollwitzer, 1999). Using the family trip example, parents who form the general intention 'to pack a bag for Jack' are assuming that as they begin to pack the bag, all of Jack's necessary items will easily come to mind. But, as Gollwitzer (1999) and many other researchers have found, people who form general intentions often later fail to remember to perform those intentions. People are more likely to succeed if they form very specific intentions, such as 'I need to pack a bag that includes the blue pacifier, apple slice snacks, *Kodi* the stuffed animal, and the big firetruck toy' (see Chen et al., 2015). Therefore, parents who invest more top-down processes at intention formation to encode specific intentions may earn a return on their investment in terms of fewer items being forgotten and a more enjoyable family trip.

There is a clear advantage to prospective memory retrieval when intentions are specifically encoded, but specific encoding may not always require top-down elaborative processing. Instead, some intentions may be encoded either implicitly or 'in passing'. For example, when a person removes their watch to take a shower, they typically do not consciously or elaboratively encode the intention to put that watch back on their wrist after the shower, yet most people remember to do so with ease (Kvavilashvili et al., 2013). Furthermore, when one thinks of packing toiletries, not every person will effortfully generate a list of as many toiletry items as possible. Instead, simply thinking of the overarching category of 'toiletries' can trigger automatic spreading activation in semantic networks (Collins & Loftus, 1975) to pack the toothbrush, deodorant, floss, and other items.

We tested the above views of encoding across eight experiments in which participants were told to remember to press the Q key if they saw a word belonging to the category 'fruits' (Scullin et al., 2018). Immediately after encoding, participants were asked what was on their mind: 25% of the participants were not thinking about the prospective memory task at all (e.g. mind wandering), 25% of the participants were thinking of specific possible exemplars of fruits (apple, banana, etc.), and 50% of the participants were generally thinking about the overarching category of 'fruits' very broadly. Consistent with the view that some encoding can occur 'in passing', there were no differences in encoding duration between specific encoders ($M = 22$ sec) and general/broad encoders ($M = 23$ sec).

These individuals also did not differ in measures of working memory capacity. However, they did differ in later prospective memory performance: participants who generated specific exemplars detected more target cues (69%) than participants who only broadly thought about the target cues (41%). Interestingly, the specific encoders achieved this higher prospective memory performance with no ongoing task costs. Thus, forming specific intentions is better than forming general intentions, and specific-intention encoding may be accomplished by top-down elaborative processes, bottom-up spreading-activation processes, or in some cases, both.

The manner in which prospective memory intentions are consolidated before retrieval is an important extension of understanding encoding. Most intentions are not performed immediately after encoding, but hours or days later. For example, before leaving on the road trip, you may put some apple snacks in the refrigerator that you then re-encode as needing to take with you the next morning. Importantly, processes occurring during sleep have been shown to benefit the consolidation of episodic memories (Rasch & Born, 2013). Does sleep serve a similar role for prospective memories? An emerging body of literature suggests that healthy sleep of 7–9 hours increases the strength of the association between encoded cues and their corresponding intended actions, thus improving bottom-up mechanisms of retrieval (see Scullin & McDaniel, 2010; Diekelmann et al., 2013; Barner et al., 2017). On the flip side of that coin, sleep restriction is related to worse prospective memory functioning (Esposito et al., 2015).

We recently had younger and older adults encode a focal prospective memory intention in the evening and tested them the following morning after undergoing polysomnography-monitored sleep (Scullin et al., 2019). One hypothesis was that individual- and age-related differences in slow-wave activity and sleep spindles, which are typically associated with episodic (retrospective) memory consolidation, would be associated with better morning prospective memory performance. An alternative hypothesis was that prospective memory performance would be associated with levels of rapid eye movement (REM) sleep, which has been implicated in procedural memory consolidation, emotional processing, and binding memory associations. Even after controlling for age, we found that the duration of REM sleep was more strongly related to prospective memory performance than slow-wave activity or sleep spindle density. In summary, current research suggests that one of the main benefits of sleep in prospective remembering is the increase in strength between encoded cue–action associations, which leads to easier retrieval of those intentions in the future. It seems that a good night's sleep (particularly REM-filled sleep) can be the difference between remembering or forgetting to grab that bag of road trip snacks.

RETRIEVAL ERRORS

The family truckster is now all packed, and you are barrelling down the road towards your fun-filled destination. After a few hours, you are enticed by a billboard to stop at the 'best roadside snack shop in Texarkana' about 30 miles ahead at exit 253. How will you remember to take this exit? The simplest approach would be to make a 'mental note' (i.e. encode) to exit the highway when you encounter the sign for exit 253. When the exit sign appears, you may suddenly retrieve your intention to grab snacks and successfully take the exit. This would be an instance of *spontaneous retrieval*, which is a less cognitively demanding strategy than engaging effortful top-down processes such as monitoring. However, it is also a probabilistic process and therefore fallible. For example, spontaneous retrieval is heavily dependent on noticing cues relevant to the prospective memory intention, such as noticing the highway sign for exit 253. As such, it is susceptible to various forms of interference that can lead to prospective memory forgetting.

One way that retrieval errors can occur is from a failure to notice or adequately process the target cue. Failure to notice cues, naturally, precludes the retrieval of any associated intentions. Harrison et al. (2014) found that divided attention, which decreases the likelihood of noticing target cues, exacerbated forgetting when people were relying on spontaneous retrieval. It is easy to conceive that while driving down the road, you may fail to exit for the Texarkana snack shop while being distracted by a conversation with your spouse, by noisy kids arguing in the back seat, or by a focus on the speedometer when seeing a police car ahead. In laboratory settings, Kidder et al. (1997) found that participants performed significantly worse on prospective memory tasks that were performed under high cognitive load relative to tasks under low cognitive load (see also Meier & Zimmerman, 2015; Ballhausen et al., 2017). Similarly, Marsh et al. (1998, 2002a) found that prospective memory errors were more likely in a dual-task context when participants switched between different ongoing demands as compared to when they performed a demanding single task. Using eye-tracking, both West et al. (2007) and Hartwig et al. (2013) found that approximately half of retrieval failures were due to not fixating on the target cues at all. The other half of failures were associated with fast, inadequate processing of the target cues. Together, these data indicate that failure to retrieve a prospective memory intention results from a failure to notice or sufficiently process an associated cue in the environment.

Consider another scenario: you're driving down the road and notice the sign for exit 253. Suddenly you are reminded that there was something special about that exit (*hint*: the snack shop!), which leads you to search your memory and (hopefully) remember that you wanted to stop for a bite. This series of events describes the *discrepancy-plus-search* process of prospective memory retrieval. The 'discrepancy' portion is an automatic process of noticing some difference between a current stimulus (the sign for exit 253) and previous stimuli (the past few exit signs). When a discrepancy occurs, this initiates a resource-demanding search through memory for the source of the discrepancy. Breneiser and McDaniel (2006) and Guynn and McDaniel (2007) manipulated discrepancy by varying pre-exposure to either target cues (e.g. exit 253) or related lures (other exits). They found that as discrepancy between familiarity of cues and lures increased, so did prospective memory performance. Lee and McDaniel (2013) found similar results using an odd-ball paradigm with anagrams that varied in difficulty: performance was better when there was greater discrepancy between the difficulty of target cues and lures. Further evidence comes from neuroimaging research using electroencephalography (EEG). West et al. (2003) found that the N300 (an ERP measure of target cue processing; West, 2011) was larger on trials where the target cues were more distinct from lures, and memory was better for more distinct trials. These results suggest that retrieval errors can occur when the target cues are not sufficiently different in processing fluency from other stimuli that do not have any prospective relevance.

In situations where prospective memory cues are not salient or focal to the processing of ongoing events, it can be beneficial to engage in effortful retrieval processes. Smith (2003) provided evidence for such a benefit across three experiments. She found that having to perform six prospective memory tasks caused slower responding on non-target ongoing task trials (i.e. *cost*). Moreover, individuals who performed better on the prospective memory task demonstrated greater costs on the ongoing task. Additional studies have supported the idea that effortful monitoring for target cues can help to reduce retrieval errors (e.g. West et al., 2006; Smith et al., 2007; Shelton & Christopher, 2016). Using functional magnetic resonance imaging (fMRI), researchers have observed that when prospective memory cues are non-focal to ongoing task performance, sustained activation of regions related to top-down allocation of attention (the rostral-lateral PFC and dorsal attention network) is linked to prospective remembering (for a review see McDaniel et al., 2015).

A key factor that influences whether people will engage in effortful retrieval is the likelihood of a prospective memory cue occurring in a given context (Marsh et al., 2006). For example, during the aforementioned family road trip, if you are currently driving in Louisiana you are probably not going to monitor for an exit that you know to be located in Texas. In our lab (Scullin et al., 2013) we found that participants would only engage in effortful retrieval processes when they encountered contextual cues indicating that the target cue was likely to appear (see also Kuhlman & Rummel, 2014; Bowden et al., 2017). While contextual information can prove useful, it can also lead to retrieval failures when target cues occur outside of expected contexts (e.g. Bugg & Ball, 2017). For example, if you miss the sign that says 'Welcome to Texas', you will likely fail to initiate monitoring for the snack-shop exit sign. This phenomenon is related to the concept of *habit capture* (Dismukes, 2012). In habit capture, individuals need to make some adjustment to a normal routine, like picking up kids 1 day of the week from the soccer fields instead of from school. Errors occur when people become preoccupied with other ongoing demands and forget to make the adjustment from their normal routine. While context and routines can be helpful for accomplishing prospective intentions, they are not foolproof.

Both automatic and effortful processes are important to prospective remembering (McDaniel & Einstein, 2007; Braver, 2012). In a recent study conducted by our lab (Lewis-Peacock et al. 2016), we found evidence that both processes can support successful performance in different situations. Participants were engaged in an ongoing lexical-decision task while also performing a picture-recognition task (see Figure 5.1a). Participants' prospective memory strategies were biased by manipulating the memory

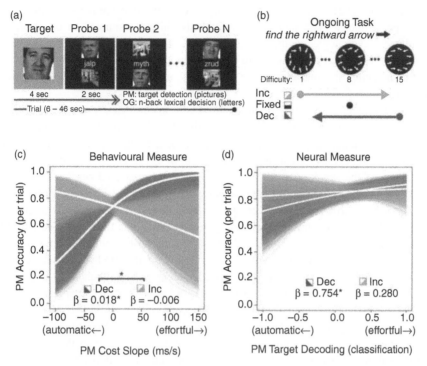

Figure 5.1 The efficacy of effortful and automatic retrieval strategies for prospective intentions is related to contextual factors of the current environment, such as target discrepancy and the cognitive demands of ongoing tasks (data were adapted from Koslov et al., 2019)

load of the lexical-decision task and the difficulty of the picture task such that participants were encouraged to use effortful retrieval strategies in one condition and automatic retrieval strategies in another. The level of effortful processing devoted to the prospective memory task was quantified in two ways. Firstly, we measured reaction time costs that were associated with performing the ongoing task with an added prospective memory intention (versus ongoing task alone). Secondly, fMRI data were used to measure the degree of effortful processing for the target cues.

In the effort-biased condition, greater levels of both the behavioural and neural measures of effort were associated with fewer errors. However, in the automatic-biased condition, there were no such relationships. In a follow-up experiment, this design was modified so that ongoing task difficulty could be incrementally adjusted over the course of each trial to observe how people shifted between effortful and automatic retrieval strategies (Koslov et al., 2019; see Figure 5.1b). On trials where difficulty decreased, both behavioural and neural measures of effortful processing were predictive of prospective memory performance. The more that individuals shifted resources to be engaged in effortful retrieval strategies on these trials, the more successful they were (see Figure 5.1c in dark grey). However, on trials where difficulty increased, engaging effortful strategies was either no better or sometimes worse than relying on automatic retrieval strategies (see Figure 5.1d in light grey).

Along with ongoing task difficulty, individuals update their prospective memory-retrieval strategies in response to meta-cognitive beliefs about the difficulty of their intention. For instance, if you know that the sign for the best snack spot is notoriously easy to miss, you may allocate a significant amount of effort into monitoring for the sign. Alternatively, if the snack spot has multiple signs that are spaced across several miles, you may feel secure in relying on spontaneous retrieval processes. Rummel and Meiser (2013) found that participants who were given instructions that a prospective memory task would be difficult demonstrated significantly greater costs than those who were told that it would be easy, even though they performed the same task. Similarly, Lourenço et al. (2015) asked participants to indicate when an animal word appeared while they performed a lexical decision task. Some participants were given atypical animals as exemplars (e.g. walrus and raccoon), thereby tacitly establishing a belief that the prospective memory task would be difficult. Other participants were given typical animal exemplars (e.g. dog and mouse), creating a tacit belief that the task would be easy. Individuals in the high-demand condition showed significantly greater monitoring costs than those in the low-demand condition. These results showed how meta-cognitive beliefs about task demands can greatly impact how one attempts to complete a prospective memory task.

The studies reviewed here demonstrate that in high-probability, low-demand environments, using effortful retrieval strategies greatly benefits prospective remembering. However, these effortful processes are costly, and may decrease performance on ongoing tasks. In other words, you might remember to exit at sign 253, but rehearsing that intention could come at the cost of reduced focus on the road and speedometer (followed by the monetary cost of a speeding ticket). Luckily, there are situations where effortful strategies need not be engaged as automatic processes may be just as good, or even better, for prospective remembering.

DEACTIVATION ERRORS

Older adults in the United States take an average of four prescription medications every day (Charlesworth et al., 2015). That represents not only a high load of prospective memory intentions, but also a significant meta-cognitive demand on remembering. In other words, individuals are constantly tasked with tracking whether their prospective memory intentions have been completed. *Commission errors* involve incorrectly performing a prospective memory task either after it has been completed or in the improper context (contrast this with *omission errors*, which involve *failing* to perform a prospective memory task in the correct context). For example, an older adult may take their daily medication, but not put the pill bottle away. They then leave the room and come back later, notice the pill bottle and spontaneously retrieve the intention that they should take their medicine. Patients who then 'double dose' can experience a number of ill-effects, such as increased risk of bleeding when double dosing on warfarin (Kimmel et al., 2007).

Commission errors, or the repetition of a prospective memory action after an intention has been cancelled or completed, are just one form of *deactivation errors*. Deactivation errors can also manifest as performing the prospective memory action during the wrong context (e.g. during a block in which the intention is suspended, also known as *false alarms*), or as slower response times to target cues that were relevant to previous intentions (i.e. before the intention was cancelled or completed; see Walser et al., 2012). Similar to retrieval errors, deactivation errors are thought to be related to failures of both automatic and effortful processes.

In general, many of the factors that lead to better spontaneous retrieval of intentions also lead to more commission errors. Bugg et al. (2013) found that greater encoding strength for prospective memory intentions led to subsequent increases in commission errors. Similarly, Walser et al. (2017) found increased after-effects, in the form of increased commission errors and retrieval-related slowing, when new prospective memory intentions were related to previous target cues. Additionally, errors of commission and response slowing to target cues are heightened when target cues are salient (Hefer et al., 2017). Collectively, these studies point to a failure in a deactivation of the cue–intention association (which should minimise spontaneous retrievals) as an explanation for many errors of commission.

On the other hand, there is evidence that errors of commission are not simply related to over-eager bottom-up automatic retrieval processes. In our previous work (Scullin et al., 2012), we found that participants made more commission errors to salient cues only when encountered in an ongoing task that was originally paired with the prospective memory intention. That finding by itself would implicate spontaneous retrieval processes as the source of the commission errors. However, they also found that the probability of making commission errors was related to inhibitory control, with less control (and also greater perseveration) related to more commission errors. These associations suggested that there is also a top-down, effortful component involved in errors of commission. Older adults, who often exhibit impaired cognitive control, commit more commission errors, providing further correlational evidence for top-down effects on this type of memory failure. Furthermore, Bugg et al. (2016) found that older adults made more commission errors than younger adults when there was a higher memory load, suggesting that effortful processes are necessary for sufficient deactivation. Only by training an association between cues and a no-go response did they observe a decrease in commission errors; simply instructing participants to mentally prepare to ignore the reappearance of prospective memory cues was insufficient. Thus, the collective results suggest that both effortful and automatic processes are important for successful deactivation of intentions.

A less common form of deactivation errors gives rise to errors of omission due to an individual mistakenly thinking they have completed an intention. Such errors may occur more often for habitual prospective memory tasks. For example, oftentimes pills are set out to be taken, and then some interruption, like a phone call, occurs. When returning to the pill bottles, the intention to take pills is successfully retrieved, but then incorrectly identified as already having been completed. Marsh et al. (2002b) tracked deactivation errors of omission on a prospective memory task and found that participants' reporting on whether they had actually completed the prospective memory task was unreliable. Research on these types of deactivation errors is limited, but it seems plausible to apply existing theoretical frameworks: an environmental cue triggers a spontaneous retrieval of the intention to perform a habitual action, followed by a failure of top-down processing to evaluate whether it is the correct context in which to do so.

In summary, deactivation errors are commonplace, are rooted in both top-down and bottom-up mechanisms, and are just as consequential as more frequently studied retrieval errors. Future work is still needed in this area, however, to (a) determine why deactivation does not occur rapidly and completely, (b) identify the neural mechanisms that lead to deactivation-related memory errors, and (c) devise approaches to mitigate the negative behavioural impact of these errors, particularly in healthcare settings and clinical groups.

PREVENTING PROSPECTIVE MEMORY FAILURES

One of the ultimate goals of any form of basic science, including the topic of prospective memory, is to translate laboratory findings into the real world. For example, many studies have been designed to combat the increasing prevalence of prospective forgetting that occurs with normal ageing (Hering et al., 2014). In this next section, we outline interventions aimed at improving prospective remembering. These interventions fall into three general classes: (1) improve retrospective memory and monitoring with *cognitive training*; (2) improve spontaneous retrieval processes with an *implementation intention* strategy; or (3) circumvent all retrieval processes with *technology-assisted reminders*.

One approach is to give participants several sessions of training on a prospective memory task, with each session increasing in difficulty (e.g. number of intentions to complete). As with all cognitive training studies, performance on the trained task improves across sessions (Hering et al., 2014). However, there is considerable debate as to whether training on a single task will 'transfer to' (show benefits on) other untrained tasks (Boot et al., 2013). Rose et al. (2015) had 23 healthy older adults train on a prospective memory task for 12 sessions across 1 month. Each session was adaptive in that it increased in the number and complexity of prospective memory tasks according to each participant's performance during the previous session. Relative to a no-contact control group (n = 18) and a group that spent 1 month in a music training programme (n = 14), participants in the prospective memory training group showed successful transfer, that is, better post-training performance on a range of prospective memory tasks that were not previously trained.

Prospective memory training studies often produce positive results, but most of these studies have not addressed why the training is beneficial. One possibility is that training emphasises the importance of performing prospective memory tasks, increasing the probability that participants will engage in monitoring or rehearsal of the intention. Across a 4-week protocol, Kliegel and colleagues manipulated whether healthy older adults worked on intention formation (imagery training) or intention retention (rehearsal training; see Ihle et al., 2018). They found that training participants to rehearse the prospective memory cues periodically during the retention interval increased the probability that the target cues would be detected, but at the cost of slower ongoing task response times. Given that prospective memory training appears to increase the requirement of attentional resources allocated (rather than make prospective remembering more efficient), it is perhaps not surprising that training benefits do not persist at 3- or 6-month follow-up tests (Zhao et al., 2019) and are not effective for patients with cognitive impairment (Bahar-Fuchs et al., 2013).

Another approach to preventing prospective memory failures is to target improving spontaneous retrieval processes. Research shows that using the *implementation intention* strategy effectively increases spontaneous retrieval processes in healthy adults (Brandstätter et al., 2001; Chasteen et al., 2001; Scullin et al., 2017). The implementation intention strategy involves verbally specifying an external cue, for example, by stating 'When I sit down at the breakfast table [*external cue*], then I will remember to take my medication' (Gollwitzer, 1999). In studies of healthy adults, the implementation intention strategy has increased remembering to take vitamins, attend physician appointments, eat recommended foods, adhere to prescribed rehabilitative exercises, and get flu and other vaccinations (for a review, see Chen et al., 2015). Figure 5.2 illustrates that, relative to

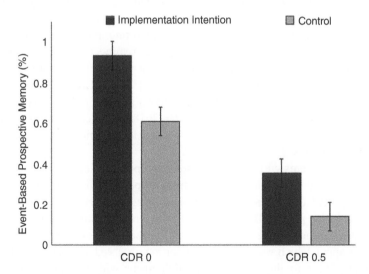

Figure 5.2 Implementation intentions can improve event-based prospective memory in healthy older adults (Clinical Dementia Rating [CDR] = 0) and adults with mild cognitive impairment (CDR = 0.5) (data were adapted from Shelton et al., 2016)

age-matched controls, prospective memory is greatly impaired in the early stages of Alzheimer's disease; but interestingly, the implementation intention strategy bolstered prospective memory performance even in this cognitively impaired group (Lee et al., 2016; Shelton et al., 2016).

Despite the benefits of implementation intentions in some settings, people typically stop using the implementation intention strategy over time even if it is initially effective (Insel et al., 2016). Furthermore, though the implementation intention strategy is beneficial, it only partially remediates prospective memory difficulties in cognitively impaired individuals (Burkard et al., 2014). A potential solution is to leverage technology to 'off-load' intentions (McDonald et al., 2011; Gilbert, 2015). The idea here is to circumvent age- and disease-related difficulties with retrieval processes (monitoring, rehearsal, and/or spontaneous retrieval) and sleep-related memory consolidation processes (Scullin & Bliwise, 2015), allowing the technological device to store and retrieve the intention at the correct time or location.

Indeed, there is a long history of studies that had participants offload their prospective and retrospective memories onto pagers, digital voice recorders, and other devices. These *electronic memory aid* studies yielded positive results in healthy adults and in patients with traumatic brain injury or dementia (Jamieson et al., 2014). However, these studies were all limited by participant non-adherence, largely because pagers and voice recorders have few other functions (and no social/emotional reinforcing functions; see Svoboda et al., 2015). By contrast, smart technology devices serve many reinforcing functions, including taking and viewing photos, connecting with friends and family, and enabling entertaining and informative dialogues with personal assistants (e.g. Apple's Siri; Benge & Scullin, 2020). More directly relevant to supporting prospective memory, many smartphone devices can store intentions and provide reminders to perform the intention at pre-specified times (via alarms and calendars), at pre-specified locations (via GPS), and with pre-specified individuals (via contacts list). In the United States, virtually all millennials now own smartphones, and more than two-thirds of older adults from the baby boomer generation do too (Pew Research Center, 2018). In other words, most individuals have technology – literally at their fingertips – that could be harnessed to support everyday prospective memory tasks.

Even geriatric patients with cognitive disorders report owning smartphones and using them frequently. Figure 5.3 illustrates data from 40 patients visiting a neuropsychology clinic who reported owning a smartphone and using it every day for email, internet browsing, and taking photos (Benge et al., 2020). More interesting was that 30% of these patients reported using the cognitive-aid features of their phones every day (e.g. calendar and reminder apps), which was triple the proportion observed in an age-matched healthy control group. These findings indicate that individuals with cognitive impairment can use smart technology, and that many of them are already using this technology to assist with everyday prospective memory tasks (Ferguson et al., 2015; El Haj et al., 2017). What is needed are studies that objectively measure the outcomes of technology-assisted

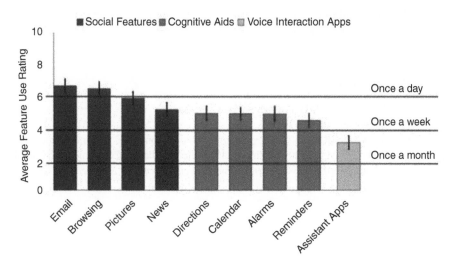

Figure 5.3 Reported use of social, cognitive, and voice interaction apps amongst cognitively impaired patients who own smartphones (data were adapted from Benge et al., 2020)

prospective memory, and studies that can identify the best means to train patients and caregivers who do not already have expertise with the cognitive-supportive features of smartphones. Furthermore, while technology-based reminder studies would seem well-suited to prevent omission errors, they may unintentionally increase risk for commission errors (e.g. receive a technology-supported reminder after having performed the intention earlier than expected). Such technology-supported behavioural clinical trials are currently underway (e.g. NCT03384043).

CONCLUSION

A combination of top-down and bottom-up processes is necessary in order to encode, retrieve, and deactivate prospective memory intentions. Without the successful coordination of such complex processes, we fail to pack what is needed for trips, we miss highway exit signs, and we double-dose on medications (or omit them altogether). Certainly, there are many ways in which prospective memory can 'go wrong', yet lost in the focus on prospective memory forgetting is that most intentions *are remembered*, even those intentions in which there are hours or days interleaved between formation and retrieval, and without any explicit external prompting to try to remember. Furthermore, there are many routes to improving prospective memory – from mnemonic strategies, to training, to technology-supportive devices – and these approaches are showing benefits even in clinical populations. Thus, the future is bright for both the mechanistic and translational investigation of how we 'remember to remember'.

Further Reading

Kliegel, M., & Martin, M. (2003). Prospective memory research: Why is it relevant? *International Journal of Psychology*, 38(4), 193–194.

Rummel, J., & McDaniel, M. A. (2019). *Prospective Memory*. Abingdon: Taylor & Francis.

Shelton, J. T., & Scullin, M. K. (2017). The dynamic interplay between bottom-up and top-down processes supporting prospective remembering. *Current Directions in Psychological Science*, 26, 352–358.

6

POSTHYPNOTIC AMNESIA

Using hypnosis to induce forgetting

John F. Kihlstrom

Following an appropriate suggestion and the termination of hypnosis, some people cannot remember the things they did or experienced while they were hypnotised. Along with eye closure and the generally relaxed appearance of the typical subject, this posthypnotic amnesia (PHA) helped give hypnosis its name, by analogy to amnesia for the events that transpire during a night's sleep. The analogy is imperfect, however. PHA does not occur spontaneously, and it can be cancelled by the administration of a pre-arranged reversibility cue. Along with hypnotic analgesia, PHA is perhaps the most thoroughly studied of all hypnotic phenomena (for earlier reviews, see Cooper, 1979; Kihlstrom & Evans, 1979; Spanos, 1986; Huesmann et al., 1987; Coe, 1989; Mazzoni et al., 2014).[1]

PHA most closely resembles the 'functional' amnesias, occurring in the absence of palpable brain insult, injury, or disease. Historically associated with 'hysteria' (Kihlstrom, 1994), these syndromes now go under the general rubric of the dissociative disorders (Kihlstrom, 2005a). In dissociative amnesia, formerly known as psychogenic amnesia, the patient cannot consciously remember events from some period in his or her past. In dissociative fugue, patients lose the entirety of their autobiographical memories, and lose or change their identity as well. In dissociative identity disorder, formerly known as multiple personality disorder, the patient embodies two or more identities, which alternate in control of conscious experience, thought and action; each 'alter ego' comes with its own fund of autobiographical memories; the amnesia which separates the different identities may be symmetrical or asymmetrical. Genuine instances of these functional disorders of memory are rare and often evanescent – Thigpen and Cleckley, who famously described *The Three Faces of Eve*, never saw another convincing case of multiple personality disorder (Thigpen & Cleckley, 1984). Still, dissociative amnesia has been a source of fascination since the time of William James (James, 1890/1980, 1902/1985; see also Taylor, 1983), and PHA has served as a sort of laboratory model for understanding its underlying processes (Kihlstrom, 1979; Kihlstrom & McGlynn, 1991; Oakley, 1999; Barnier, 2002).

SPONTANEOUS AND SUGGESTED POSTHYPNOTIC AMNESIA

The roots of modern hypnosis lie in the practices of Franz Anton Mesmer (1734–1815), a German physician who employed a technique he called 'animal magnetism' to treat various illnesses. In 1784, Mesmer's theory was discredited by two investigations commissioned by King Louis XVI of France – one of which, consisting of members of the Royal Academy of Science and the Faculty of Medicine of the University of Paris, and chaired by Benjamin Franklin, conducted what may have been the first controlled psychological experiments (*avant la lettre*, as psychology was not considered to be a science at the

---

[1] PHA frequently (but not necessarily) accompanies response to posthypnotic suggestions – so that, in the classic case, the subjects involved do not know what they are doing, or why (Sheehan & Orne, 1968; Barnier & McConkey, 1998).

time), and concluded that the effects of mesmerism were due to 'imagination' rather than any physical force (Kihlstrom, 2002b). But Mesmer's cures were not discredited, and so 'mesmerism' and 'animal magnetism' continued to be practised on the Continent, and in Britain, and America (Tinterow, 1970; Gauld, 1992). The Franklin Commission took no note of amnesia, which was first described by the Marquis de Puysegur, a disciple of Mesmer's, only later in 1784 (Laurence & Perry, 1988). But the second commission, composed of representatives of the Royal Academy of Medicine, did. A minority report concluded that some of the effects of mesmerism, including amnesia for events occurring during the mesmeric trance, could not be attributed to imagination.

James Braid, the British physician who coined the term 'hypnosis' and offered the first psychological theory of the phenomenon (Kihlstrom, 1992; Yeates, 2018a, 2018b), observed amnesia, along with eyelid catalepsy and insensitivity to external stimuli, during a demonstration of animal magnetism by Charles LaFontaine (1803–1892), an itinerant mesmerist, in 1841. Charles Richet (1850–1935), the Nobel Prize-winning physician who is credited with initiating modern interest in hypnosis, claimed that amnesia was characteristic of the state of *somnambulism provoke*, in which the subject is highly responsive to suggestion. Similarly, Jean-Martin Charcot (1825–1893), the great French neurologist, asserted that amnesia was characteristic of somnambulism, the third and deepest stage of *grand hypnotisme*.

In each of these instances, PHA appeared to occur spontaneously, without any specific suggestion being made by the hypnotist. Even Hippolyte Bernheim (1840–1919), a French physician who opposed Charcot's physiological ideas, and argued that most hypnotic phenomena were the product of suggestion, nevertheless believed that amnesia was an exception. Still, Joseph Delboeuf (1831–1896) and J. Milne Bramwell (1852–1925), two prominent turn-of-the-century authorities, both argued that 'spontaneous' amnesia usually occurred as a result of indirect or subtle suggestion – including what we would now call the 'demand characteristics' (Orne, 1962) of the hypnotic situation. Their view has come to prevail. In his pioneering experimental work, Young (1926) performed a direct comparison, finding that PHA was denser following direct suggestion. Reviewing the then-nascent experimental literature on hypnosis, he concluded that PHA was a product of suggestion, including autosuggestion (Young, 1927, 1928, 1931), a position endorsed by Hull (1933).

On the standardised scales now used to measure hypnotisability, PHA is much more likely to occur as the result of suggestion (Hilgard & Cooper, 1965). When it does appear to occur spontaneously, this is likely due to the subject's misunderstanding of instructions, or to pre-existing beliefs about hypnosis (including the analogy to sleep), and the resulting expectation that amnesia will occur. Alternatively, the subject may inadvertently have fallen asleep during the hypnotic session – especially in group hypnosis, with its necessarily limited monitoring by the hypnotist. Patients with chronic schizophrenia appear to respond positively to suggestions for PHA, but their initial forgetting does not reverse, and is more likely a result of distractibility or some other attentional impairment (Lieberman et al., 1978). Such instances are properly classified as 'pseudoamnesia', and should not be confused with the real thing.

The fact that PHA occurs as a result of suggestion does not impeach the memory failure as counterfeit. Hypnotic analgesia also occurs only as a result of suggestion, but very few investigators doubt that it is genuine. The fact is that all of the phenomena in the domain of hypnosis occur as a result of suggestion (Hilgard, 1973; Kihlstrom, 2008), which is why hypnosis is grist for the mills of both cognitive and social psychologists (Kihlstrom, 1978, 1986, 2003).

POSTHYPNOTIC AMNESIA AND HYPNOTISABILITY

Even those 19th-century authorities who believed that amnesia occurred spontaneously acknowledged that it was characteristic only of the 'deepest' level of hypnosis. The introduction in the mid-20th century of standardised scales for the assessment of hypnotisability enabled different laboratories to compare their results directly with each other, and helped put the study of hypnosis on a firm empirical foundation. The most commonly used instruments for this purpose are the individually administered Stanford Hypnotic Susceptibility Scales, Forms A, B, and C (SHSS: A, B, C), and the Harvard Group Scale of Hypnotic Susceptibility, Form A (HGSHS: A), a modification of SHSS: A for group administration. All of these scales begin with a formal induction of hypnosis, usually including suggestions for eye fixation, relaxation, and eye closure, followed by a series of suggestions for various hypnotic phenomena. Response to each of these suggestions is scored according to objective behavioural criteria. Prior to the termination of hypnosis, the subjects receive a suggestion that they will be unable to remember what they did or experienced during hypnosis, until the experimenter gives a reversibility cue, such as 'Now you can remember everything'. After the termination of hypnosis, subjects are asked to recall the various test suggestions twice: once while the amnesia suggestion is in effect, and again after the amnesia has been cancelled. According to the standardised objective scoring criterion, subjects pass PHA if they report three or fewer items (out of nine on SHSS: A/B or HGSHS: A; out of eleven on SHSS: C) on the initial amnesia test. Taking account of performance on the reversibility test, of course, helps distinguish suggested PHA from mere forgetfulness and other forms of pseudoamnesia (Kihlstrom & Register, 1984).

PHA, so measured, is highly correlated with hypnotisability (Hilgard, 1965; Kihlstrom & Register, 1984). As depicted in Figure 6.1, subjects who are classified as high in hypnotisability recall fewer items during PHA than those who score in the low range. The correlation between hypnotisability and initial recall falls to zero in the absence of an amnesia suggestion (Hilgard & Cooper, 1965) – clear evidence that spontaneous amnesia does not belong in the domain of hypnosis, and likely reflects little more than ordinary forgetting. Even when hypnotisable subjects recall enough items to fail the standard criterion for amnesia, their memories often have a vague, fragmentary, generic quality to them (e.g. 'Something about my hands'), lacking particular details of the event in question (Kihlstrom & Evans, 1978).

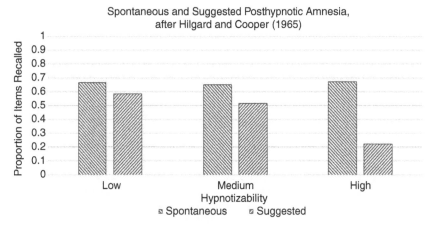

Figure 6.1 Initial test of posthypnotic recall, with and without suggestions for amnesia, after Hilgard and Cooper (1965)

PHA is induced by suggestion, and it is also cancelled by suggestion, in the form of the pre-arranged reversibility cue (Kihlstrom & Evans, 1976). Figure 6.2 shows that, on a subsequent reversibility test, hypnotisable subjects recover more new memories than insusceptible ones do. This is not simply due to suppressed performance on the initial amnesia test, a kind of regression artefact. This is because lows who nonetheless pass the criterion for initial amnesia (for whatever reason) show less recovery than highs do. In addition, subjects who showed generic recall during amnesia are now able to remember their experiences in more detail (Kihlstrom & Evans, 1978).

Despite reversibility, there sometimes remains a residual amnesia, which is also more prominent in hypnotisable than insusceptible subjects (Kihlstrom & Evans, 1977). As Figure 6.2 also shows, even after reversibility hypnotisable subjects who passed the test for initial amnesia recall fewer hypnotic experiences than those who did not. It is unlikely that this difference reflects ordinary forgetfulness, because response to amnesia suggestions is uncorrelated with performance on a battery of standard tests of short- and long-term memory (Kihlstrom & Twersky, 1978). If anything, hypnotisable amnesic subjects show superior performance on long-term memory compared to their nonamnesic counterparts.

While amnesia is routinely assessed in the context of the standardised hypnotisability scales of hypnotisability, it is also possible to employ standard verbal-learning paradigms in which subjects study a list of words while hypnotised. This strategy loses some of the ecological validity that may attend memories for actual hypnotic experiences, but it avoids other potential problems. For example, memory for hypnotic suggestions may be affected by whether subjects are surprised, pleased, or disappointed by their responses to particular suggestions, resulting in Zeigarnik or Von Restorff effects (Hilgard & Hommel, 1961; Pettinati et al., 1981). Nevertheless, suggestions for PHA are as effective with wordlists as they are with actual hypnotic experiences, provided that the subjects are highly

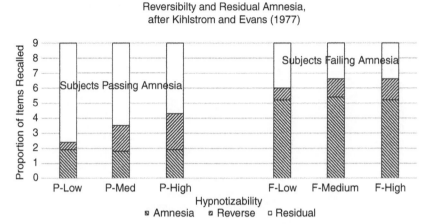

Figure 6.2 Posthypnotic amnesia, reversibility, and residual amnesia in subjects classified by hypnotisability and initial amnesia, after Kihlstrom and Evans (1977)

hypnotisable. This allows investigators to employ standard paradigms from the literature on human learning and memory in the study of PHA.

Figure 6.3 shows the results of an experiment in which subjects memorised a list of 15 familiar words to a strict criterion of learning, and then received a suggestion for PHA (Kihlstrom, 1980). An initial free-recall test revealed a dense PHA on the part of the more hypnotisable subjects, and little memory impairment in subjects of low or medium hypnotisability; after the amnesia suggestion was cancelled, full memory was restored to the hypnotisable subjects. In this experiment, and many others using verbal-learning paradigms, there was no residual amnesia, probably owing to the strict criterion of learning achieved during the study phase.

Aside from administering the pre-arranged reversibility cue, is there anything that can be done to gain access to the memories forgotten during PHA? To some extent, PHA may dissipate over time: if a second test is inserted after the initial amnesia test, but before administration of the reversibility cue, some new memories are often recovered – though still more are recovered after the reversibility cue (Kihlstrom et al., 1980, 1983). However, this gain in memory may not be time dependent. Rather, it may be a variant on the well-known testing effect, by which an initial test of memory improves performance on later tests.

Exhortations to recall more items, and instructions for honesty in reporting memories, have no more effect than a simple uninstructed retest (Kihlstrom et al., 1980). Some breaching of amnesia does occur in subjects who expect that such attempts will be successful (Spanos et al., 1984; Silva & Kirsch, 1987). Breaching also occurs in subjects who rate themselves as voluntarily controlling recall (Howard & Coe, 1980; Schuyler & Coe, 1989), but such individuals are a minority among highly hypnotisable subjects

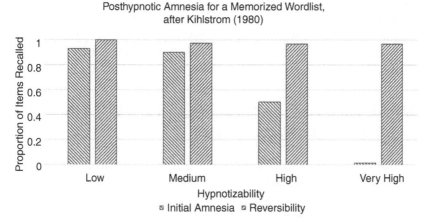

Figure 6.3 Free recall of wordlist memorised during hypnosis, during suggested amnesia and following the reversibility cue, after Kihlstrom (1980, Experiment 1)

(Bowers, 1981, 1982; Bowers et al., 1988). Like other hypnotic phenomena, PHA is usually experienced as an involuntary 'happening', rather than a voluntary 'doing' (Sarbin, 2002), so that subjects are often surprised when it occurs (Shor et al., 1984). Honesty demands have little effect on response to hypnotic suggestions in general, though they can have profound effects on other conditions to which hypnosis is often compared (Bowers, 1967; Bates, 1992).

Characterisation of hypnosis as an altered state of consciousness (Kallio & Revonsuo, 2003; Gruzelier, 2005; Kihlstrom, 2005b, 2018) has sometimes prompted the suggestion that PHA is a form of state-dependent memory (SDM). Consistent with the encoding specificity principle in memory, there is some evidence that suggestions for PHA are more effective for material learned before, rather than during, hypnosis (Smith et al., 1998). However, the reversibility cue does not re-induce hypnosis, and subjects do not show enhanced suggestibility or other signs of hypnosis while executing other posthypnotic suggestions (Reyher & Smyth, 1971). Some researchers have studied *hypnotic* rather than *posthypnotic* amnesia, giving suggestions for amnesia that are tested while subjects are still hypnotised (Spanos & Bodorik, 1977), and it is also possible to give suggestions of amnesia for events that occurred before hypnosis was induced (Barnier et al., 2001). These procedural variants produce effects that are equivalent to traditional PHA for events occurring during hypnosis: taken together, they suggest that PHA is not an instance of SDM. Empirically, the re-induction of hypnosis has no effect on memory in amnesic subjects, over and above a simple retest conducted posthypnotically (Kihlstrom et al., 1985).

Ordinarily, an experimenter would not let a subject leave the laboratory until all hypnotic and posthypnotic suggestions had been cancelled. Nevertheless, the question of the persistence of posthypnotic suggestions endures in the literature. PHA has been reported to last for as long as one year (Wells, 1940). However, the duration of the effect, as with all hypnotic and posthypnotic suggestions, will depend on the hypnotisability of the subject, the precise wording of the suggestion, the subject's understanding of the experimenter's intent, the cognitive load imposed by the suggestion, and other considerations (Damaser et al., 2010).

COMPARISON TO DIRECTED FORGETTING AND THOUGHT SUPPRESSION

There is a long history of comparing hypnosis with a 'task-motivation' condition in which unhypnotised subjects are exhorted to think and imagine with the themes of the suggestions they are given, and to try their best to do what is asked of them (Barber, 1969). This body of research includes some studies of PHA (Barber & Calverley, 1966; Thorne, 1969; Spanos et al., 1980), but task-motivation instructions and similar procedures are known to be heavily laced with behavioural compliance (Bowers, 1967; Spanos & Barber, 1968; Bowers & Gilmore, 1969; Bates et al., 1988; Bates, 1992), and will not be considered further here.

In some respects, PHA resembles the 'directed', 'instructed', or 'positive' forgetting (DF) observed in the normal waking state (Bjork, 1978; Golding & MacLeod, 1998; Sahakyan et al., 2013; see also Groome, Eysenck, & Law in Chapter 9 of this volume). A number of studies have compared PHA and DF, but various procedural differences between PHA and the various forms of DF make direct comparison difficult (Kihlstrom, 1983; Kihlstrom & Barnhardt, 1993). The DF paradigm most closely resembling PHA involves post-input cuing by item sets, which appears to involve some sort of retrieval inhibition (Anderson & Levy, 2009). In a head-to-head comparison, depicted in Figure 6.4, Basden and her colleagues found that PHA produced more forgetting than DF; forgetting in PHA, but not in DF, was correlated with hypnotisability, and after PHA was cancelled hypnotisable subjects produced more new target memories than their counterparts did after the DF instruction was cancelled (Basden et al., 1994). David and colleagues also found that PHA was correlated with hypnotisability, but DF was not (David et al., 2000).

A related phenomenon is thought suppression (TS), except that what is being suppressed is an idea rather than an episodic memory. In a series of provocative experiments, *Wegner and his colleagues* found that asking subjects to suppress a thought – for example, not to think about a white bear – led to a paradoxical enhancement of thoughts concerning the proscribed topic, and a further increase after the injunction was lifted – a phenomenon called 'ironic rebound' (Wegner, 1992; Abramowitz et al., 2001). However, in another comparative study, Bowers and Woody (1996) found that subjects given hypnotic suggestions for thought suppression displayed neither paradoxical enhancement nor ironic rebound (see Figure 6.5). In contrast to the hypnotic condition, nonhypnotic thought suppression was not correlated with hypnotisability. Whereas subjects in the thought

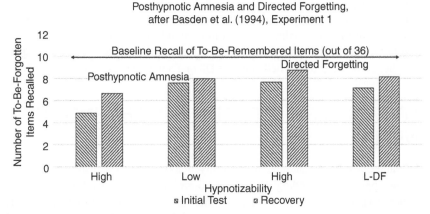

Figure 6.4 Comparison of posthypnotic amnesia and directed forgetting for subjects classified by hypnotisability, after Basden et al. (1994, Experiment 1)

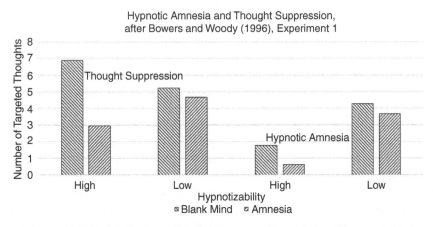

Figure 6.5 Comparison of posthypnotic amnesia and thought suppression for subjects classified by hypnotisability, after Bowers and Woody (1996, Experiment 1)

suppression condition reported that they experienced considerable difficulty in keeping the unwanted thoughts out of mind, the hypnotic subjects had little trouble doing so. Taken together, these findings indicate that PHA, DF, and TS are very different phenomena, with different underlying mechanisms.

Interestingly, PHA enhances performance on an attention-demanding random-number-generation task. When asked to generate random numbers, subjects tend to make some consistent errors, such as not repeating digits frequently enough – a phenomenon known as 'repetition avoidance'. However, Terhune and Brugger (2011) found that a posthypnotic suggestion to forget previously generated digits improves performance for a subset of highly hypnotisable subjects who also report a strong tendency to have dissociative experiences – mostly by reducing repetition avoidance. Repetition avoidance was observed in the absence of the amnesia suggestion, and it returned when the suggestion was cancelled. It is not known whether either DF or TS would provide the same advantage.

RETRIEVAL DISRUPTION IN POSTHYPNOTIC AMNESIA

Residual amnesia notwithstanding, reversibility marks PHA as a disruption of memory retrieval, as opposed to encoding or storage – a problem of accessibility, not availability (Orne, 1966; Evans & Kihlstrom, 1973). To understand the mechanisms underlying PHA, a number of researchers turned to information-processing theories of memory. Both traditional two-stage theories of retrieval (e.g. Watkins & Gardiner, 1979) and levels-of-processing theory (Lockhart et al., 1976) motivate a comparison of recall and recognition testing. According to two-stage theory, successful recall requires both the generation and recognition processes, while recognition testing obviates the generation process. In levels of processing theory, the more cues presented at the time of retrieval, the higher the probability of finding overlap with those features processed at the time of encoding. According to Tulving's (1976) theory of 'episodic ecphory', recall and recognition differ only quantitatively, in terms of the informational value of the retrieval cues presented to the subject.

In any event, research is unanimous that PHA is densest when assessed with free recall as opposed to cued recall or recognition tests (Williamsen et al., 1965; Kihlstrom & Shor, 1978; Allen et al., 1995, 1996). Remarkably, however, some hypnotisable subjects remain amnesic even after viewing a videotape of themselves responding to a series of hypnotic suggestions – what must be the most informative retrieval cues imaginable (McConkey et al., 1980; McConkey & Sheehan, 1981).

Figure 6.6 shows the results of an experiment in which subjects memorised a list of 16 words consisting of four items from each of four categories, followed by tests of free recall, cued recall, and recognition conducted during PHA, and a final test of free recall following administration of the reversibility cue (Kihlstrom, 2019b). A control group who learned the material, and were tested, in the normal waking state scored perfectly on each test. The initial recall test revealed a dense amnesia. Memory during amnesia progressively improved with the provision of additional retrieval cues, but was fully restored to free recall only following the reversibility cue – a variant, perhaps, on the recognition failure of recallable words.

Interestingly, subjects who have been instructed to simulate hypnosis perform worse on recognition tests than real hypnotic subjects do – even scoring below chance levels (Williamsen et al., 1965; Barber & Calverley, 1966; Spanos et al., 1990). The demand characteristics of the hypnotic situation are clear: subjects are not supposed to remember what they did during hypnosis, and it should not matter how their memory is tested. That recognition is

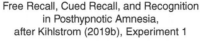

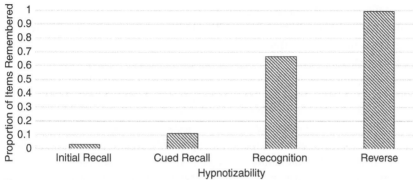

Figure 6.6 Comparison of initial free recall, cued recall, recognition during posthypnotic amnesia, and free recall following the reversibility cue, after Kihlstrom (2019b, Experiment 1)

superior to recall during PHA reassures us on two points: first, that hypnotic subjects are doing something other than responding to the demand characteristics of the experimental situation; and second, that even PHA does not violate the basic principles of memory.

ORGANISATION OF MEMORY IN POSTHYPNOTIC AMNESIA

The discovery of organisation in recall, whether by associative or categorical clustering or some other subjective relationship, was one of the signal events in the cognitive revolution in the study of human learning and memory. According to at least some versions of generate-recognise theory, recall succeeds to the extent that it is organised. However, testing the hypothesis that retrieval is disorganised in PHA entails a sort of paradox: when amnesia is complete, the subjects do not recall enough material to test for organisation. Accordingly, this line of research has focused on subjects who recall at least some of the to-be-remembered material – but who, by virtue of their relatively high hypnotisability, can be assumed to be experiencing at least the partial effects of the amnesia suggestion.

Initial studies of disorganised retrieval focused on temporal organisation – that is, the tendency of subjects to recall events in the order in which they occurred. This organisational rubric seems natural for a sequence of events, such as the items of the standardised scales of hypnotisability. In recounting their experiences while hypnotised, after all, subjects are essentially constructing a narrative – a story with a beginning, a middle, and an end. Moreover, the wording of the amnesia test on the standardised scales

('Please tell me everything that happened since you began looking at the target') implies that subjects should begin at the beginning and proceed through to the end. As Figure 6.7 shows, hypnotisable subjects are less likely, compared to subjects of low or moderate hypnotisability, to recall the test suggestions in the order in which they occurred (Evans & Kihlstrom, 1973; Kihlstrom & Evans, 1979). If the amnesia suggestion has been omitted from the scale, there is no difference between the groups in temporal organisation if the amnesia suggestion (Kihlstrom & Evans, 1979).

Embedding standard verbal-learning procedures in a hypnotic context permits examination of the fate of other forms of organisation in PHA. Figure 6.8 compares serial organisation with category clustering and subjective organisation. Consistent with the findings from the standardised scales, subjects who organised the list sequentially during the memorisation phase showed a disruption in temporal sequencing during PHA, which was restored after the amnesia suggestion was cancelled (Kihlstrom & Wilson, 1984). However, the same pattern was not observed with category clustering or subjective organisation (Wilson & Kihlstrom, 1986).

Taken as a whole, these results suggest that there may be something special about temporal organisation and its disruption in PHA. At the same time, some controversies remain with regard to the organisation of recall in PHA (Kihlstrom & Wilson, 1988; Spanos et al., 1988). Some studies have failed to find the disorganisation effect on seriation, while another study found a decrement in subjective organisation, once overlearning enabled subjects to achieve higher levels of organisation prior to the amnesia suggestion. Other studies have found disorganised clustering. Another set of experiments found that

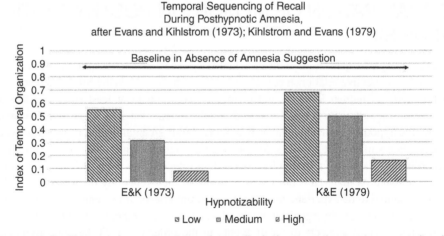

Figure 6.7 Temporal sequencing of recall during posthypnotic amnesia, for subjects classified by hypnotisability. Left panel: after Evans and Kihlstrom (1973); Right panel: after Kihlstrom and Evans (1979). Baseline temporal sequencing, without amnesia suggestion, after Kihlstrom and Evans (1979).

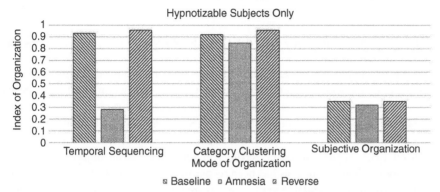

Figure 6.8 Organisation of recall for wordlists memorised during hypnosis. Left panel: temporal sequencing, after Kihlstrom and Wilson (1984). Centre panel: category clustering; Right panel: Subjective organisation, both after Wilson and Kihlstrom (1986).

suggestions to forget only one category of items had no effect on recall, or clustering, of the remaining items, suggesting that categorical organisation remained intact (Davidson & Bowers, 1991). At present, methodological differences among the studies preclude firm conclusions about the fate of organisation during PHA.

In its original formulation, the disorganisation hypothesis did not distinguish between seriation and other forms of organisation, such as clustering. Given the availability of large amounts of data from the standardised scales, and the item-by-item structure of the typical experience of hypnosis, temporal sequencing was simply a convenient – not to mention ecologically valid – place to begin understanding the mechanisms underlying genuine retrieval failure. An alternative 'social-cognitive' view construes hypnosis as a special case of strategic role-enactment: subjects respond positively to amnesia suggestions by failing to attend to appropriate retrieval cues, failing to employ appropriate retrieval strategies, or simply failing to report items that they remember perfectly well – all in the service of presenting themselves as 'good' hypnotic subjects (Wagstaff, 1977; Spanos, 1986). The social-cognitive account of PHA would seem to be indifferent to the particular form of organisation being studied. On the other hand, the failure of Wilson and Kihlstrom (1986) to find a disruption in either category clustering or subjective organisation, despite the use of procedures identical to those that yielded a substantial effect on seriation (Kihlstrom & Wilson, 1984), suggests that temporal disorganisation may play a special role in PHA. Even subjective organisation can sometimes involve temporal organisation: linking unrelated items into a story or image is a familiar mnemonic device with an underlying temporal structure; and alphabetisation, another popular form of subjective organisation, counts as a special form of seriation.

Perhaps subjective organisation is disrupted when it is essentially serial in nature, but not otherwise. This hypothesis remains to be tested.

IMPLICIT MEMORY IN POSTHYPNOTIC AMNESIA

It is one thing to fail to remember something, but quite another for the forgotten material to continue to dynamically influence experience, thought, and action, even in the absence of conscious recollection. It turns out that PHA impairs conscious recollection, but spares what has come to be known as implicit memory (Schacter, 1987; Kihlstrom et al., 2017). Hints of a dissociation between explicit and implicit memory appeared even in the earliest research on PHA, which employed savings in relearning as an objective measure of memory. Savings in relearning, as has been recognised since its invention by Ebbinghaus, is sensitive to memories available in storage that are not consciously accessible. In the first study of the type, Young (1926) noted that hypnotic subjects typically showed substantial savings in relearning material which they could not remember learning during hypnosis. Strickler, working in Hull's laboratory, confirmed Young's findings in a more extensive and thoroughly documented study (Hull, 1933). While hypnotised, subjects mastered a list of paired-associate nonsense material presented on the memory drum that Hull himself invented (Kihlstrom, 2004). On a 'reinstatement-recall' test, hypnotic subjects gave the correct response to only about 3% of items, on average, compared to about 84% correct for a control series studied and tested in the normal waking state. Nevertheless, these densely amnesic subjects showed approximately 48% savings in relearning, versus 98% for the waking control series.

Other experiments from Hull's laboratory yielded much the same results (for a comprehensive overview, see Hull, 1933). Coors obtained about 38% savings in relearning of a stylus maze compared with 83% in control subjects. Patten found that a period of practice in hypnosis, covered by PHA, did not interfere with cumulative practice effects in mental addition, while Life obtained similar findings for rehearsal effects on memory for nonsense syllables. Mitchell discovered that PHA did not abolish retroactive interference effects. Scott found no effect of PHA on conditioned responses acquired during hypnosis. The amplitude of the conditioned response was somewhat reduced, but this was likely confounded with extinction during repeated testing of response to the conditioned stimulus.[2]

Interpretation of all these experiments is complicated by the fact that during these experiments amnesia was not specifically suggested to the subjects. But only a little: as Hull

---

[2] Stern, Edmonston, and their colleagues found that PHA abolished habituation to a tone stimulus, as measured by the electrodermal orienting response (Stern et al., 1963). Although thus would seem to contradict Scott's findings, it appears that most of Stern et al.'s subjects were not actually amnesic. Instead, they distorted either their memory of the habituation stimulus, or their perception of the test stimulus – for example, by transforming the tone into a buzzer.

himself noted (p. 133, fn. 2), all of these subjects were highly selected for hypnotisability. All had demonstrated suggested PHA in previous laboratory sessions, so it can be assumed that the subjects expected to be amnesic during the experiments in question, and Hull makes clear that all of the subjects in his group's experiments showed complete PHA as tested by recall.

Subsequent research employing explicit suggestions for PHA has generally confirmed the findings of the earlier experiments. In a study of retroactive inhibition, Graham and Patton (1968) had subjects learn a list of adjectives in the normal waking state. Two groups then learned a second list while hypnotised, followed by suggestions either for complete amnesia or complete recall; a third group learned the interpolated list in the normal waking state, with no suggestion. Compared to control subjects who had no exposure to the second list, all three experimental groups showed a significant diminution of savings in relearning the original list; the amount of loss did not differ significantly among them (Figure 6.9). Coe et al. (1976) also observed substantial levels of retroactive interference during PHA.

Source amnesia, another expression of implicit memory, was initially discovered and named in the context of research on PHA. Evans and Thorn (1966) found that some amnesic subjects retained world knowledge which they had learned incidentally during hypnosis (e.g. the colour an amethyst turns when exposed to heat, or the difference between the antennae of moths and butterflies), although they did not remember the circumstances in which they acquired this information. It is possible to suggest source amnesia (Cooper, 1966), but in the initial study by Evans and Thorn, the phenomenon occurred spontaneously in subjects who had been given the usual suggestion for PHA. In a later study, Evans (1979) showed that source amnesia did not occur in insusceptible subjects who simulated hypnosis and PHA. Although the methodology of Evans' study has

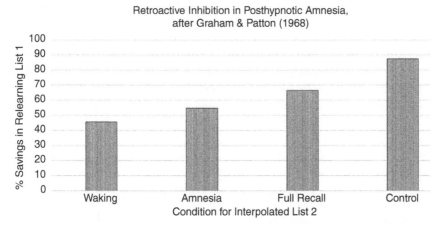

Figure 6.9 Retroactive inhibition during and after posthypnotic amnesia, compared to waking and control conditions, after Graham and Patton (1968)

been criticised (Coe, 1978; Wagstaff, 1981; Spanos et al., 1988), most of these criticisms pertain to the real–simulating comparison, and do not undermine the phenomenon itself. Along with the notion of demand characteristics (Kihlstrom, 2002a; Orne, 1962), source amnesia is one of the most salient examples of a concept emerging from hypnosis research that has become part of the common parlance of psychological theory.[3]

Source amnesia might be implicated in research by Huesmann et al. (1987) on PHA. In their first experiment, hypnotised subjects solved a series of problems adapted from the Luchins 'water jar' paradigm, followed by a suggestion for PHA. Despite recalling very little of the learning experience, they displayed a clear problem-solving set on test items, employing an algorithm learned during hypnosis, even though a simpler algorithm would have sufficed. In another experiment, subjects listened to a story about either baseball or a cave; following a suggestion for PHA, they were asked to free-associate to homographs such as *bat*. Examination of their responses indicated that their interpretation of the homographs was biased by the story they had heard, even though they could not remember the story itself.

Research employing psychophysiological measures of memory also indicates that implicit memory is spared during PHA. Bitterman and Marcuse (1945), working with only a single subject over multiple trials in a lie-detector situation, suggested PHA for single words presented during hypnosis. Experienced polygraphers were able to identify the target words on a majority of trials – on all trials, in fact, allowing for second guesses. This outcome does not necessarily mean that the subject was being deceptive; indeed, as the authors noted, the results might indicate a 'dissociation' (p. 251) between conscious recognition and autonomic indices of memory that operate outside conscious awareness. This possibility is strengthened in a study by Kinnunen et al. (1994), who examined skin conductance responses during a posthypnotic interview. They concluded that hypnotic subjects were being truthful when discussing their responses to hypnotic suggestions, including PHA, while subjects simulating hypnosis typically showed physiological signs of deception.

In the most extensive psychophysiological investigation of PHA to date, Allen and his colleagues (Allen et al., 1995; Schnyer & Allen, 1995) examined five peak components of the event-related potential (ERP). They found a pattern of response during PHA that distinguished highly hypnotisable, amnesic subjects from both insusceptible, nonamnesic subjects and simulators; the latter two groups did not differ significantly. The differences

---

[3] Source amnesia had been famously observed in an amnesic patient by Claparede (1911/1951; see also Kihlstrom, 1995), but not named as such. Evans and Thorn (1966) also noted that their findings had been anticipated by Banister and Zangwill (1941a, 1941b), who used hypnotic suggestion to produce visual and olfactory 'paramnesias' in which subjects recognise a previously studied item but confabulate the context in which it has been studied. Even earlier, Young (1926, p. 352) had noted that one of the subjects in his experiment on savings in relearning 'retained all the associations but did not remember when he had learned them'. Another subject, remarking on his ability to produce the correct associations, said that 'they just come'.

between amnesic and nonamnesic subjects disappeared after the amnesia suggestion was cancelled. Taken together with differences in response latencies between amnesic subjects and simulators, Allen et al. suggested that their findings were indicative of 'recognition without awareness' (p. 427), analogous to the psychophysiological findings common in studies of prosopagnosia.

Savings in relearning, retroactive (and proactive) interference, source amnesia, classical conditioning, and physiological response all count as examples of implicit memory, because none of them require conscious access to the episodic memories which give rise to these effects. But as the concept of implicit memory has evolved, priming has emerged as the gold standard. Priming occurs when one task, such as studying a word (the prime), influences performance on another task, such as free association (the target). When the one task facilitates task performance, we speak of positive priming; negative priming occurs when the first task impairs performance on the second. Most research on implicit memory in general, and all of the research on implicit memory in PHA, has involved positive priming.

Priming as an aspect of implicit memory in PHA was first observed, though not labelled as such, in a pair of studies employing free-association and category-generation tasks (Kihlstrom, 1980; see also Kihlstrom, 2019a). Figure 6.10 depicts the major results. In the first experiment, hypnotised subjects memorised a list of words, such as *girl*, that were strong associates of other words, like *boy*, followed by a suggestion for PHA. Highly hypnotisable subjects performed very poorly on a free-recall test administered while the amnesia suggestion was in effect, but continued to use the list items as responses on a word-association test. In a second experiment, in which subjects memorised lists

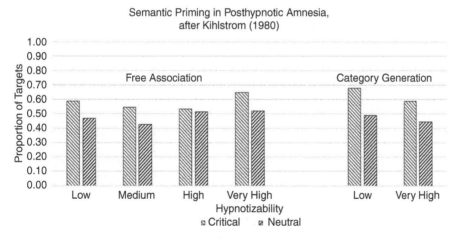

Figure 6.10 Semantic priming on free association and category generation tests during posthypnotic amnesia for subjects classified by hypnotisability, after Kihlstrom (1980, Experiments 1 and 2)

consisting of highly salient category instances, such as *foot*, highly hypnotisable subjects were densely amnesic on the test of free recall, but still used the list items when asked to generate instances of categories such as *part of the human body*. More important, the amnesic subjects were *more likely* to generate list items as free associates and category instances, compared to carefully matched items that had not been learned.

This study had been explicitly modelled on an earlier experiment by Williamsen et al. (1965), who observed, but did not comment on, similar priming effects in both free association and partial-word completion (Figure 6.11). Barber and Calverley (1966), in a replication and extension of Williamsen et al., likewise found, but did not comment on, spared priming in partial-word completion. Later studies found preserved priming on a free-association test (Spanos et al., 1982), and on a homophone-spelling test (Bertrand et al.,1990), confirming the earlier results. They also showed that an alternative suggestion, that subjects would be 'unable to bring these words to mind, unable to think of or remember them in any way' (p. 568), actually suppressed the production of target items, and increased the response latency for those that were produced. This effect on semantic memory, as opposed to episodic memory, is more properly termed *agnosia* rather than amnesia. Hypnotic agnosia is an understudied phenomenon that warrants treatment in a different chapter, in a different book.

Priming comes in two general forms. Repetition priming is based on a perception-based representation of the prime, and is mediated by its physical resemblance to the target. Semantic priming is based on a meaning-based representation, and is mediated by semantic similarity. While most research on implicit memory in the amnesic syndrome and other forms of 'organic' amnesia focuses on repetition priming, the studies of priming in free association and category-generation tasks entail semantic priming.

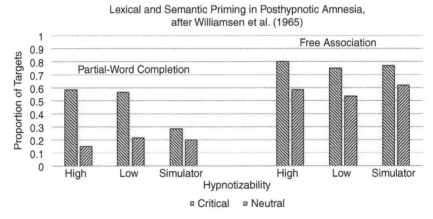

Figure 6.11 Lexical (partial-word completion) and semantic priming (on free association) during posthypnotic amnesia for hypnotisable and insusceptible subjects, and insusceptible simulators, after Williamsen et al. (1965)

Partial-word completion is often considered to be an instance of repetition priming, but in the Williamsen et al. and Barber-Calverley studies, the situation is somewhat ambiguous. In both experiments, the items were presented for study aurally, but the completion test was visual. Given the cross-modal nature of the situation, the priming might better be construed as lexical in nature, based on abstract stored representations of the items in question – in any event, something more complex than repetition priming.

Although these priming effects appear to demonstrate a dissociation between explicit (conscious) and implicit (unconscious) memory, they are not completely definitive. Simply comparing priming with free recall entails a confound: free-recall tests involve very minimal retrieval cues which specify only the time and place the target event occurred; but free-association and category-generation tests provide additional cues, in the form of the free-association stimuli or category labels. The most convincing demonstration of explicit-implicit dissociations come from studies where the two tests are matched for the informational value of the cues provided to the subjects. Such closely matched tests of explicit and implicit memory were not built into the design of these early studies.

The criticism is muted somewhat by the fact that many of these studies found that recognition, which involves highly informative 'copy cues', was also impaired during PHA. Barnier and her colleagues examined both repetition and conceptual priming in a study that kept modality of presentation (visual) constant between encoding and retrieval, and employed matched cues for the tests of explicit and implicit memory (Barnier et al., 2001). As Figure 6.12 shows, the hypnotisable subjects showed a substantial deficit on a cued-recall test of explicit memory, but normal levels of priming on free-association and fragment-completion tests of implicit memory.

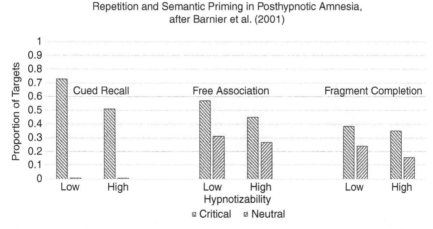

Figure 6.12   Repetition and semantic priming compared to matched test of cued recall, after Barnier et al. (2001)

Even though priming is generally considered to reflect unintentional retrieval of stored information concerning a prior episode, conscious recollection may still contribute to performance on tasks such as fragment completion, free association, and category generation. Following up on preliminary research reported by Dorfman and Kihlstrom (1994), David and his colleagues (2000) performed a more definitive experiment using the Process Dissociation Procedure (PDP) to assess the differential contributions of automatic, unconscious and controlled, conscious processes to the priming effects observed during PHA. While the traditional PDP distinguishes only between controlled (voluntary, conscious) and automatic (involuntary, unconscious) memory-retrieval processes, David et al. employed a variant which further distinguished between two forms of conscious memory: voluntary, such as deliberate recall or recognition, and involuntary, as in Proust's 'madeleine episode', where a conscious recollection comes involuntarily to mind. In their experiment, subjects received suggestions for amnesia covering only half the studied items, and then completed both a stem-cued recall test of explicit memory and a stem-completion test of implicit memory. As shown in Figure 6.13, both hypnotisable and insusceptible subjects showed a mix of voluntary conscious, involuntary conscious, and involuntary unconscious memory for the to-be-remembered (TBR) items; this mix was also evident for the to-be-forgotten (TBF) items in the insusceptible subjects (who, after all, did not experience PHA) and for controls who were not hypnotised. For the hypnotisable subjects, however, the TBF items – that is, those covered by PHA – showed quite a different pattern. The two consciously controlled components were very weak, with performance during PHA dominated by involuntary unconscious memory.

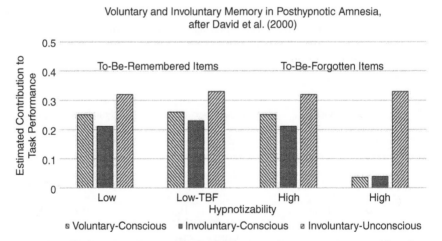

Figure 6.13 Estimates of controlled and automatic processing, and involuntary-conscious memory, during posthypnotic amnesia, after David et al. (2000)

RECOLLECTION AND FAMILIARITY IN POSTHYPNOTIC AMNESIA

The study by David et al. (2000) supports the hypothesis that spared priming in PHA reflects a dissociation between explicit and implicit memory, but leaves open the question of whether amnesic subjects can capitalise on a priming-based feeling of familiarity to support performance on explicit memory tasks such as recognition. In fact, it is now understood that recognition by both amnesic and nonamnesic subjects can be supported by both conscious recollection and a priming-based feeling of familiarity (Mandler, 1980; Yonelinas et al. 2010). For example, Tulving (1985) distinguished between two forms of recognition memory: recognition-by-remembering entails retrieval of an episodic memory as part of one's personal past (what Tulving called 'autonoetic consciousness'), while this personal connection is absent in recognition-by-knowing, which allows a person to know about a past event without actually remembering it. Although Tulving likened 'knowing' to semantic memory, it has become popular to interpret 'knowing' in terms of a priming-based feeling of familiarity. Unfortunately, Tulving's 'Remember-Know' paradigm has not been employed in research on PHA (hint, hint). Any such study should take care to distinguish 'knowing', which Tulving construed as analogous to retrieval from semantic memory, from the intuitive 'feeling' of familiarity (Kihlstrom, 2020). The contribution of priming to episodic recognition is almost certainly represented by the latter, not the former.

Recent studies of recognition memory suggest that familiarity plays a role in whatever success amnesic subjects have on recognition tasks (Kihlstrom, 2019b). These studies have substituted a continuous measure of recognition confidence for the traditional, dichotomous, 'Yes/No' ratings. For example, in the study illustrated in Figure 6.6, subjects made recognition judgements on a 1–4 scale, which yields three different criteria for recognition: a strict criterion, counting only items receiving a rating of 4; a moderate criterion counting items that received ratings of 3 or more; and a liberal criterion counting even those items that received a rating of 2. The value for recognition given in Figure 6.6 reflects the moderate criterion.

Figure 6.14 shows more detailed findings from that experiment (Kihlstrom, 2019b, Experiment 1). The subjects studied a list of 16 items, four drawn from each of four taxonomic categories. The recognition test consisted of 64 items: the 16 'critical targets'; 16 'critical lures' drawn from the same categories and matched to the targets; 16 'neutral targets' matched to the critical targets; and 16 'neutral lures' matched to the neutral lures (and, perforce, to the critical targets and critical lures as well). Recognition was quite poor under the strict criterion. As the criterion for recognition was loosened, recognition of critical targets increased progressively, but remained less than perfect even after application of the loosest criterion.

Even with an increase in false alarms, d' increased as the analysis shifted from the strict to the moderate criterion; d' dropped off somewhat with the liberal criterion, but was still higher than under the strict criterion. Similar findings were obtained with patients who were amnesic following electroconvulsive therapy, when they were encouraged to loosen

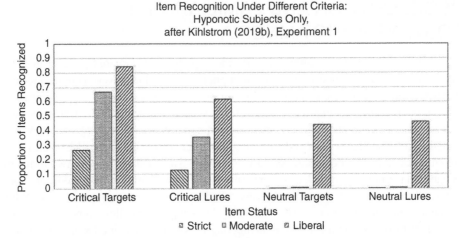

Figure 6.14 Item recognition under different criteria for critical and neutral categories, and targets and lures within categories, after Kihlstrom (2019b, Experiment 1)

their criterion for recognition (Dorfman et al., 1995). In both cases, it appeared that the subjects were able to capitalise on the priming-based feeling of familiarity to improve their performance on the recognition test.

As the criterion for recognition was loosened, the increase in hits was accompanied by an increase in false alarms, especially to distractor items that were conceptually related to, or semantically associated with, targets. In addition, amnesic subjects had difficulty identifying the particular list on which recognised items were presented for study (Experiment 2), or the correct order in which targets appeared on the study list (Experiment 3). All of these findings support the conclusion that successful recognition during PHA is more likely to be mediated by a priming-based feeling of familiarity than conscious recollection.

The role of priming-based familiarity in recognition may help explain the findings of an experiment by Smith et al. (2013). In a variant on the standard priming paradigm, hypnotisable subjects performed a free-association test, and then received a suggestion for amnesia covering both the fact of the test and the responses they had given. On a second free-association test, which contained the same cues as the first one, plus some additional cues, these subjects showed about 47% overlap between the two sets of responses. By contrast, unhypnotised control subjects instructed to generate different responses on the second test showed only about 3% overlap, while another control group, given no particular instruction, showed about 89% overlap. Interestingly, the amnesic subjects displayed longer response latencies on the second test, compared to the first, and the increase in response latencies was correlated with the number of novel responses given. This suggests that the amnesic subjects recognised some of the cues from the second list as repetitions from the first list, and edited their responses accordingly – resulting in the lengthened response latencies. Smith et al. rejected conscious withholding as an explanation for their findings, but suggested that the targeted material is *unconsciously* blocked from further processing. Another possibility is that the subjects responded to a priming-based feeling of familiarity by producing a second response which did not seem familiar.

NEURAL CORRELATES OF POSTHYPNOTIC AMNESIA

Although recent years have seen an upsurge of neuropsychological and neuroimaging studies of hypnosis (Halligan & Oakley, 2013; Kihlstrom, 2013; Oakley & Halligan, 2013; Landry & Raz, 2015), so far only one of these has focused directly on PHA. Mendelsohn et al. (2008) began by showing highly hypnotisable subjects a documentary film in the normal waking state; a week later, they entered an fMRI scanner, were hypnotised, received a suggestion for PHA, and were queried about the events depicted in the film. Compared to controls, the subjects showed a clear impairment in (cued) recall for the events of the film; however, they showed no deficit in memory for incidental details of the context in which they had viewed the film. Whole-brain analysis of the fMRI image revealed a substantial reduction in activity, compared to the control group who viewed the same film but received no suggestion for PHA. The changes particularly affected portions of the left temporal pole and extrastriate cortex, regions thought to be involved in memory retrieval. There was also increased activity in the left rostrolateral prefrontal cortex, a region thought to be involved in the regulation of memory-retrieval strategies. These shifts were reversed when the suggestion for PHA was cancelled.

The finding of altered activity in fronto-temporal regions during PHA is broadly consistent with neuroimaging studies of other forms of top-down memory inhibition, including various forms of directed forgetting (Anderson & Hanslmayr, 2014) and dissociative amnesia (Bell et al., 2011; Staniloiu & Markowitsch, 2014). However, this area of research is in its infancy, and any definitive conclusions are precluded by the vast differences in paradigms employed in the various studies. Nevertheless, the ease with which PHA can be induced in hypnotisable subjects suggests that continued neuroimaging research on PHA and other phenomena of hypnosis will shed light on the neural mechanisms of not only hypnosis, but also the fascinating, but frustratingly rare, dissociative disorders.

AUTHOR NOTES

Research by the author cited here was supported by Grant #MH35856 from the National Institute of Mental Health. For a more comprehensive list of references, see an expanded version of this chapter posted on www.ocf.berkeley.edu/~jfkihlstrom/PDFs/2010s/2019/PosthypnoticAmnesia2019_uned.pdf

Further Reading

Kihlstrom, J. F. (2008). The domain of hypnosis, revisited. In M. R. Nash and A. J. Barnier (eds), *Oxford Handbook of Hypnosis: Theory, research, and practice* (pp. 21–52). Oxford: Oxford University Press.

McConkey, K. M. (2008). Generations and landscapes of hypnosis: Questions we've asked, questions we should ask. In M. R. Nash and A. J. Barnier (eds), *Oxford Handbook of Hypnosis: Theory, research, and practice* (pp. 53–80). Oxford: Oxford University Press.

7

ORGANIC AMNESIA

The contribution of patient studies to theories of memory and forgetting

Melissa C. Duff
and Neal J. Cohen

Memory failure is common. We all experience everyday failures of memory, such as not recalling where we placed our keys, associating a famous actor with the wrong movie, or struggling to remember how or in what context we came to learn what is now a highly familiar face. There are also catastrophic failures of memory, or amnesia, associated with brain injury and disease (e.g. Alzheimer's disease) that prevent individuals from learning new information and can strip them of previously acquired knowledge. Thus, forgetting, or memory loss, is part of the human condition and studies of human memory loss, ranging from everyday forgetting to the more extreme versions of amnesia, have played a critical role in the development of memory theory.

When we were invited to contribute a chapter to this volume on memory failure in the context of patient studies, it caused us to reminisce about the history of such work and the current trajectory of work on amnesia and where it fits into current day cognitive neuroscience. While patient studies have long been a critical arm of the converging methods approach to understanding human cognition and memory (Corkin, 2002; Roden & Karnath, 2004; Chatterjee, 2005; Rosenbaum et al., 2005; Poldrack, 2006), it can, at times, feel as though many of the highly lauded examples of what is new and exciting in the memory literature come from the newest imaging technique or findings from animal studies. Yet close attention to the history of the scientific study of memory, and its failures, suggests that many of the most significant advances stem from, or were confirmed by, patient findings. In this chapter we review the critical contribution of patient studies to the theoretical advances on memory and memory failures. As we will discuss, relational memory representations have a more powerful and pervasive impact on our everyday lives than previously appreciated, and the consequences of amnesia are more far-reaching than traditional studies of memory and memory failure have suggested. Finally, we suggest that new findings on the breadth of disruptions in cognition observed in hippocampal amnesia challenge our current thinking of what it means to remember and to forget.

STAGES OF MEMORY

Much of the early experimental work on amnesia used as its starting point models emerging from the study of normal memory (and normal forgetting), using these models to understand the nature of the impairment in amnesia. The major theories of the day had distinguished between short-term, or working, memory versus long-term memory, and also distinguished among various stages of memory, or of information processing – encoding, storage, and retrieval. Applying these ideas to amnesia, the work focused on identifying the *locus* of the deficit, that is, whether amnesia could best be understood as disruption of either short-term or long-term memory, and/or disruption of any particular stage of memory.

Evidence from amnesic patients, as reported by multiple investigators, consistently supported the identification of the locus of memory impairment in amnesia to long-term memory as opposed to short-term memory, and indeed many authors of the day argued that amnesia findings provided the strongest evidence for the theoretical distinction between short-term and long-term memory stores or systems. However, as we will see in a subsequent section, amnesic patients show impairment even at delays on the timescale of short-term or working memory if tested on memory for the relations among items, rather than just memory for items.

Work on whether amnesia could also be identified with impairment specific to one or another stage of memory proved more problematic. Various lines of evidence were adduced by different investigators with different groups of amnesic patients pointing to disruption of encoding or storage/consolidation or retrieval processes. That patients, or patient groups, might differ in which stage of memory might be disrupted ended up steering discussion away from the issue of what is the fundamental deficit in amnesia, and instead towards discussion of the idea that amnesia should not be considered a homogenous condition. Rather, this work raised interesting questions about whether amnesia consequent to damage to the hippocampus and medial temporal lobe structures was fundamentally different, in terms of the locus of impairment, from amnesia consequent to damage to midline diencephalic regions of the brain (thalamic and hypothalamic nuclei).

One important line of work on this theme explored the possibility that amnesias differed in their rate of forgetting, with some instances of amnesia showing an accelerated forgetting rate compared to others. The examination of forgetting rates raises important questions about what, if anything, memory failures can tell us about the nature of memory. If amnesia(s) is (are) a deficit focal to long-term memory, leaving short-term or working memory intact, then all instances of amnesia will show an abnormal rate of forgetting, with memory performance comparable to that of neurologically intact participants at a short enough delay but (increasingly) poorer-than-normal performance at (increasingly) longer delays. But the question addressed was whether there was a form of amnesia, perhaps that associated with medial temporal lobe damage, which was truly a forgetting deficit, that is, a disruption of memory storage or consolidation processes resulting in loss of memories at an abnormally fast rate over time. To get at this experimentally, they 'equated' performance of amnesic patients to that of matched comparison participants when assessed at a modest delay after learning (e.g. 10 min), typically by giving the patients extra exposure time to study the to-be-learned materials, and then assessed whether the patients nonetheless went on to show an accelerated rate of forgetting.

The results were hotly debated at the time. But it has become increasingly clear that memory is a *final common pathway*, and that a deficit in any of the stages of memory, whether of the quality of memory encoding, the robustness of memory storage, or the ability to access memories at the time of retrieval, will result in increasingly poor memory performance as time passes, namely, increasing forgetting. Here, 'forgetting' means no more than 'memory failure', with little insight into the locus of the processing disruption causing memory failure. One of the studies in that vein showed that patient HM could show a 'normal' rate of forgetting across a 24-hour delay, but required study exposure 20 times as long as that given to the comparison participants (Freed et al., 1987). That the procedures required to equate HM's performance to that of matched comparisons participants were so extreme speaks volumes to the magnitude of his memory deficit, but says much less about the cause of his profound forgetting.

To this day, it remains unresolved whether (some) amnesias can be characterised as a 'forgetting' deficit, in terms of a specific deficit to memory storage or consolidation, or whether we can only talk about 'forgetting' in amnesia in the more generic sense of memory failure. Critically, as we will see in the next section, there came a time in the history of this field when there was a radical shift away from studying the nature of the deficit, to instead focus on preserved memory abilities. This shift had enormous impact because now data from amnesic patients were being use to learn about the nature and organisation of normal memory – in this case, about how memory must be organised in order for there to be an orderly distinction between preserved versus impaired memory abilities in the face of amnesia.

IDENTIFICATION OF MULTIPLE MEMORY SYSTEMS

Memory refers to knowledge that is stored in the brain and to the processes associated with acquiring, encoding, storing, and retrieving this information. Separate from the various stages of memory (e.g. encoding vs retrieval), it has long been appreciated that there are different forms or kinds of memory. Philosophers and psychologists dating back nearly 100 years pointed to a distinction between a form of memory that is accessible to conscious introspection (e.g. knowing that; also referred to as representative memory, secondary memory, memory with record) and a form of memory that is not accessible to consciousness (e.g. knowing how; also referred to as mechanical memory, habits, memory without record) (di Bian, James, Ryle, Bruner). While these functional distinctions were intuitive, a key ambition of memory research in the 20th century was to localise memory in the brain in the same way that language had been localised by Broca and Wernicke. Specifically, researchers were interested in determining whether there were specific brain areas, regions, or systems that were reliably associated with or critical for memory. Karl Lashley (1950) famously conducted a series of cortical ablation studies in rats to localise memory in the brain. While the size of the lesion was related to lesion-induced impairment in the animals, the location of the lesion was not. Lashley concluded:

> I sometimes feel, on reviewing the evidence on the localization of the memory trace, that the necessary conclusion is that learning is just not possible. It is difficult to conceive of a mechanism which can satisfy the conditions set for it. Nonetheless, in spite of such evidence against it, learning does sometimes occur.

Only 7 years later, Scoville and Milner (1957) reported on the seminal case of HM who underwent an experimental operation resecting the medial temporal lobes bilaterally to treat epilepsy. While the surgery was considered a success in terms of managing the seizure disorder, an unexpected consequence was a severe and irreversible memory loss characterised by severe and global anterograde memory impairment (i.e. profoundly disrupted ability to form new memories) and a temporally graded retrograde amnesia (i.e. loss of previously acquired memory, with greater deficit in the time period close to the surgery and better memory moving back in time). The subsequent neuropsychological and neuroanatomical descriptions of HM have provided significant insight into the organisation of human memory and its instantiation in the brain (see also Corkin et al., 1997; Corkin, 2002). From HM, and from other cases of amnesia, we have learned that damage to the hippocampus and related medial temporal lobe regions, whether by surgical resection, as in HM, or following anoxia or other neurological insult, results in a profound yet circumscribed amnesia.

The specificity of the observed impairment in HM was of critical importance. The impairment was specific *to* the domain of memory, as well as specific *within* the domain of memory. The impairments are seen in aspects of memory function, disproportionate to any deficits in general cognitive or intellectual abilities. HM had not lost the capacity for speech and language (i.e. he did not have aphasia) and his other cognitive abilities were intact including attention, problem solving, and reasoning. Moreover, the observed impairment in HM affected only certain aspects, or forms of memory. Evidence accumulated that the crux of anterograde amnesia due to hippocampal damage is a deficit in the ability to form and retain new long-term memories (Cohen, 1988; Squire, 1992b; Cohen & Eichenbaum, 1993; Eichenbaum & Cohen, 2001), including acquiring new vocabulary and facts (semantic memory) and memory for time- and place-specific experiences that are personal or autobiographical in nature (episodic memory); that is, HM was profoundly impaired in his ability to form new memories regarding the details and events of his daily life, including his own activities during the day, the names of people he came into contact with, or major historical events (Corkin, 2002), and was unable to learn the meanings of new words (Gabrieli et al., 1988).

Yet other forms of memory appeared intact. HM's working memory appeared intact as he was able to complete digit span tasks (e.g. reciting strings of numbers of increasing length), and was able to follow and implement instructions and participate in conversations over short periods of time. HM's remote declarative memory also appeared intact as he was able to provide detailed accounts of episodic memory from his childhood. He was also able to acquire new skills. Milner et al. (1968) investigated HM's ability to acquire the sensorimotor skill of mirror drawing. In this task, HM viewed a line drawing containing two concentric outlines of a star and could only view his hand by way of a mirror. The task required drawing a pencil line within the outlines of the star. An error was counted each time the pencil made contact with one of the outline borders. Because of the difficulty imposed by only being able to view the line drawing through the mirror, even normal participants require several trials in order to have no or only a few errors. The number of errors was recorded for 10 trials across three successive days. HM demonstrated a decrease in the number of errors across the 3 days and showed considerable savings across sessions, making few errors on any given trial on day three compared to nearly thirty errors on trial one of day one. Although HM was successful in acquiring this sensorimotor skill, he was unable to recall learning the task or any of the testing sessions. Thus, there was a striking dissociation between spared learning and impaired memory abilities observed in HM. Given that this early demonstration of spared learning in amnesia was tied to a motor task, there was an assumption that this preserved learning was tied to the motor system.

Cohen and Squire (1980) demonstrated that the dissociation between sparing and impairment of memory was not an exception to HM and not exclusively within the domain of motor learning. Rather, they demonstrated that this dissociation constituted a large domain of spared learning in amnesia in general that included but was not limited to motoric learning. Cohen and Squire (1980) showed that a group of amnesic patients were able to acquire, retain, and express perceptual skills, such as the reading of mirror-reversed words. Although their patients were able to demonstrate intact skilled performance, they were impaired at both recognising the words employed during training and remembering the training experience itself. This pattern of spared skill and perceptual learning in the absence of conscious recollection provided further support for distinct forms of memory.

The striking dissociation between spared and impaired memory abilities observed in HM has been replicated across numerous other cases of amnesia (e.g. Cohen & Squire, 1980; Squire, 1987; Wilson & Wearing, 1995; Tranel et al., 2000; Rosenbaum et al., 2005). Findings from patients with amnesia have been revolutionary in advancing our understanding of the organisation of memory systems. Patient studies revealed what previous animal studies alone had failed to demonstrate – that memory is not a unitary system but rather manifested in multiple functionally distinct memory systems supported by anatomically distinct brain systems. Specifically, the study of patients with profound failures of memory led to the development, and subsequent testing, of a taxonomy for classifying the distinct forms of long-term memory and their neural correlates that are still in widespread use today. Repeated observations of distinct and replicable patterns of memory sparing and loss lead to the classification of declarative memory and nondeclarative memory. Declarative memory, the memory system impaired in amnesia, supports the conscious reflection and introspection of autobiographical events (episodic) and knowledge about the world and words (semantic), and the flexible use and deployment of such knowledge in novel contexts and settings (Cohen & Squire, 1980; Cohen, 1984). Nondeclarative memory, the form of memory spared in patients with amnesia, refers to changes in performance (i.e. speed or preferences) that directly result from experience, although these changes are characterised as slow and incremental. These distinct forms of memory have unique and separable neural correlates, with the declarative memory system depending critically on the hippocampus and related medial temporal lobe structures (damaged in patient HM and other patients with amnesia), and nondeclarative memory depending on the striatum, neocortex, and cerebellum (largely preserved in most cases of amnesia) (Squire & Zola-Morgan, 1996; Milner et al., 1998).

The study of patients with hippocampal amnesia and identification of multiple memory systems in the brain laid the critical groundwork for many subsequent advances in the study of memory across methods. For example, the work on multiple memory systems has been extended and replicated in animals (e.g. Morris et al., 1982; Squire, 1992a; Alvarez et al., 1995; Packard & Goodman, 2012). The identification of specific neural systems (e.g. the hippocampus and medial temporal lobes) for different forms of memory inspired subsequent anatomical studies (Davachi, 2006; Eichenbaum et al., 2007; Diana et al., 2008; Davachi & Preston, 2014). Beyond determining the boundaries of distinct memory systems and their functional processing features, researchers went on to examine the conditions in which these memory systems cooperate or compete, using behavioural, neuroimaging and computational methods (McClelland et al., 1995; Poldrack & Packard, 2003; Poldrack & Rodriguez, 2004; Schapiro et al., 2017). Finally, we should note that while patients with hippocampal amnesia who have highly specific patterns of memory loss and focal neurological damage are rare, findings from such patients have informed our understanding of the neurobiology of other disorders where hippocampal dysfunction and memory loss are hallmarks of the condition (e.g. stroke, schizophrenia, Alzheimer's disease, TBI).

AMNESIA IS A DEFICIT IN RELATIONAL MEMORY

Work with patients has been instrumental in the development, testing, and refining of theories of memory. Over the last 20–30 years, advances in cognitive neuroscience research have emphasised the relational nature of declarative memory and demonstrated that at the heart of the declarative, or relational, memory deficit following hippocampal damage and amnesia is an impairment in relational memory binding. Relational memory theory, proposed by Cohen and Eichenbaum (1993; Eichenbaum & Cohen, 2001; see also Rubin & Cohen, 2017; Schwarb et al., 2017), emphasises two hallmark features of the hippocampus in relational memory: (1) the *binding* of arbitrary relations between the elements of experience into durable representations of events or scenes; and (2) the *flexible* expression of these representational bindings in novel settings, namely, those contexts different from the original encoding context; this allows for the search, reconstruction, and recombination of the information contained within them (as opposed to a 'video-camera'-like recapitulation of prior events) and for use in novel situations (Konkel & Cohen, 2009). Thus, the compositional nature of relational memory representations allows for the retrieval or reactivation of individual or even multiple configurations of associations that exist among the rich and complex experiences of our daily lives, and for the flexible use of this knowledge across a broad range of conditions (Eichenbaum & Cohen, 2014). For instance, relational memory representations permit us to learn the names of new acquaintances (completely arbitrary relations that cannot be appreciated *a priori* or inferred upon the initial encounter), to remember where and at what time to go for a new appointment (relying on representations previously created from past learning experiences and flexibly using them prospectively in service of a new goal), and even to facilitate new learning of information (Rigon et al., 2019; Rubin et al., 2017). Relational memory theory also predicts that any representation (spatial, temporal, etc.) that requires the binding of the constituent elements of a scene or event will place demands on the hippocampus.

A seminal study demonstrating the relational binding deficit in amnesia monitored eye movements to assess memory for scenes (Ryan et al., 2000). The use of eyetracking was a particularly novel advancement in assessing memory in amnesia, as it did not require a verbal response and researchers could ensure that the critical elements of the stimuli were perceived by all participants. The individuals with amnesia and neurologically intact comparison participants viewed real-world scenes (e.g. girls on a footbridge over a creek; a boy with a group of kittens) on a computer monitor while their eye movements were recorded. Participants viewed three types of scenes: novel scenes (seen once); repeated scenes (seen three times); and manipulated scenes (addition of a new object, deletion of an object, or left–right shifting of the objects). Each scene was viewed twice in the original form and then seen in a manipulated form during the critical block. The comparison participants exhibited a relational manipulation effect, an increase in viewing of the regions where manipulations of relations among scene elements had occurred. For manipulated scenes compared to novel or repeated, the comparison participants displayed a greater proportion of fixation on the manipulated region and a greater number of transitions to and from the manipulated region. In contrast, the amnesic participants failed to show the relational manipulation effect. Thus, memory representations of scenes contain information about relations among elements of the scenes, at least some of which is not accessible to verbal report. This failure to show any demonstrable memory for relations among the constituent elements of scenes suggests that amnesia demonstrates the fundamental deficit in relational memory processing in amnesia.

As an aside, it is important to note while patient studies continued to focus on and confirm the critical role of the hippocampus in relational memory processes, the animal literature approached questions about the role of the hippocampus from a different perspective. Whereas the human work largely focused on studies that linked the hippocampus to explicit remembering and conscious recollection, phenomena that are hard to study in animal models, the animal work focused on mapping and navigating spatial environments and the identification of place cells in the hippocampus (e.g. O'Keefe & Dostrovsky, 1971; O'Keefe & Nadel,1978; Muller et al., 1987; O'Keefe & Burgess, 1996; Shapiro et al., 1997; Hafting et al., 2005; Moser et al., 2008). The animal work led some to the conclusion that memory representations of space had special status in the hippocampus and that amnesia was primarily a deficit of spatial representations. More recent attempts to reconcile these interpretations across literatures argues that spatial relations are just one type of relational memory representation across both human and non-human animals and that amnesia impairs all manner of relations including but not limited to spatial relational representations (Crystal & Smith, 2014; Eichenbaum, 2017; see Eichenbaum & Cohen, 2014, for discussion).

In a study of patients with hippocampal amnesia, Konkel and colleagues (2008) provided evidence that the hippocampus contributes to relational binding of all manner of relations, including, but not limited to, spatial relations. In that study, patients and matched comparison participants were presented with computer-generated stimuli constructed to be odd shapes of different colours, all roughly the same size, but with different textual patterns, so each one was clearly distinguishable from the others. Shapes were presented one at a time, sequentially, each in one of three consistent locations on the screen (upper left, upper right, and bottom centre). Any given shape could appear in any of the three temporal slots and any of the three spatial locations. A blank screen was presented in between sets of three stimuli to encourage the temporal grouping of stimuli into triplets. The study consisted of sets of several triplets, followed by corresponding test displays in which triplets were presented in different layouts to allow for the separate and unconfounded assessment of either spatial relations (correct assignment of the three stimuli to their studied spatial locations), or temporal relations (correct assignment of the three stimuli to their studied temporal order), or associative relations (correct assignment of the three stimuli as having co-occurred in the same studied triplet, independent of spatial location or temporal order). Importantly, participants were encouraged to represent all types of relation at study, as the type of relation to be assessed at test time was only apparent upon presentation of the test display. Additional test displays presented individual stimuli for the assessment of item memory, in order to disambiguate any observed deficits in memory for relations among items from any deficits in memory for the items themselves. Consistent with predictions of relational memory theory, findings showed that patients with damage to the hippocampus were impaired for each of the types of relations (spatial, temporal, and associative) relative to the comparison participants. These findings provide strong support for the contribution of the hippocampus to relational memory, across all manner of relations.

The theoretical and experimental work elucidating the relational binding and processing provided by the hippocampus in support of the encoding of rich and complex representations of our daily lives, and how hippocampal damage impairs such processes, has provided critical insights into the compositional nature of relational memory representations for creating and reconstructing memory across time and space. Just as the work in patients with hippocampal amnesia was critical for understanding multiple memory systems and hippocampal pathology in other conditions, understanding amnesia as a deficit in relational memory has influenced characterisations of the nature of memory impairment in other populations as a deficit in relational memory (e.g. schizophrenia; see Öngür et al., 2006; traumatic brain injury; see Rigon et al., 2019).

EXTENDING THE REACH OF THE HIPPOCAMPUS ACROSS TIMESCALES AND COGNITIVE DOMAINS

Recent discoveries from patients with hippocampal damage and amnesia have expanded the breadth of hippocampal functionality beyond its role in long-term memory. A growing body of work from patients reveals deficits in relational memory processes when there are minimal delays, and even when there are no delays at all (i.e. all the necessary information is immediately available) (Warren et al., 2011; Hannula et al., 2006; Olsen et al., 2006; Barense et al., 2007; Sharger et al., 2008; also see Ranganath & D'Esposito, 2001; Hannua & Ranganath, 2008 for converging fMRI data). For example, Hannula et al. (2006) compared the performance of individuals with hippocampal amnesia and healthy comparison participants on a relational memory task for face–scene pairings. Study and test trials were intermixed so that participants were tested on face–scene pairings they had just studied (a lag of 1 and a delay of only a few seconds), or face–scene pairings that were from nine trials earlier. For study trials, participants viewed a scene for two seconds, and then a face was superimposed for three seconds. On test trials, participants viewed a studied scene for two seconds then three previously studied faces were superimposed on the scene, and participants were asked to indicate the face that matched the scene with a key press. Critically, while all three faces were previously studied (and equally familiar), only one face had been previously presented with the particular scene. As expected, the patients with amnesia were significantly impaired at the long delay. However, in striking contrast to earlier studies of intact working memory in amnesia, the patients were also impaired relative to the healthy participants on memory for face–scene relations at the short lag condition, a delay of just a couple of seconds.

The finding that patients with amnesia are impaired on relational memory processing on timescale of working memory and short-term memory tasks is significant for several reasons. First, amnesia, and the role of the hippocampus to memory, had long been characterised as exclusively the domain of long-term memory (recall that HM performed like healthy individuals on working memory tasks like digit span). These new findings suggest that new hippocampal-dependent representations are available rapidly enough to influence ongoing processing when new information is perceived; old information is retrieved; and representations are held in-line to be evaluated, manipulated, integrated, and used in service of behavioural performance. Thus, the role of the hippocampus in memory may have less to do with the distinction between long-term and short-term memory and more to do with the distinction between relational memory (e.g. face–scene pairings) and memory for single times (e.g. single faces or digits) (Hannula et al., 2005); that is, the hippocampus seems to be recruited in the processing of relations irrespective of the timescale.

Second, these studies implied that the hallmark relational binding, flexibility, and integration of hippocampal-dependent representations can be deployed and are rapidly available when information is processed in the moment and in an ongoing fashion. These findings had significant implications for a role of the hippocampus in cognitive abilities outside the domain of memory. Indeed, our labs and others have now demonstrated that patients with hippocampal amnesia have far-reaching deficits beyond memory, including in future thinking and imagination (e.g. Hassabis et al., 2007; Race et al., 2013; Kurczek et al., 2015), creativity (e.g. Duff et al., 2013; MacKay & Goldstein, 2016; Warren et al., 2016), decision-making (e.g. Gupta et al., 2009; Palombo et al., 2019), empathy and social cognition (e.g. Croft et al., 2010; Davidson et al., 2012; Beadle et al., 2013) and in discourse and language processing (e.g. Duffy et al., 2007; Rubin et al., 2011; Duff & Brown-Schmidt, 2012; see also Rubin et al., 2014, for a review). Not only have these studies been informative in understanding the expanding breath of the hippocampus in cognition and the scope of the deficit in amnesia beyond memory, but they have also inspired and led to a significant expansion in research and theory on the expanded role of hippocampal dependent memory representations (Addis et al., 2007; Buckner & Carroll, 2007; Addis & Schacter, 2008; Zeithamova et al., 2012; Spreng, 2013; Shohamy & Daw, 2015; Kumaran et al., 2016; Hannula & Duff, 2017; Moscovitch et al., 2016).

How do we reconcile the well-established role of the hippocampus in memory with its role in other cognitive domains? The characteristic processing features of the hippocampus, namely its ability to form representations of arbitrary relations and permit the flexible use of such representations, that are critical in the (re)construction of relational memory representations, are also called upon in service of meeting the demands of other cognitive abilities with overlapping processing demands. We have come to understand that neural structures seldom act alone, but rather are part of, and participate in, broader neural networks that support all domains of cognition. We have also come to understand that the hippocampus participates in a number of neural networks and thus in a broad array of cognitive abilities. For example, just as we have come to understand that the full capacity and expression of memory depends critically on a network of brain structures, including but not limited to the hippocampus and MTL (e.g. Buckner & Carroll, 2007; Ritchey et al., 2015; Wang et al., 2015; Moscovitch et al., 2016), other cognitive domains also depends on a disturbed, and often partially overlapping, network of brain structures that can, depending on processing demands, include the hippocampus (e.g. language use and processing, Covington & Duff, 2016; Piai et al., 2016). Patient studies reveal that the hippocampus provides for an extraordinarily powerful system capable not just of encoding and retrieving enduring memories of the past but of guiding a wide range of behavioural choices and actions in the world. Thus, the powerful and pervasive impact of relational memory representations on our everyday lives is far more consequential than previously appreciated.

WHAT IS MEMORY FOR AND WHAT DOES IT MEAN TO FORGET? EVIDENCE FROM FAILURES OF RELATIONAL MEMORY

Working on this chapter and documenting the role patient studies played in our understanding of memory and its failures has also caused us to think deeply about what it means to have a memory failure or to forget. On the surface, amnesia seems like a disorder of forgetting. These individuals move through their daily lives yet have little in the way of a tangible record of their experiences that they call on to reminisce, introspect, or declare to others. Yet, and as pointed out earlier in the studies of forgetting rates with HM, in controlled studies patients with amnesia often acquire so little information this makes it difficult to study forgetting rates. Patient studies suggests that that learning and forgetting are inextricability linked. We often see abnormal forgetting in contexts when learning was also abnormal. We also often see that when the learning rate is comparable to healthy individuals, so are rates of forgetting. For example, Duff, Hengst, Tranel, and Cohen (2006) reported an intact rate of learning for semantic information in patients with hippocampal amnesia, when the to-be-learned information did not require the acquisition of new arbitrary relations, but instead could be accomplished using pre-existing semantic information for the stimuli. The long-term retention of this new learning at 30 minutes, 6 months, and even 2 years for one participant, did not differ between patients and comparison participants. While learning and forgetting are inextricably connected, 'forgetting' is often the term applied, both by lay people and scientists alike, to examples of when an individual experienced an event but does not have a whole or complete memory representation for it (whether it had been successfully encoded or not). For the sake of discussion, below, we will use the term 'forgetting' in the same manner.

The advances, however, in our understanding of amnesia as a deficit in relational memory, and of the expanded reach of the hippocampus across timescales and cognitive domains, cause us to re-examine what it means to have a memory failure or to forget in amnesia. One source of data to consider comes from the studies on future thinking, imagination, and creativity. Numerous studies have reported that patients with amnesia are not only impaired at recall and reconstructing their pasts, but are also impaired in their ability to think about, project themselves into, or imagine future events and episodes (Hassabis et al., 2007; Race et al., 2013; Kurczek et al., 2015). Across studies, participants are typically given a neural cue word (tree, restaurant) and asked to (re)construct events across time (past, future); the verbal descriptions are then analysed for the amount of episodic detail (temporal, spatial, perceptual relations) they contain. The interpretation across studies is that in the same way the hippocampus plays a role in the relational binding and subsequent retrieval of the temporal, spatial, and relational content that forms our mental representations of real past events, it plays the same role in constructing events that are imagined or in the future by retrieving and combining temporal, spatial, and relational content in new ways. These studies again highlight the compositional nature of relational memory representations and their flexibility in service of cognition that is not strictly memory or recalling the past. Yet this literature often discusses this ability (or lack thereof in patients) as 'memory for the future' (e.g. Schacter, 2012). Given that the underlying mechanism of the memory failure in patients in future thinking and imagination is the same as the memory failure in thinking about or recalling the past, can we consider both examples of forgetting?

A similar example comes from studies demonstrating deficits in creative thinking in amnesia. Like future thinking and imagination, creativity would seem to require hippocampal contributions as creativity requires re-activating relational representations of previous experience and knowledge, as well as flexibly recombining their elements (critically dependent on the property of compositionality, which is fundamental to relational representations) to generate new, novel, products or ideas. Duff and colleagues (2013) evaluated the performance of patients with hippocampal damage on a well-validated, standardised measure of creativity, the Torrance Tests of Creative Thinking (TTCT). The TTCT is comprised of both verbal and figural measures of creativity, in which a written prompt is provided and then participants have between 5 and 10 minutes to generate the most creative responses they can imagine, either by writing or drawing on the respective forms. For example, one prompt asked to generate creative uses for cardboard boxes during a 10-minute period, whereas an example from the figural form consisted of participants being presented with a filled-in oval shape and asked to draw a picture, adding new ideas, to make the picture tell as interesting and exciting a story as possible, also within a 10-minute period. The patients with amnesia scored significantly worse than comparison participants, producing both fewer and impoverished (less detailed) responses. The deficit in creativity shares its underlying mechanisms and stems from the same impairments in relational memory as failures of recalling previously experienced events. We agree one might be hard pressed to interpret a lack of creativity as forgetting using traditional frameworks. Yet if we can have memory for events we have not yet or may never experience (as is the case in future thinking and imagination), is the impairment in such memory an example of forgetting?

As the emerging evidence on the nature of amnesia and the scope of hippocampal contributions to cognition forces us to expand our thinking about the boundaries of memory, and our terminology to describe its phenomena, it also forces us to re-examine our notions of what memory is actually for. Whereas evolutionary accounts of memory have highlighted its role in our ability to learn about our environment to determine and avoid threats, and later to experience the personal and social rewards of reminiscing around a campfire, what we have learned from cases of amnesia is that memory has a far more significant and far-reaching purpose than remembering. Relational memory representations permit us the ability to create and reconstruct the full record of our experience, the past, the future, the widely imagined, not just for introspection but so that we can act in and on our current world as we create and build our futures.

While many of the advances from patient studies that challenged our conceptualisation of memory failure and forgetting come from the domain of thinking about and imagining the future (i.e. forgetting in the absence of experience), other challenges come from memory failures and forgetting in the domain of remote semantic memory (i.e. forgetting despite a lifetime of experience). There has been overwhelming consensus that remote semantic knowledge, the general knowledge about words and the world acquired long before the onset of hippocampal pathology, becomes independent of the hippocampus via neocortical consolidation (McClelland et al., 1995) and is intact in amnesia. This view has been supported by data from patients with hippocampal amnesia on tests of linguistic knowledge: patients with amnesia do not have aphasia or semantic dementia, and they perform within normal limits on neuropsychological measures of vocabulary knowledge and naming (Kensinger et al., 2001). That patients with amnesia could still name common objects and provide definitions of objects (e.g. a lemon is a yellow fruit) was taken as evidence that hippocampal damage does not lead to loss or forgetting of remote knowledge.

Our knowledge of words and their meanings, however, is not static but rather grows and is refined with a lifetime of use. Klooster and Duff (2015) examined how much information is associated with highly familiar words that were previously acquired in patients with amnesia and healthy and brain-damaged comparison participants. The tasks included a word associates test (identifying synonyms and common collocates), a word senses task (naming all the senses of a word; e.g. lemon can be a fruit, a colour, a defective automobile), and a word features task (naming all of the features of a word; e.g. lemon tastes sour, is native to Asia, is used in tea). Patients with amnesia performed significantly worse than healthy and brain-damaged comparison groups (i.e. patients with ventromedial prefrontal cortex damage) on all three measures of word knowledge. For example, patients with amnesia generated, on average, only half the number of features for common words (e.g. shirt) as comparison participants. The deficit in remote semantic memory was even evident on tasks where all the information was in view of the participants. For example, when provided with a word (e.g. sudden) and asked to endorse possible synonyms (e.g. beautiful, quick, surprising, thirsty), all of which were written on paper in view of the participants, individuals with amnesia were significantly less likely to identify the correct responses. Furthermore, this deficit was evident despite showing no differences from comparison participants on self-reported rates of familiarity (scoring familiarity on a 9-point scale) of words used in the word features and senses tasks. Using tasks and measures that assess semantic richness, or depth of semantic knowledge, this study showed that patients with hippocampal amnesia have impoverished remote semantic memory, suggesting the possibility that the hippocampus plays a long-term role in maintaining semantic representations across the lifetime. This finding raises several interesting interpretations regarding the mechanisms of deficit.

On one hand, the deficit could be a failure to update existing semantic presentations with new information over the course of the more than 20 years of living with amnesia. On the other hand, the deficit could be an example of attrition of knowledge or forgetting. In either case, it is interesting to note that these patients have daily social interactions and experience with language, and some even extensive daily experience through communication and reading. Thus, whether they are failing to associate new information or forgetting previously acquired information, they are doing so having experienced the information but in the context of hippocampal damage to not seem to benefit from the experience. It would be remarkable if future studies were to confirm that despite normal acquisition of knowledge about objects, concepts, and words, and with normal levels of engagement and experience with that knowledge, hippocampal damage results in that the store of information fading away over time. Such a finding would be suggestive of an expanding retrograde amnesia. This decoupling of learning, experience and memory might also suggest that deficits in future thinking and imagination in amnesia be considered examples of forgetting. While offered as a bit of a thought experiment, data from patient studies reveal that the concepts of amnesia, memory, and forgetting are more far reaching than traditional studies and terminology around memory failure and forgetting have suggested.

IMPORTANCE OF PATIENT STUDIES FOR THE FUTURE OF THEORIES OF MEMORY AND FORGETTING

The field of cognitive neuroscience has been incontrovertibly enhanced and the course of discovery unquestionably accelerated by patient studies. The studies of patients with amnesia have been crucial in providing insights into the aspects of memory supported by the hippocampus, and the influence of the hippocampus and relational memory on aspects of performance that challenge the traditional view of memory and forgetting. We would be remiss to forget the critical contribution of these patient studies to memory theory, and the promise of new discovery and breakthrough, as the field (and funding agencies) grapple with issues of reproducibility, replication, and generalisation. Whether from HM, other single case studies, or small groups of patients with hippocampal amnesia, at nearly every stage of significant advancement in the cognitive neuroscience of memory, it was a finding from a patient study that was critical in revealing the nature and structure of memory, its organisation in the brain, and the surprisingly long reach of the hippocampus into aspects of cognition beyond the domain of memory.

In the age of the replication crisis there are calls for larger samples, and there can even be some doubt or suspicion regarding the value of what can be learned from a single observation in a single patient. Let us remember that many of the most significant advances in our understanding of human memory and learning have their roots in a small number of patient studies of hippocampal amnesia, and such work should be an active arm in the converging methods approach to memory research. Indeed, personalised or precision, medicine (the practice of using valid and reliable medical and behavioural information of a single individual to make tailored diagnostic and treatment decisions) is often touted as the future of medicine and clinical science. As history has already shown, patient studies are undoubtedly going to play a continued and critical role in the future of memory research. We as individuals and all members of the cognitive neuroscience community owe a deep debt to the individual patients for all they have shared and taught us about normal memory and forgetting.

Acknowledgements

This work was supported by NIH R01NS110661 to MCD and NJC.

Further Reading

Eichenbaum, H. (2015). Amnesia: Beyond Scoville and Milner's (1957) research on HM. In M. W. Eysenck and D. Groome (eds), *Cognitive Psychology: Revisiting the classic studies.* London: SAGE.

8

FORGETTING AND COGNITIVE INHIBITION

Inhibitory processes in episodic memory

Karl-Heinz T. Bäuml, Magdalena Abel
and Oliver Kliegl

Memory is vulnerable to forgetting. Indeed, results from a vast amount of literature clearly demonstrate that, under certain circumstances, retrieval of encoded information can fail. The circumstances under which such forgetting can arise include a number of factors that over the years have been identified to impair memory performance (for an overview, see Baddeley et al., 2015). The two most prominent factors are the retention interval between study and retrieval and the interference level at retrieval. When the delay between study and retrieval is increased, retrieval is typically impaired, reflecting so-called time-dependent forgetting (Ebbinghaus, 1885). When additional information has been encoded before retrieval, be it prior to or right after study of some target information, retrieval of the target information can suffer, reflecting so-called proactive interference (prior encoding of additional information; see Underwood, 1957) and retroactive interference (subsequent encoding of additional information; see Müller & Pilzecker, 1900).

But there are further factors beyond retention interval and the encoding of additional material that can induce forgetting. For instance, forgetting can arise when there is a mismatch between the temporal contexts at study and retrieval. Temporal context refers to the current pattern of activity in an individual's mind, which can differ between study and retrieval, for instance when the physical environment or an individual's mood has changed between the two phases (Godden & Baddeley, 1975; Eich, 1989). Because memory performance benefits from a match between the contexts at study and retrieval (Tulving & Thomson, 1973), retrieval can be impaired under such circumstances, causing so-called context-dependent forgetting. Finally, even the retrieval process itself can cause forgetting. Corresponding evidence has arisen from studies on retrieval-induced forgetting, showing that the selective retrieval of a subset of studied information can impair retrieval of other, nonretrieved information (Anderson et al., 1994).

All these factors share the characteristic that forgetting occurs incidentally and is not the result of an individual's intention to forget. However, people can also forget when cued to do so. Evidence for this proposal, for instance, has arisen from studies on directed forgetting and think/no-think impairment. Research on list-method directed forgetting has shown that providing a forget cue between the study of two lists can improve later recall of the second list items, but induce forgetting of the first list items (Bjork, 1972). Research on the think/no-think procedure has shown that when instructed to not let a previously encoded item enter consciousness, later recall of the item can be impaired (Anderson & Green, 2001). Forgetting, therefore, can arise incidentally as well as intentionally.

Over the years, a number of cognitive mechanisms have been suggested to mediate these forms of episodic forgetting, the two most prominent being retrieval competition and context change. Retrieval competition refers to the idea that memories that share a common cue – be it a temporal, semantic, or emotional cue – compete for conscious recall when this cue is provided, and as a result show reduced recall performance (McGeoch, 1932; Rundus, 1973). Retrieval competition can easily explain retroactive and proactive interference when assuming that the target information and the additionally encoded related (nontarget) information share a common retrieval cue, and thus compete for conscious recall. The proposal can also account for time-dependent forgetting, if during the delay between study and retrieval further (related) material is encoded. But retrieval competition may also explain retrieval-induced forgetting. Indeed, if retrieval competition was strength-dependent (i.e. contents with a stronger memory representation create higher interference levels than contents with a weaker memory representation: see Rundus, 1973; Raaijmakers & Shiffrin, 1981), then selective retrieval should make the retrieved items stronger competitors for the remaining nonretrieved items, and thus induce forgetting of the nonretrieved material (Roediger & Neely, 1982; Raaijmakers & Jakab, 2012).

Context change is a second prominent mechanism. It refers to the idea that changes in the physical or mental context after study can induce a difference in contexts between study and retrieval and thus impair recall performance. Obviously, this proposal can explain typical context-dependent forgetting, such as the ocurrence of forgetting when the environment or individuals' mood has changed between study and retrieval. It can account for time-dependent forgetting when supposing that context drifts during the retention interval (e.g. Estes, 1955; Bower, 1972). It can also explain list-method directed forgetting. Here the assumption is that the presentation of a forget cue after study can induce a change in people's mental contexts, and the resulting contextual mismatch between study and retrieval impairs recall of the to-be-forgotten memory contents (Sahakyan & Kelley, 2002). More recently, context change has also been suggested to underlie retrieval-induced forgetting. Here the proposal is that the retrieval process itself creates context change (Shiffrin, 1970; Jang & Huber, 2008). Selective retrieval may therefore change people's internal contexts and thus reduce their chances to recall previously encoded nonretrieved items (Jonker et al., 2013). Retrieval competition and context change thus offer explanations for a wide range of forgetting findings.

Although retrieval competition and context change provide promising explanations of episodic forgetting, it has repeatedly been argued in the memory literature that retrieval competition and context change cannot capture the whole variety of forgetting findings and there is an additional role of inhibition in some situations. Evidence for the role of inhibition has arisen mainly in retrieval-induced forgetting, list-method directed forgetting, and think/no-think impairment. In retrieval-induced forgetting the suggestion is that during selective retrieval the nonretrieved items interfere and are inhibited to reduce the interference, which can impair later retrieval of the nonretrieved items (Anderson, 2003). In list-method directed forgetting, the proposal is that the forget cue inhibits access to the original study context and thus impairs recall of the items studied in this context (Geiselman et al., 1983). Finally, in think/no-think impairment the assumption is that, during attempts to not let some memory contents enter consciousness, the memory representation of these contents is reduced so that accessibility is lowered when it comes to later retrieval (Anderson & Green, 2010). For an overview of the three inhibition proposals, see Bäuml et al. (2010).

This chapter discusses the possible role of inhibition in retrieval-induced forgetting and list-method directed forgetting. For each of these two forms of forgetting, the chapter introduces the experimental task employed to study the respective form of forgetting and the inhibition proposal entertained to explain the forgetting. Next, an overview of basic findings of each form of forgetting is provided, with a special emphasis on findings that the inhibition view can explain but which the prominent noninhibitory accounts cannot easily explain. Then, for both forms of forgetting, shortcomings of the inhibitory view are discussed and challenges for future work on theoretical accounts of this forgetting are outlined. The chapter will end with some conclusions regarding the possible roles of inhibition in retrieval-induced forgetting and list-method directed forgetting.

RETRIEVAL-INDUCED FORGETTING

Experimental task and inhibition view on retrieval-induced forgetting

In recent years, retrieval-induced forgetting (RIF) has mostly been examined using the retrieval-practice task, which was first introduced by Anderson et al. (1994) into the literature. In this task, participants repeatedly retrieve a subset of previously studied material, to find out how retrieval practice influences later recall of the practised and unpractised material. Participants typically study exemplars from different semantic categories (e.g. FRUIT-*orange*, FRUIT-*banana*, FURNITURE-*table*), before, in a subsequent retrieval-practice phase, they are asked to repeatedly retrieve half of the exemplars from half of the categories using a word stem completion task (e.g. FRUIT-*or___*). Finally, recall of all initially studied exemplars is tested after some delay (see Figure 8.1a). The retrieval practice phase creates three types of items: practised items, unpractised items, and control items. Practised items refer to practised items from practised categories (*orange*), unpractised items refer to unpractised items from practised categories (*banana*), and control items refer to items from unpractised categories (*table*). Unsurprisingly, recall of the practised items is typically enhanced relative to the control items. The crucial RIF finding, however, is that recall of the unpractised items is usually impaired relative to control items on the later test (see Figure 8.1b). RIF is a very general phenomenon and has been observed over a wide range of materials and experimental settings (for recent reviews, see Storm et al., 2015; Bäuml & Kliegl, 2017).

The proposal that an inhibitory mechanism mediates the forgetting of the unpractised items plays a very prominent role in the RIF literature (see Storm et al., 2015; Bäuml & Kliegl, 2017). This proposal assumes that RIF arises because the memory representation of the unpractised items is inhibited during retrieval practice. In particular, the account suggests that during retrieval practice of some of the studied items, related unpractised items interfere and compete for conscious recall. To reduce the interference and facilitate selection of the to-be-practised items, the memory representation of the unpractised items is suppressed. For instance, when subjects are cued with FRUIT-*or___* during the retrieval-practice phase, other studied fruits, like *banana*, may come to mind and compete for conscious recall. To reduce the interference from *banana* the memory

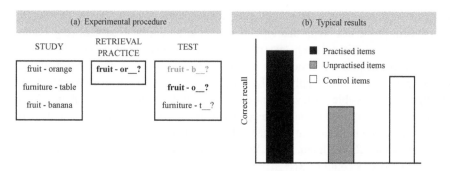

Figure 8.1 Retrieval-induced forgetting. a) Initially, participants study items from different semantic categories. In an ensuing retrieval-practice phase, only some of the items from some of the categories are repeatedly retrieved and thereby practised. On a final memory test, participants are asked to recall all items from the initial study phase. b) Practised items (e.g. fruit - orange) usually show enhanced recall, whereas unpractised items from the same practised categories (e.g. fruit - banana) show reduced recall relative to control items from categories that were not subject to retrieval practice (e.g. furniture - table).

representation of the item is suppressed, and, as a result, recall of that item on the subsequent final test is impaired.

CRITICAL RIF FINDINGS THAT INHIBITION CAN EXPLAIN

Testing format

The inhibition account assumes that suppression directly affects the representation of the unpractised items themselves, so that all retrieval routes to the inhibited item should become less effective and forgetting should therefore be observed across a wide range of memory tests. Research has largely confirmed this prediction, for instance showing that RIF occurs with category-cued recall and when category cues together with additional item-specific cues – like the items' unique initial letters or word stems – are exposed as retrieval cues at test (e.g. Anderson et al., 1994). But RIF has also been found in item recognition, both when using yes–no recognition testing (e.g. Hicks & Starns, 2004) and when using receiver-operating-characteristic analysis to examine whether selective retrieval impairs recognition of unpractised items (e.g. Spitzer & Bäuml, 2007).

Another suggestion arising from the view that RIF is due to inhibition is that RIF should still emerge when a novel test cue that was not present during study is provided at test.

Anderson and colleagues tested this cue-independence assumption by developing the independent-probe test. With this type of final test, an unpractised item (e.g. *banana*) is not tested with its original study cue (FRUIT-*b___*) but with a novel test cue (YELLOW-*b___*). The argument behind this procedure is that the presence of the novel retrieval cue may prevent participants from applying the original study cue to retrieve the practised item, thus bypassing possible retrieval competition arising from the practised items. A number of studies have examined the cue-independence assumption over the years, and the results from this research indicate that RIF can still arise when novel retrieval cues are employed at test (Anderson & Spellman, 1995; Weller et al., 2013). These findings provide support for the inhibition account of RIF.

Retrieval specificity

A further prediction of the inhibition account is that RIF should be retrieval specific, that is, only a practice phase that involves active retrieval of previously studied items should reduce recall of the unpractised items, whereas passive restudy of the same material should not. The reason is that retrieval practice, but not restudy of the practised items, should induce interference and inhibition of the unpractised items. Early research addressing the issue used two variants of the retrieval-practice task: restudy and noncompetitive retrieval practice. In both variants, the to-be-practised items are re-exposed intact with the goal of strengthening the items' associations to their cue without inducing interference and inhibition of the unpractised items. When employing the restudy method, some of the originally studied category–item pairs are re-exposed (e.g. FRUIT-*orange*) and participants are asked to study the word pairs once again (e.g. Ciranni & Shimamura, 1999; Bäuml & Aslan, 2004). When employing the noncompetitive retrieval practice method, some of the originally studied items are re-exposed and participants are asked to recall the items' category label when the category's word stem is provided as a retrieval cue (e.g. FR___- *orange*; Anderson et al., 2000; Hanslmayr et al., 2010). The typical finding with these methods was that RIF arose in the (competitive) retrieval-practice condition, but no RIF-like impairment was observed following restudy or noncompetitive retrieval practice, which suggests that RIF is retrieval specific.

The influence of secondary tasks

In recent years, a number of studies have sought to determine the nature of the inhibitory mechanism presumed to mediate RIF. Anderson (2003), for instance, suggested that the type of inhibition that selective memory retrieval can trigger belongs to a more general family of executive processes that also operate to control overt behaviour or ignore irrelevant stimuli. In contrast, some other authors have championed the view that inhibition is mostly an automatic mechanism that acts whenever irrelevant information is co-activated during attempts to retrieve relevant information by suppressing the irrelevant information (Conway & Fthenaki, 2003). Putting these two versions of the inhibition account to a test, Román et al. (2009) reduced participants' attentional resources during the retrieval-practice phase with a secondary, concurrent updating task. The idea was that if the suppression mechanism underlying RIF needs executive control, then overloading attentional resources with a secondary task during retrieval practice should impair the action of the suppression mechanism and thus reduce RIF. On the other hand, if the suppression mechanism was mainly an automatic process, then overloading subjects' attention during retrieval practice should not affect RIF. The results showed that, relative to a standard retrieval-practice condition, there was no RIF effect when the secondary task was performed during retrieval practice, but there was reliable facilitation of the practised items. Overall, these findings align with the view that RIF requires attentional control, thus supporting the executive-control version of the inhibition account.

Neural correlates

Thus far, a number of studies have provided evidence for the inhibition account of RIF by examining neural correlates of the forgetting effect during the retrieval-practice phase. According to Anderson's (2003) executive-control version of the inhibition account, frontally mediated executive control processes should be recruited to suppress competing items during retrieval practice, so enhanced activation in such frontal areas during retrieval practice should be observable. Employing electrophysiological measures of brain activity (electroencephalogram – EEG), one study did find that stronger positivity over frontal electrodes was elicited in the retrieval-practice condition relative to a restudy condition, and the stronger positivity was correlated with the amount of RIF arising at the final test (Johansson et al., 2007). A more recent fMRI (functional Magnetic Resonance Imaging) study reported even more direct evidence for a critical role of inhibition in RIF, by demonstrating that selective retrieval practice measurably reactivates competing (unpractised) items and then progressively suppresses those interfering competitors (Wimber et al., 2015).

A few studies also searched for neural markers of RIF during the final memory test (Wimber et al., 2008; Spitzer et al., 2009). On the basis of the inhibition account, one might expect to find neural markers of RIF that reflect the suggested reduced memory strength signal of the unpractised items. One study found the retrieval of unpractised items to be associated with increased activation in the left anterior region of the ventro-lateral prefrontal cortex (Wimber et al., 2008). This finding is consistent with the inhibition account because prior neuroscientific work was able to demonstrate that increased activity in this region reflected the retrieval of weak memory traces (Badre & Wagner, 2007). Overall, the findings from both fMRI and EEG studies suggest that inhibitory processes operate during retrieval practice, inducing RIF at the final memory test.

Developmental findings

One prominent view in research on both cognitive development and cognitive ageing is that inhibitory cognitive control capabilities are highly efficient in younger adults, but considerably less efficient in children and older adults (Hasher & Zacks, 1988; Bjorklund & Harnishfeger, 1990). Aslan and Bäuml (2010) examined RIF in kindergartners, second graders, and young adults, using both category-cued recall and item recognition. Results revealed that although all three age groups showed significant RIF in recall, only adults and second graders, but not kindergartners, showed forgetting in item recognition. Because inhibition-based RIF should be present in recall and recognition, these findings indicate that in adults and second graders, but not in kindergartners, RIF is mediated by (efficient) inhibition, supporting the proposal of an inhibitory deficit in kindergartners', but not school-aged children's, selective memory retrieval.

Prior research on RIF has provided evidence for an inhibitory deficit not only in preschool children, but also in adults above the age of 75 years. Aslan and Bäuml (2012) compared a group of 'young-old' adults (individuals between the ages of 60 and 75 years) with 'old-old' adults (individuals older than 75 years). They employed the retrieval-practice task with item recognition at test. In doing so, Aslan and Bäuml replicated earlier findings of intact RIF in the group of young-olds (e.g. Aslan et al., 2007; Ortega et al., 2012) but found an elimination of the effect in the group of old-olds, indicating that RIF may be a late-declining capability. Taken together, the findings from both children and older adults are in line with the proposal that inhibitory control processes mediate the forgetting. These control processes may develop during childhood, but then remain intact for most of the lifespan.

RIF FINDINGS THAT RETRIEVAL COMPETITION AND CONTEXT CHANGE CANNOT EASILY EXPLAIN

While the inhibition account assumes that RIF arises due to an inhibitory process that acts to overcome interference, the retrieval-competition and context-change accounts of RIF suggest that noninhibitory mechanisms underlie this form of forgetting.

Retrieval competition assumes that the associations between the practised items and their category cues are strengthened during retrieval practice, so that on the final test the (strengthened) practised items interfere and block access to the (non-strengthened) unpractised items, thus impairing memory for these items. For instance, successful retrieval of *orange* in the retrieval-practice phase may lead to a stronger association between *orange* and its category label FRUIT. When participants attempt to retrieve another initially studied exemplar from the category FRUIT on the final test (like *banana*), *orange* may then interfere and block successful recall of *banana*, thus creating RIF (Raaijmakers & Jakab, 2012).

In contrast, the context-change account of RIF argues that the act of retrieval in the retrieval-practice phase introduces a shift in the subjects' internal context, creating distinct study and practice contexts. During the final test, subjects are then presumed to access the practice context when searching for the (practised and unpractised) items of the practised categories but access the study context when searching for the control items, so that due to the induced context change, memory for the unpractised items may be impaired relative to the control items and RIF may arise (Jonker et al., 2013).

The finding that RIF arises over a wide range of final-test formats and is even present in item-recognition and independent-probe tests (e.g. Anderson & Spellman, 1995; Hicks & Starns, 2004) is hard to explain on the basis of the retrieval-competition account of RIF. Indeed, the account assumes that strengthening some exemplars through retrieval practice (e.g. FRUIT-*orange*) impairs the recall of related exemplars (e.g. FRUIT-*banana*) on a subsequent test because the presentation of their shared cue (FRUIT) causes the strengthened item (*orange*) to come to mind constantly and block the weaker item. Therefore, if RIF reflected the effects of retrieval competition, RIF should be present when the items' category cues are provided as retrieval cues at test. In contrast, RIF should be absent with item recognition or independent-probe testing, in which the effects of (strength-based) retrieval competition should be largely reduced, if not eliminated (see Ratcliff et al., 1990; Rupprecht & Bäuml, 2016). The context account of RIF has been argued to be able to explain the presence of RIF in item recognition, at least when the recognition task is unspeeded (Jonker et al., 2013). The argument is that when the studied item *banana* is presented at test without its category label, participants reactivate the category label FRUIT together with the context in which the label was previously provided. In the case of practised categories (like FRUIT), this context may be the practice context, whereas for control categories, it may be the study context, thus inducing RIF. Although the context account may thus explain the presence of RIF in item recognition (but see Rupprecht & Bäuml, 2017), the account cannot explain the presence of RIF in independent-probe tests. Indeed, novel cues should eliminate the suggested context effects and thus eliminate RIF.

The demonstration that RIF arises after standard (competitive) retrieval practice but not after restudy practice (e.g. Ciranni & Shimamura, 1999; Bäuml & Aslan, 2004) and not after noncompetitive retrieval practice (e.g. Anderson et al., 2000; Hanslmayr et al., 2010) is also difficult to reconcile with the two noninhibitory accounts of RIF. On the basis of retrieval competition, standard retrieval practice, restudy practice, and noncompetitive retrieval practice should all strengthen the cue–item associations of the practised items, thus impairing recall of the unpractised items on the later memory test. The context account is challenged by the finding that noncompetitive retrieval practice does not induce RIF. Because retrieval practice should create a change in mental context regardless of whether the task is competitive or noncompetitive in nature, RIF should arise after both types of retrieval. The account, however, is consistent with the finding that no RIF arises after restudy practice because, unlike retrieval practice, restudy should not induce a change in mental context, thus precluding RIF.

Román et al.'s (2009) finding that a secondary task during the retrieval-practice phase can eliminate RIF is inconsistent with retrieval competition. Because, in this study, selective retrieval practice led to successful strengthening of the practised items regardless of whether attention was divided during retrieval practice or not, memory of the unpractised items at test should have been impaired both when the secondary task was present and when it was absent during practice. The finding can also not easily be explained by the context account. On the one hand, proponents of the account may argue that a secondary task can attenuate retrieval-induced context change, thus reducing or even eliminating RIF, which is what Román et al. found. On the other hand, however, one might expect the presence of the secondary task to enhance the change in subjects' internal context and thus increase the size of RIF. In its current form, the account may be largely silent on this critical finding.

The observation that RIF is absent in preschool children and old-old adults (Aslan & Bäuml, 2010, 2012) is consistent with the inhibition account of RIF but is difficult to explain on the basis of retrieval competition. Because the two studies by Aslan and Bäuml found selective retrieval practice to induce successful strengthening of the practised items regardless of subjects' age levels, memory for the unpractised items should have been impaired on the final test in all these subject groups, which is not what the results showed. In contrast, the context account may be consistent with these developmental findings. Because previous work indicates that, in both younger children and older adults, memories are less well associated with context information than in young adults (Foley et al., 1983; Billingsley et al., 2002), one could argue that, when these two age groups attempt to retrieve an unpractised item on the final test (e.g., FRUIT-*o*___), the presentation of the category label FRUIT may trigger less of a tendency than in young adults to reinstate the context in which the label was last encountered (i.e. the practice context). Instead, these age groups may also recover the (more adequate) study context, which would reduce the RIF effect.

Possible shortcomings of and challenges for inhibition

While the inhibition account can explain a wide range of RIF findings, there are also findings that challenge the account. As was pointed out above, early findings consistently suggested that RIF exhibits retrieval specificity and arises in response to retrieval practice but not restudy trials (e.g. Ciranni & Shimamura, 1999; Anderson et al., 2000), which is well in line with the inhibition view. However, the results of more recent studies indicate that at least some re-exposure formats can induce RIF-like forgetting. Raaijmakers and Jakab (2012), for instance, employed a more demanding noncompetitive retrieval-practice task, in which the word stems of the category labels were absent during re-exposure (e.g. ___-*ball*) and exemplars with a relatively low frequency within their categories were used, which was supposed to enhance the strengthening of the associations between practised items and their category labels.

Verde (2013) re-exposed studied category–exemplar pairs during practice but asked subjects questions about each single pair (e.g. '*Is the category presented the best to classify the exemplar?*'), again with the intention of strengthening category–exemplar associations. Finally, in Jonker et al. (2013), mental imagination tasks preceded the restudy trials to simulate context change as it may be induced by the retrieval process itself during retrieval practice. And indeed, in all these cases, restudy impaired recall of the unpractised items, thus mimicking the typical RIF effect. These findings challenge retrieval specificity and therefore challenge the inhibition account. Rupprecht and Bäuml (2016, 2017) recently replicated all these findings but showed that the findings were restricted to recall testing. In fact, when item recognition was employed on the final test, (competitive) retrieval practice induced forgetting, whereas none of the employed reexposure formats did. Retrieval specificity thus seems to depend on testing format.

Another finding that is difficult to reconcile with the inhibition account is the observation that unpractised items seem to be shielded from the effects of retroactive interference. Abel and Bäuml (2014) employed a retrieval-practice task in which participants studied a categorised list and were then engaged in retrieval practice of some of the exemplars from some of the categories, before they were asked to learn a second categorised list, using the same categories as were employed in the first study list but with new category exemplars. The researchers found that the interpolated learning of the new category exemplars impaired recall of the control items, which replicates the standard finding of retroactive interference. In contrast, however, no such impairment arose for the recall of the practised and unpractised items, indicating that interpolated learning can reduce or even eliminate RIF. Arguably, on the basis of the inhibitory account, the unpractised items may be spared from interference effects because the learning of the related interpolated material may induce release processes on the inhibited information. While reexposure of the inhibited items following retrieval practice can diminish RIF (Storm et al., 2008), it is far from clear whether exposure of new, related material can induce the same release processes and thus eliminate the possible effects of retroactive interference.

The effects of prolonged delay on unpractised items constitute another puzzle for the inhibition account of RIF. Using retention intervals of 24 hours or longer between practice and test, a number of studies examined the role of prolonged delay for RIF. The results of the studies were mixed: while many studies reported intact RIF after the short delay but no RIF after the long delay (e.g. MacLeod & Macrae, 2001; Abel & Bäuml, 2014), a few other studies reported intact RIF also after the long delay (Garcia-Bajos et al., 2009; Storm et al., 2012). Interestingly, despite the difference in results, the findings from all these studies seem to converge on the pattern that the size of the RIF effect decreases with delay, with more time-dependent forgetting for the control items than the unpractised items (for a more extended discussion, see Bäuml & Kliegl, 2017). The role of retention interval for the unpractised items therefore shows a remarkable parallel to the role of retention interval for the practised items, which, both in the RIF studies and in studies on the testing effect (e.g. Roediger & Karpicke, 2006), typically show reduced time-dependent forgetting as well. As a whole, retrieval practice thus seems to insulate both practised and unpractised items against the effects of time-dependent forgetting and retroactive interference. These findings impose important empirical restrictions on theories of RIF, challenging the inhibition account of RIF as well as all other current accounts.

Final remarks on the role of inhibition in RIF

Many findings in the RIF literature are in line with the proposal that RIF is mediated by inhibitory processes. This account assumes that during selective retrieval the not-to-be-retrieved items interfere and are inhibited to reduce this interference. Such inhibition is proposed to weaken the items' memory representation, so that memory for these items is impaired over a wide range of memory tests, which correlates with the empirical findings. The inhibition account is also consistent with the findings that RIF is often retrieval specific and disappears in the presence of secondary tasks, and it agrees with a number of further findings as well (see Storm et al., 2015; Bäuml & Kliegl, 2017). However, not all findings in the RIF literature can be explained by inhibition. In particular, the presence of RIF-like forgetting in recall tests when certain restudy formats are employed for practice disagrees with the account, and may point to an additional role of retrieval competition in RIF (see Rupprecht & Bäuml, 2016, 2017).

Along these lines, a two-factor account of RIF has recently been suggested, which assumes that both inhibition and retrieval competition can contribute to RIF (Rupprecht & Bäuml, 2016; see also Anderson & Levy, 2007; Aslan & Bäuml, 2010; Schilling et al., 2014). This account assumes that inhibitory processes are triggered during retrieval practice and, in addition, retrieval competition can operate at test. While inhibition should induce a retrieval-specific reduction in the unpractised items' memory representation that can be measured over a wide range of memory tests, retrieval competition is assumed to not be retrieval specific and to play a role primarily in tests in which item-specific cues are reduced, like free recall or category-cued recall. In contrast, retrieval competition should hardly play a role in item recognition, in which the items themselves are presented as cues, and with independent-probe testing. Consequently, even though both inhibition and retrieval competition may contribute to RIF in general, the particular test format may influence the relative contributions of the two mechanisms.

LIST-METHOD DIRECTED FORGETTING

Experimental task and inhibition view on list-method directed forgetting

In experiments on list-method directed forgetting (LMDF; Bjork, 1970, 1989), participants typically study two lists of items. Between studying the two lists, they are either cued to remember the just studied first list for a later memory test (*remember condition*), or they are cued to forget the studied list – pretending that it was just presented for practice or by error (*forget condition*). In both conditions, participants are asked to memorise the second list, which is presented immediately after the remember cue or the forget cue were provided. After study of the second list, all participants recall *both* lists of items, irrespective of whether they received a remember or a forget cue for the first list (see Figure 8.2a). The results typically show two distinct effects of the forget cue relative to the remember cue condition: a recall impairment of list-1 items, often termed 'directed forgetting' of the first list items; and a recall improvement of list-2 items, often termed 'recall enhancement' of the second list items (see Figure 8.2b). Both effects of the forget cue are very general findings and have been demonstrated over a wide range of materials and experimental conditions (for reviews, see Bäuml et al., 2010; Sahakyan et al., 2013).

The proposal that an inhibitory mechanism mediates directed forgetting of list-1 items is one of the most discussed, and still current, theoretical accounts in the LMDF literature. The proposal assumes that a forget cue activates an inhibitory control process that reduces access to the list-1 study episode (Geiselman et al., 1983; Bjork, 1989). Thus, in contrast to RIF, inhibitory processes are assumed not to directly affect the memory representations of the single items but to impair retrieval routes to the whole list-1 study context. Such inhibition, for instance, might operate during list-2 encoding, when the previously studied list-1 items may get reactivated and interfere with the encoding of list-2 items (Conway

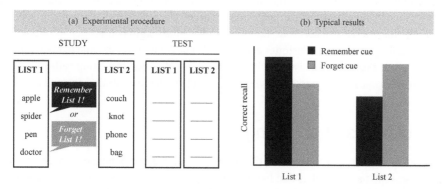

Figure 8.2 List-method directed forgetting. a) Participants study two lists of items and, after studying list 1, are cued to either keep on remembering the list for a later test or to try to forget the list, pretending that it would not be tested later. After studying list 2, all participants are asked to recall both previously studied lists, irrespective of which cue they received for list 1. b) Relative to participants who received a remember cue for list 1, participants who received a forget cue show reduced recall of list 1 and enhanced recall of list 2.

et al., 2000; Pastötter & Bäuml, 2007; Bäuml et al., 2008).[1] Critically, the inhibited access to list 1 can not only account for the reduced recall of list-1 items but can also accommodate the finding of the enhanced recall of list-2 items. Indeed, if the interference from list 1 is reduced after a forget cue has been provided, then recall of list-2 items should benefit and show higher recall in the forget condition than in the remember condition (see also Bjork & Bjork, 1996; Bäuml & Kliegl, 2013).

CRITICAL LMDF FINDINGS THAT INHIBITION CAN EXPLAIN

Testing format

A central assumption of the inhibition account is that inhibition does not directly impair the representation of the to-be-forgotten items in memory, but reduces access to the whole list-1 study episode. This assumption suggests that the presence of list-1 forgetting should depend on the type of test used to assess memory. For instance, whereas in free recall no retrieval cues are provided that can help reinstate the original study context, re-exposure of the list items during item recognition may reinstate context. Consistent with these expectations, list-1 forgetting has typically been found to be present with free-recall testing (e.g. Bjork, 1989) and to arise also when weak item-specific cues, such as the items' unique initial letters, are provided as retrieval cues at test (e.g. Bäuml & Samenieh, 2010). In contrast, with recognition testing, list-1 forgetting has typically been found to be absent, both when using yes–no recognition testing (e.g. Geiselman et al., 1983) and when using receiver-operating-characteristic analysis to examine whether the forget cue influences recognition of the to-be-forgotten items (Pastötter et al., 2016). The findings on the role of testing format for LMDF are therefore consistent with the view that directed forgetting reflects reduced access to the original study context, a view compatible with the inhibition account of LMDF.

The role of list-2 encoding

Another finding of high relevance to the continuing theoretical debate on which cognitive mechanisms mediate LMDF is that list-1 forgetting depends on subsequent list-2 encoding. Following an original finding by Gelfand and Bjork (cited in Bjork, 1989), Pastötter and Bäuml (2007) varied in whether, after study of list 1 and the presentation of the forget or

---

[1] In its original version, the inhibition account is completely silent on exactly when the suggested inhibition processes should operate, thereby raising at least two possibilities: one possibility is that the proposed inhibitory processes may be activated immediately after the forget cue has been provided, and the other possibility is that the proposed inhibitory processes may be activated later during encoding of the second list items.

remember cues, subjects were asked to study a second list of items or were engaged in an unrelated distractor task. Results showed list-1 forgetting when the second list had been studied, but did not show any forgetting of the first list when the second list had not been studied. In a follow-up study, Pastötter and Bäuml (2010) additionally showed that the amount of list-1 forgetting is directly related to the amount of list-2 encoding; that is, the more items that are studied during list-2 encoding, the more pronounced the forgetting of list 1 is. These findings are consistent with the view that control processes unfold during list-2 encoding that reduce possible interference from list-1 items by inhibiting access to the whole list-1 study context. Importantly, the degree of the involvement of such control processes should depend on between-list interference: when there is no or only little interference arising from list 1 during study of list 2, no or only little cognitive control should be required and no list-1 forgetting should arise. Results by Conway et al. (2000) are consistent with this proposal.

The influence of secondary tasks

A natural prediction arising from the proposal that the mechanism mediating directed forgetting is inhibitory in nature, and relies on cognitive control and executive processes, is that its involvement should be resource dependent. A few studies examined this proposal by introducing secondary tasks during list-2 encoding. If inhibitory control was resource dependent and operated during list-2 encoding, then secondary tasks during list-2 encoding should reduce the inhibitory control, thus attenuating list-1 forgetting. Macrae et al. (1997) were the first to address the issue, asking subjects to count vowels during the presentation of list-2 items. Conway et al. (2000) revisited the issue, asking subjects during list-2 encoding to keep in mind a list of digits. Both studies found the secondary task to reduce or even eliminate list-1 forgetting. These findings are consistent with the assumption of an inhibitory control process that is active during list-2 encoding and downregulates interference from intruding list-1 items.

Effects on incidental learning

Another prediction arising from the inihibition account of LMDF is that all contents that were encoded into memory during list-1 encoding should show directed forgetting, regardless of whether they were subject to the forget instruction or not. Indeed, according to inhibition, access to the study episode as a whole should be impaired, and thus all the contents that were part of this episode should show forgetting. In a seminal study by Geiselman et al. (1983), this prediction was put to the test by presenting intermixed study and judge items in each of the two item lists. For study items, subjects were asked to memorise them for a later test, but for judge items, subjects were merely asked to provide pleasantness ratings; in particular, subjects did not anticipate being tested on these judge items later. Intentionally encoded study items were generally remembered better than incidentally encoded judge items, but reduced recall of list 1 and enhanced recall of list 2 after the forget cue compared to the remember cue were nevertheless present for both item types (for a replication, see Abel & Bäuml, 2019). This finding is consistent with the view that the forget cue triggers inhibition of the whole list-1 study episode, not differentiating between an episode's intentionally and incidentally encoded contents.

Neural correlates

To date, two studies have been reported in the literature investigating the neural mechanisms underlying LMDF. Both studies measured neural correlates during list-2 encoding and thus were based on the view that the mechanisms mediating this form of forgetting operate during postcue encoding (Conway et al., 2000; Pastötter & Bäuml, 2007, 2010). Measuring EEGs and analysing subjects' oscillatory brain activity, Bäuml et al. (2008) found that the forget cue induces two effects relative to the remember cue condition: an increase in power and a decrease in phase coupling, both observed in the upper alpha frequency band (11–13 Hz). Whereas the increase in alpha power predicted the enhanced recall of list-2 items, the decrease in alpha phase coupling predicted the forgetting of list-1 items. Because phase coupling between electrode sites is often regarded a measure of the synchrony between distant neural assemblies and coherent firing between distant neuronal populations has been interpreted as a mechanism subserving binding processes, the decrease in alpha phase coupling could reflect the inhibitory unbinding of list-1 items and the deactivation of the retrieval routes to list 1.

In the second study, Hanslmayr et al. (2012) measured participants' brain activity by simultaneously recording EEG along with fMRI. EEG analysis again revealed a decrease in phase coupling in the upper alpha frequency band (11–13 Hz), whereas fMRI analysis additionally showed a simultaneous BOLD signal increase in the left prefrontal cortex. Moreover, direct repetitive Transcranial Magnetic Stimulation (rTMS) of the dorsolateral prefrontal cortex during list-2 encoding enhanced directed forgetting and phase desynchronisation, establishing a causal link between neural activity in the dorsolateral prefrontal cortex and list-1 forgetting. These findings go well with prior work on other forms of voluntary forgetting, which indicated that memory control may be mediated by the dorsolateral prefrontal cortex (see Anderson & Hanslmayr, 2014). Overall, the reports on neural correlates of LMDF are consistent with the view that frontally mediated executive control processes underlie directed forgetting.

Developmental findings

Following the view that cognitive control capabilities should be less efficient in children and older adults than in young adults (e.g. Hasher & Zacks, 1988; Bjorklund &

Harnishfeger, 1990), another line of research has examined directed forgetting across the lifespan. Regarding children, this work indicates that the mechanisms underlying directed forgetting seem to be maturing during childhood. In fact, several studies reported directed forgetting in older elementary school children, like fifth graders, that was indistinguishable in size from the forgetting in young adults, whereas the directed forgetting in younger elementary school children, like first graders, was reduced or even eliminated (e.g. Harnishfeger & Pope, 1996; Aslan et al., 2010). This holds while first graders may also show typical LMDF – but only if a forget cue is employed that places very high emphasis on the need to forget (see Aslan et al., 2010a).

Regarding older adults, results indicate that the mechanisms mediating directed forgetting remain rather stable across large parts of adulthood. In comparing LMDF in younger adults with LMDF in older adults with an age range between 65 and 75 years, results consistently showed directed forgetting in older adults that was comparable in size to that in young adults (Sego et al., 2006; Zellner & Bäuml, 2006). Above 75 years of age, however, older adults' directed forgetting seems to dissipate. Consistent with this view, Aslan and Bäuml (2013) reported typical LMDF in young-old adults (up to 75 years) but reduced LMDF in old-old adults (above 75 years). LMDF thus seems to be a late-declining capability. Taken together, the findings from both young children and older adults are in line with the proposal that inhibitory control processes mediate the forgetting. These control processes may evolve during middle childhood, but then remain intact for most of the lifespan, only becoming inefficient when we reach very old age.

LMDF FINDINGS THAT CONTEXT CHANGE CANNOT EASILY EXPLAIN

The inhibition account of LMDF assumes that directed forgetting is due to the involvement of an inhibitory control process that downregulates the interference from list 1 by inhibiting access to the list as a whole. In contrast, the context-change account of LMDF assumes that the forget cue induces a change in people's mental context after study of list 1. This context change should lead to a mismatch between the context present at test and the context present during list-1 study, which should reduce recall of list-1 items (Sahakyan & Kelley, 2002). Like inhibition, this account not only provides an explanation of list-1 forgetting, but can also explain list-2 enhancement. Indeed, because the suggested reduced access to list 1 should decrease the list's interference potential during recall of list-2 items, not only list-1 forgetting but also list-2 enhancement should arise.

The finding that LMDF arises mostly in free recall and cued recall but not in item recognition tests (e.g. Geiselman et al., 1983) is not easily explained on the basis of the context-change view of LMDF. The reason is that results on the effects of context change in item recognition in the literature are mixed. Whereas some context-change studies reported evidence for context effects in item recognition (e.g. Bodner & Lindsay, 2003), other studies did not find any reduction in recognition performance after context change (e.g. Smith et al., 1978). Apparently, the circumstances that surround a context change determine whether context change reduces item recognition. What exactly the circumstances in LMDF are that may prevent the forgetting of list-1 items to show up in item recognition is unclear to date.

The finding that list-2 encoding is a necessary precondition for directed forgetting to arise, together with the finding that the amount of forgetting increases with the amount of postcue encoding (Pastötter & Bäuml, 2007, 2010), provides another challenge for the context-change account. The reason is that, in a number of classic context-change studies, manipulations that decreased access to study context at test have been shown to reduce recall even in the absence of further encoding after the context change (e.g. Godden & Baddeley, 1975; Smith et al., 1978). On the other hand, when relatively weak context-change manipulations had been used, like simple room changes or manipulations of internal states, such as mood induction, context change sometimes failed to induce a context effect (e.g. Eich, 1985; Fernandez & Glenberg, 1985). Mental context change as induced by a forget cue may thus represent such weak context change, requiring subsequent learning of further material to enhance the contextual effect. Results from Pastötter and Bäuml (2007) showing context-dependent forgetting, as induced by a mental context change task, in the presence but not the absence of subsequent encoding, are consistent with such a proposal.

The finding that secondary tasks during list-2 encoding can reduce or even eliminate directed forgetting (Macrae et al., 1997; Conway et al., 2000) is also not easily explained by the context-change account. Indeed, if the forget cue triggered mental context change, what exactly happens subsequent to the context change might not matter much, and list-1 forgetting might arise regardless of whether attention was divided during list-2 encoding or not. Alternatively, one may argue that secondary tasks may well influence context change. For instance, the encoding of the list-2 context may require attentional resources, and when these resources are taxed by a secondary task, context encoding may become less efficient, thus reducing the contextual change and the forgetting of list-1 items (e.g. Sahakyan et al., 2013). In contrast, the presence of the secondary task might create further context change on its own regardless of whether there was prior forget cue-induced context change or not, in which case list-1 forgetting would not depend much on the presence of the secondary task. Obviously, in its current form, the context-change account is largely silent on the possible role of secondary tasks in LMDF.

Probably the currently strongest challenge for the context-change account of LMDF is provided by the recent finding that list-1 forgetting is lasting (Abel & Bäuml, 2017, 2019). Indeed, it is a relatively straightforward prediction of the context-change account that LMDF should not be lasting. The reason is that internal context is generally assumed to change over time (e.g. Estes, 1955; Bower, 1972), so that experimentally induced context change should lose much of its relevance when the retention interval between study and test is prolonged and mental context thus has changed due to the sheer passage of time. Results by Divis and Benjamin (2014) provide direct support for this claim by showing that context-change effects can be present immediately after study but be absent

15 minutes later. Against this background, the findings of Abel and Bäuml (2017, 2019) on the persistency of LMDF are important. These researchers conceptually replicated Divis and Benjamin's (2014) result that context-change effects are transient, reporting intact context-dependent forgetting after a 3-minute retention interval but no forgetting after a prolonged retention interval of 20 minutes. More important, Abel and Bäuml showed that a forget cue can create forgetting that is still present after delays of 20 minutes and even 24 hours. Critically, the difference in results between context-dependent forgetting and directed forgetting after prolonged retention interval arose, although the two forms of forgetting showed equivalent forgetting after the short 3-minute retention interval. These findings are clearly at odds with the context-change account of LMDF.

Possible shortcomings of and challenges for inhibition

While the inhibition account is basically consistent with a wide range of LMDF findings, a general critique of advocates of noninhibitory accounts of LMDF is that the account suffers from conceptual shortcomings and a certain degree of theoretical vagueness. Indeed, in itself the account makes relatively few specific predictions that can be tested directly, and quite often the account provides a post hoc explanation of findings only. One example is the issue of when exactly inhibition in this paradigm operates. As mentioned above, a priori there are at least two possibilities, and inhibition may operate either immediately after the forget cue has been provided or later during list-2 encoding. It is the finding that LMDF presupposes list-2 encoding (e.g. Pastötter & Bäuml, 2007, 2010), which indicates that inhibition may operate during list-2 encoding. Another example is the issue of whether LMDF is transient or persistent. In its original version, the account makes no prediction on the issue at all. It is the finding of persistent LMDF which suggests that inhibition should be assumed to be lasting (for a discussion, see Abel & Bäuml, 2019). Obviously, the concept of inhibition in LMDF is still underspecified and requires further conceptual work in order to create a larger number of specific predictions.

Like the context-change account of LMDF, the inhibition account assumes that list-1 forgetting and list-2 enhancement are the two sides of the same coin. Because the forget cue reduces the accessibility of list-1 items, interference of list 1 during list-2 recall should be reduced and recall of list-2 items should thus be enhanced. However, results from a number of studies have shown that the two effects of the forget cue do not always arise together. Accordingly, list-1 forgetting has been found in the absence of list-2 enhancement, and list-2 enhancement has been found in the absence of list-1 forgetting (e.g. Sahakyan & Delaney, 2003; Benjamin, 2006; Pastötter & Bäuml, 2010; Aslan & Bäuml, 2013). As a result, it has been suggested that the two effects of the forget cue might be partly mediated by different mechanisms, with the forgetting being caused by inhibition or context change, and the enhancement being mediated by (additional) improved encoding. Sahakyan and Delaney (2003), for instance, suggested that list-2 enhancement might be due to a switch to more efficient encoding strategies from list 1 to list 2. Pastötter and Bäuml (2010) argued that encoding efficiency decreases with increasing amounts of incoming information, and the forget cue then prompts a reset of the encoding process for list-2 items. In both cases, the inhibition account would have to be complemented with a second (encoding) mechanism in order to be able to explain the findings of dissociations between list-1 forgetting and list-2 enhancement.

Another challenge for the inhibition account of LMDF is provided by Lehman and Malmberg's (2009) finding that LMDF as it occurs in the original (two-list) task differs from LMDF as it occurs in a three-list variant of the task. In the three-list variant, before studying lists 1 and 2, subjects study an additional list (list 0), and after studying list 0 and list 1 they are then cued to either remember or forget the two previous lists.[2] Unfortunately, LMDF in the three-list task differs fundamentally from LMDF in the two-list task. Above all, when using the three-list task, the forgetting of list-1 items is present in item recognition, whereas it is typically absent in the two-list task (for further dissociations between tasks, see Abel & Bäuml, 2019). This finding provides a challenge to the inhibition account, which assumes that forgetting should be absent in item recognition. Why results seem to change from the two-list task to the three-list task is an open issue. Getting an answer on this issue is important and may inform us on whether different mechanisms mediate the forgetting in the two types of tasks.

Final remarks on the role of inhibition in LMDF

Many findings in the LMDF literature are consistent with the proposal that LMDF is mediated by inhibitory processes. The inhibition account assumes that a cue to forget no-longer-relevant information activates a cognitive control process that reduces access to the respective study episode, and thereby downregulates the outdated information's interference potential. Critically, such inhibition is assumed to impair retrieval routes to the original episode but to not impair the memory representation of the single items. Consistently, LMDF is reliably observed on recall tests, but is usually absent on item recognition tests. On the basis of the proposal that inhibition operates during postcue encoding, the inhibition account is in line with the finding that list-1 forgetting depends on list-2 encoding and disappears when secondary tasks are introduced during list-2 encoding, as well as a number of further findings in the literature (see Bäuml et al., 2010; Sahakyan et al., 2013). Yet not all findings are easily explained by inhibition. Above all, the account suffers from conceptual shortcomings, which reduce the account's predictive power.

Accounts of LMDF are typically single-mechanism accounts and assume that list-1 forgetting and list-2 enhancement are mediated by the same cognitive mechanism. This is also true for inhibition. Results on dissociations between list-1 forgetting and list-2 enhancement challenge this view and thus also challenge inhibition. They indicate that

---

[2] This task was introduced by Lehman and Malmberg to reduce possible unwanted advantages of list 1 over list 2, which, according to the authors, may occur in the two-list task.

an additional encoding mechanism may contribute to list-2 enhancement, as is reflected in current two-mechanism accounts of LMDF, which assume that inhibition or context change mediate list-1 forgetting and an additional encoding mechanism contributes to list-2 enhancement. Whether the contribution of the encoding mechanism reflects a change in encoding strategy (Sahakyan & Delaney, 2003) or some reset of the encoding process (Pastötter & Bäuml, 2010) is an open issue that requires further research.

CONCLUSIONS

Retrieval competition and context change can explain a wide range of forgetting findings, including retroactive interference, proactive interference, time-dependent forgetting, and context-dependent forgetting. Although it has been argued that the two cognitive mechanisms can also explain RIF and LMDF – and, in concert, may even serve as a complete explanation of episodic forgetting – there is evidence that this is not the case and that neither of the two mechanisms can (easily) explain the whole range of RIF and LMDF findings. For instance, regarding RIF, both retrieval competition and context change are challenged by the findings that (i) RIF arises in item recognition and independent-probe tests, (ii) RIF can be retrieval specific, with selective retrieval (but not selective restudy) impairing recall of nonrepeated items, and (iii) RIF disappears when there is a secondary task during selective memory retrieval, although the secondary task does not affect recall of the practised items. Regarding LMDF, context change has problems to explain why (i) changes in internal context induce transient forgetting whereas a forget cue induces lasting forgetting, (ii) postcue encoding is critical for the forgetting of precue items, and (iii) a secondary task during second list encoding eliminates the forgetting of first list items. Thus, other cognitive mechanisms may operate to induce RIF and LMDF.

Indeed, there is evidence that inhibitory processes contribute to RIF and LMDF. The assumption that selective retrieval induces inhibition of nonretrieved items, for instance, can explain why (i) RIF arises over a wide range of memory tasks and is not restricted to recall tests, (ii) RIF can be retrieval specific, and (iii) RIF disappears in the presence of a secondary task. Similarly, the assumption that a forget cue inhibits access to the original study context in LMDF may explain why (i) the forgetting of to-be-forgotten items is lasting but forgetting induced by context change is not, (ii) there is a critical role of postcue encoding for the forgetting of precue items, and (iii) directed forgetting disappears in the presence of a secondary task.

However, although it is likely that inhibition contributes to RIF, there is also evidence that inhibition alone can not capture the whole range of RIF findings, as, for instance, is demonstrated by the fact that retrieval specificity typically arises in item recognition but can be absent in recall tests. Multiple mechanisms may thus underlie this form of forgetting, and a two-mechanism account, which assumes a role of both inhibition and retrieval competition in this form of forgetting, indeed seems to be able to explain a wide range of RIF findings. Whether this account is sufficient to explain RIF, or needs the inclusion of further mechanisms like context change, is unclear to date and awaits future examination.

With regard to LMDF, inhibition may be able to account for a wide range of LMDF findings, but this holds only if inhibition is assumed to be long lasting and to operate during postcue encoding. Both assumptions are post hoc inclusions into the original version of the account and, clearly, further empirical work is required to see whether these assumptions really hold. Until then, the status of the inhibition account of LMDF remains somewhat unclear, as does the answer to the question of whether multiple mechanisms may mediate LMDF, for instance, with inhibition operating in some situations (or individuals) and context change in others. Understanding the exact role of inhibition in episodic forgetting remains a challenge for future studies.

Further Reading

Bäuml, K.-H. T., & Kliegl, O. (2017). Retrieval-induced remembering and forgetting. In J. T. Wixted (ed.), *Learning and Memory: A comprehensive reference. Vol. 2: Cognitive Psychology of Memory* (2nd edn), Editor J. H. Byrne, (pp. 27–51). Oxford: Academic Press.

Sahakyan, L., Delaney, P. F., Foster, N. L., & Abushanab, B. (2013). List-method directed forgetting in cognitive and clinical research: A theoretical and methodological review. *Psychology of Learning and Motivation*, 59, 131–189.

9

MOTIVATED FORGETTING

Forgetting what we want to forget

David Groome, Michael W. Eysenck
and Robin Law

This chapter is about motivated forgetting, which is the suppression of memories that we do not want to retrieve, often because they are in some way troubling or unpleasant. We begin with a section on repression, which was the first type of motivated forgetting to be investigated. Freud (1915/1963) considered that people tend to repress memories of disturbing events, by forcing them out of consciousness and into the unconscious part of the mind. However, Freud's theory of repression was not supported by any scientific evidence. The evidence for and against the theory of repression from subsequent studies is reviewed in the section that follows. Another example of motivated forgetting is seen in the efforts made to suppress distressing and unwanted memories in those suffering from PTSD (Post-Traumatic Stress Disorder), a condition that is caused by exposure to a distressing or terrifying experience of some kind. Having discussed these examples of motivated forgetting in real-life settings, we then consider the findings of laboratory studies in which participants are asked to deliberately try to suppress memories. These studies include the investigation of Directed Forgetting (DF), in which participants are instructed to forget certain items, and the Think/No-think procedure, in which participants are instructed not to direct their thoughts to some items. These laboratory studies are included in the chapter because they help to shed light on the ways in which people can suppress memories in real life.

WHAT MOTIVATES PEOPLE TO FORGET?

Throughout most of the history of psychological research on memory, it has been assumed that forgetting is undesirable. As a result, research designed to explain forgetting has focused on factors beyond our control (see Chapter 1). However, as Anderson and Hanslmayr (2014, p. 290) pointed out, 'We are … conspirators in our own forgetting. We wield control over mnemonic processes, choosing among life's experiences, winners and losers for the potent effects of attention, reflection, and suppression'.

What motivates us to deliberately forget some of our memories? There are more answers to this question than you can shake a stick at. Here we will briefly discuss the main ones. First, and most importantly, selective forgetting of unpleasant memories can help us to be happier. The most famous advocate of this reason was Sigmund Freud, who argued that traumatic memories are often made inaccessible to conscious awareness through repression (Erdelyi, 2006). As we will see, there has been considerable controversy over the role (and even the existence) of repression. In addition, as discussed later, we sometimes use various cognitive strategies to downregulate or reduce our negative emotions.

Second, forgetting unpleasant or threatening information about ourselves can help us to preserve our self-image. Research has led to the identification of 'mnemic neglect', whereby individuals remember self-affirming feedback but selectively forget self-threatening feedback (Sedikides & Green, 2009). Of importance, there is much less mnemic neglect if individuals have previously received positive, self-enhancing feedback on a different task. As Sedikides and Green (2009, p. 1055) concluded, 'The phenomenon [mnemic neglect] is motivational: it is in the service of self-protection'.

Most individuals are also motivated to have a shared reality with other people to enhance feelings of social belongingness. This often leads us to exhibit a sharing-is-believing effect: we forget what actually happened in the past and replace it with a version of events fitting others' memories (Echterhoff & Higgins, 2018; see Chapter 1).

Third, sometimes we want to deceive other people. It is generally easier to do so if we deliberately forget information we want to keep secret. In recent years, there has been much interest in a lie-detection technique called 'brain fingerprinting'. This involves using electroencephalography (EEG) to assess brain-wave activity in response to various stimuli. Of crucial importance are individual responses to crime-related stimuli having special significance for the culprit. The focus is on an EEG component called the P300; this occurs approximately 300 ms–900 ms after stimulus presentation and reflects conscious recognition of the stimulus as significant.

If individuals cannot suppress or forget incriminating evidence, we would predict that culprits' P300 to crime-related stimuli would be greater than that of innocent individuals. It has been claimed that this is the case. However, there have been many criticisms of the evidence (McGorrery, 2017). Of most importance is a study by Bergström et al. (2013). 'Culprits' instructed to suppress their memory of crime-related stimuli had significantly smaller P300s to such stimuli than did those not so instructed. Thus, people can use retrieval suppression to evade detection.

Fourth, forgetting information inconsistent with our beliefs can facilitate us in maintaining our beliefs and attitudes. Consider views on climate change, which is currently a hot topic. The memories of many climate-change deniers are distorted. Howe and Leiserowitz (2013) tested Americans' memories of the previous summer, which had been unusually hot. Only half as many strong climate-change deniers remembered that summer as very hot compared to individuals strongly believing in human-induced climate change.

Leviston et al. (2013) reported a different memorial distortion among climate-change deniers in an Australian study. On average, they believed 43% of other people agreed with their views on climate change, whereas the actual figure was only 6%! These disbelievers in climate change thought that only 20% of Australians believed in human-induced climate change (the actual figure was 50%).

In what follows, we discuss several diverse examples of motivated forgetting. As you will see, much progress has been made in understanding the processes and mechanisms underlying these examples. As yet, however, we have no overarching theoretical framework.

Repression

The first systematic attempt to understand motivated forgetting was that of Sigmund Freud (1856–1939). Of central importance to his theoretical approach was the notion of repression: 'The essence of repression lies simply in the function of rejecting and keeping something out of consciousness' (Freud, 1915/1963, p. 86). However, matters are more complex than that quotation implies. Freud sometimes used the term 'repression' to refer to an inhibited capacity for emotional experience (Madison, 1956).

It is often thought that Freud regarded repression as being unconscious. However, that is also an oversimplification. Freud argued that repression can be an active, intentional process (Erdelyi, 2001; Boag, 2010). Unfortunately this rather wide-ranging view of repression makes it harder to assess the validity of Freud's notion of 'repression' since it can mean several different things.

It would be hard to overestimate the importance of the 'repression' concept to Freud's entire theoretical approach to psychoanalysis. He claimed repressed memories predominantly refer to extremely unpleasant or traumatic events patients could not recall consciously without experiencing intense anxiety. Psychoanalytic therapy focuses on allowing patients to retrieve their repressed memories as a prerequisite for recovery.

Most evidence on repression is based on adult patients (predominantly suffering from clinical anxiety) claiming to have recovered previously repressed memories of childhood physical and/or sexual abuse. There has been (and continues to be) huge controversy concerning how these recovered memories should be interpreted. Approximately 25% of practising clinical psychologists believe patients often have genuine repressed memories that cannot be recalled because they are so emotionally traumatic (Engelhard et al., 2019). Patihis et al. (2014) found 77% of the public in the United Kingdom and the United States agreed that traumatic experiences are frequently repressed, and 64% agreed these repressed memories can be recalled accurately in therapy. In contrast, only 9% of applied cognitive psychologists believe patients often repress their memories of trauma.

The great majority of applied cognitive psychologists argue that most recovered memories are actually false. These false recovered memories occur predominantly because of suggestions provided by their therapist. This has led many researchers to distinguish between recovered memories emerging spontaneously *outside* therapy and those emerging *inside* therapy itself. The obvious prediction from the false-memory viewpoint is that most recovered memories should emerge inside rather than outside therapy.

Evidence for the occurrence of repression

We start by considering the traditional Freudian repression account of recovered memories. This account would receive support if two conditions were met: (1) there is confirmatory evidence that the alleged childhood abuse actually happened; and (2) the individuals concerned demonstrably developed amnesia for that abuse. Pope and Hudson (1995) adopted those criteria and found there were only four applicable published studies. None of these studies satisfied both criteria. Pope et al. (1999) reviewed the relevant evidence and confirmed the lack of convincing evidence that individuals whose abuse had been corroborated had repressed (or even forgotten) their traumatic experiences.

According to Freud's theory, repression occurs as a way of reducing the intolerable anxiety associated with traumatic memories. It follows that the probability of repression occurring for memories of childhood sexual abuse would *increase* progressively with increases in the traumatic impact and distress associated with such memories. Goodman et al. (2019) obtained relevant findings from a longitudinal study on childhood maltreatment (including sexual abuse). Contrary to the Freudian account, greater traumatic impact of the abuse and greater distress associated with it were both associated with more accurate subsequent memory for the abuse.

Advocates of the false-memory perspective have carried out numerous studies showing that it is surprisingly easy to create false childhood memories under controlled laboratory conditions. Much of this research has used the 'lost-in-the-mall' technique (Loftus & Pickrell, 1995). Adults are presented with descriptions of childhood events allegedly provided by family members (e.g. parents). Of key importance, one event is false and was simply made up by the researchers. Then participants recall these childhood events on two or three occasions employing techniques used in therapy to produce recovered memories. Finally, the extent to which participants have formed a false memory is assessed by interview.

Scoboria et al. (2017) reviewed the findings from eight studies using the 'lost-in-the-mall' technique. Overall, 30% of participants developed a false memory and an additional 23% accepted the false event as genuine to some extent. These percentages were higher under certain conditions. For example, if the description of the false event included idiosyncratic self-relevant information (e.g. a teacher's name), 40% of participants formed a false memory compared to only 24% if that information was not provided.

Evidence supportive of the false-memory perspective was obtained by Lief and Fetkewicz (1995) in a study of patients who admitted that they had reported false recovered memories. Approximately 80% of these patients had had a therapist who made direct suggestions they had been sexually abused in childhood. However, it is hard to establish the truth of these retracted allegations of childhood sexual abuse (Ost, 2017).

Dramatic findings relating to the possible extent of recovered memories were reported by Patihis and Pendergrast (2019). They discovered that 4% of an age-representative sample of adult Americans reported having had recovered memories – this implies that an amazing 9 million Americans have experienced recovered memories! Their key finding was that recovered memories were 20 times more likely among those whose therapists had discussed the possibility of repressed memories than those whose therapists had not done so. These findings strongly suggest that most recovered memories are not genuine.

One of the most important studies was conducted by Geraerts et al. (2007). They identified three groups of adults who had suffered childhood sexual abuse: (1) suggestive therapy group: recovered memories initially recalled inside therapy; (2) spontaneous recovery group: recovered memories initially recalled outside therapy; and (3) continuous memory group: they had continuous memories of sexual abuse from childhood onwards.

Geraerts et al. (2007) assessed the genuineness of the memories of childhood sexual abuse by using corroborating evidence (e.g. the abuser had confessed). There were major group differences: there was corroborating evidence for 45% of the continuous memory group, 37% of the spontaneous memory group, but 0% of the suggestive therapy group. Thus, recovered memories recalled outside therapy (i.e. spontaneous memory group) are probably much more likely to be genuine than those recalled inside therapy (the suggestive therapy group).

One limitation with the above study is its somewhat simplistic dichotomy of recovered memories into those recovered inside or spontaneously outside therapy. For example, memories recovered outside therapy would not really be spontaneous if they were triggered by suggestions made by another person (Raymaekers et al., 2012).

A resolution

McNally and Geraerts (2009) and Engelhard et al. (2019) proposed a theoretical account of the findings relating to allegedly repressed memories that differs significantly from the repression and false-memory accounts. They argued that children who suffer physical and/or sexual abuse fail to interpret their experiences as traumatic at the time of their occurrence. Such non-traumatic memories are not repressed but rather not accessed over a period of years because of 'ordinary forgetfulness' (Engelhard et al., 2018, p. 92). Patients often recall these memories in adulthood when presented with relevant triggers or reminders. This can lead them to *reinterpret* their childhood experiences as having been sexually abusive and traumatic.

There is much empirical support for the above theoretical account. Clancy and McNally (2005/2006) discovered that only 8% of female patients with recovered memories perceived the relevant events as being traumatic or sexual when they occurred during their childhood. Most of these patients described their memories of those events as confusing or uncomfortable, and it is easy to understand that such memories could be subject to normal forgetting processes.

McNally (2012) discussed evidence from many patients reporting they had recalled childhood sexual abuse after many years of forgetting. The abuse described in their reports often involved fondling by someone close to them who did not threaten or harm them. They often reported having experienced confusion, disgust or anxiety, but not terror. Approximately one-third of these individuals met diagnostic criteria for post-traumatic stress disorder when they recalled the childhood abuse, and re-interpreted it accurately as morally reprehensible and indefensible behaviour by the adult concerned.

Overall evaluation

In spite of the enduring popularity of Freud's repression-based account of recovered memories among the public and many clinical psychologists, it has received little empirical support (e.g. Pope & Hudson, 1995). As McNally (2017, p. 2) argued, 'There is no convincing replicable evidence that people can encode traumatic memories, but then become incapable of recalling them, thanks to repression'.

The above findings are unsurprising from the perspective of our general understanding of long-term memory for various reasons. First, children experiencing childhood sexual abuse typically do so on many occasions, and there is compelling evidence that repeated experiences are generally remembered better than those occurring only once. Second, most research on non-traumatic memory indicates that long-term memory is superior for extremely negative events than for neutral or less emotional ones (Bowen et al., 2017).

There is much more support for Engelhard et al.'s (2018) contention that adults are most likely to have recovered memories for childhood sexual abuse when they originally interpreted that abuse in non-traumatic ways. Forgetting over a period of years afterwards is plausible if the memories are not perceived as being especially important or significant, especially if relevant cues (e.g. being in the presence of the culprit) are lacking during later childhood and early adulthood.

According to this approach, we can understand how such memories are recovered, by considering factors known to facilitate the retrieval of information from long-term memory. For example, according to the encoding specificity principle (e.g. Tulving, 1979), there is a maximal probability of retrieval when the information (e.g. cues) available at the time of retrieval matches the information within the memory trace. Geraerts (2012) reviewed research on women whose recovered memories had been recalled spontaneously outside therapy. These memories were often triggered by relevant retrieval cues (e.g. returning to the scene of the abuse).

We have seen that it is relatively easy to produce false childhood memories (Scoboria et al., 2017). What are the underlying mechanisms? Of major importance, therapists often successfully persuade their patients to have the *belief* that they suffered childhood sexual abuse even though they initially have no direct *memory* of such abuse (Ost, 2017; Scoboria et al., 2017). When patients have this belief, it often motivates efforts to retrieve relevant information from long-term memory. The therapist typically provides numerous cues, any of which can trigger false memories of childhood abuse.

It is also important to consider retrieval strategies. More specifically, when people try to recall information, they often start off using one particular retrieval strategy, but subsequently switch to different retrieval strategies (Unsworth, 2017). The potential relevance of using a variety of retrieval strategies was shown by Williams and Hollan (1981). Individuals who had finished high school several years earlier recalled the names of as many of their high-school classmates as possible over several hours. They all used several different strategies while performing this task.

What did Williams and Hollan (1981) find? On average, the participants recalled approximately 50 correct names during the first hour but eventually produced approximately 120 correct names. Of most immediate relevance, however, they also recalled approximately 25 false names in the first hour and eventually produced about 74 false names! The applicability of these findings to research on recovered memories remains to be determined. However, it is striking that prolonged retrieval periods involving several different retrieval strategies can produce ever-increasing numbers of false childhood memories.

In sum, we now have a general understanding of the main factors influencing the extent and accuracy of recovered memories. However, more remains to be discovered about the underlying mechanisms. Progress here requires more systematic application of theories of human memory to the phenomena associated with recovered memories (Roediger & Bergman, 1998).

POST-TRAUMATIC STRESS DISORDER

There are some situations in which individuals wish to suppress memories of a distressing or terrifying experience, but are unable to do so. The term 'Post-Traumatic Stress Disorder' (PTSD) describes the symptoms that can occur following extremely stressful experiences or prolonged trauma, such as natural disasters, warfare, or sexual assault. Individuals with PTSD can often experience 'flashbacks', which are particularly vivid memories of the initial traumatic event. Other memory-related symptoms include nightmares, and physical sensations such as pain, nausea, sweating or trembling.

Experiencing distressing or threatening situations is, unfortunately, not uncommon. In a large sample of older adults in the USA it was found that 90% reported encountering at least one potentially traumatic event in their lifetime (Ogle et al., 2013), while evidence from a large sample of young people from Britain found that around 30% had experienced trauma by the age of 18 (Lewis et al., 2019). The use of the word 'trauma' (from the Greek word for 'wound') to describe a mental reaction emerged only at the beginning of the 20th century (Brewin, 2003). Our understanding of mental trauma developed a great deal in the middle of the 20th century, as doctors attempted to understand the symptoms experienced by many soldiers following some of the major international wars of that period. For example, the concept of 'shell shock', introduced by Charles Myers in 1915, recognised the trauma experienced by many soldiers as an emotional, rather than simply a physical, reaction. While post-trauma stress symptoms were initially thought to have physical causes (such as the sound of exploding shells), this view changed following World War I, when it became evident that some soldiers were suffering trauma even in the absence of first-hand experience of gunfire. PTSD symptoms were described similarly during World War II, when they were usually described as 'combat fatigue'. But it was not until after the Vietnam War that PTSD first appeared in the *Diagnostic and Statistical Manual of Mental Disorders* (DSM-III; American Psychiatric Association, 1980).

From this brief summary of the history of PTSD, it is clear that our understanding of psychological trauma has developed significantly over the past century. The latest development has been the debate over the conceptualisation of PTSD as an anxiety disorder, with some arguing that it would be better understood as a disorder of memory. Indeed, in the most recent version of the DSM, PTSD is no longer listed as an anxiety disorder, but is now categorised as a 'trauma- and stressor-related disorder' (DSM-5; American Psychiatric Association, 2013).

The role of memory in PTSD

Although people often think of traumatic memories as being powerful and permanent, sometimes these memories are actually forgotten. In fact, a lot of events we experience may seem significant at the time, but may not end up being well remembered. For example, in a study by Raphael et al. (1991), participants completed monthly checklists to record personally significant life events, and after 10 months they were asked to retrospectively recall their experiences over the whole period. Of the life events recorded in the monthly checklists, participants only remembered about a quarter of these at the end of the 10-month study.

The same can be true of traumatic experiences, so that even if we do experience something traumatic, this alone does not guarantee that we will incorporate it into our autobiographical memory (Brewin, 2018). Not only can we forget one-off traumatic events, but in some cases individuals can forget about serious repetitive traumatic experiences, including even child abuse (Ghetti et al., 2006). The reason for this appears to be the way we store memory depending upon personal significance. Like other autobiographical memories, traumatic memories are more likely to be remembered if they are part of a shared social experience or perceived as having personal consequences (Brewin, 2018). It has been estimated that only around 29% of people exposed to trauma will go on to develop PTSD (Santiago et al., 2013).

One question we might want to ask at this point is why do some people develop PTSD, while other people may experience similar trauma and not develop any lasting symptoms? A possible answer to this question may be that it depends upon how well someone is able to inhibit intrusive thoughts. Some evidence to support this was provided by Catarino and colleagues (2015), who compared inhibitory control in patients with a current diagnosis of PTSD to a group of trauma-exposed individuals with no current or history of PTSD. Their results suggested that, compared to the trauma-exposed control participants, PTSD patients showed significantly reduced ability to control memory inhibition. This suggests that intrusive memories in PTSD are at least partly due to deficient memory inhibition. In other words, it would appear that executive functions involved in the way we control our memory may have some influence on our susceptibility to developing PTSD, and this might offer some potential insight for future development of new forms of PTSD prevention and treatment.

Cognitive theories of PTSD

There is growing evidence to suggest that PTSD can be considered primarily as a disorder of memory (Brewin, 2018), and some of the best-supported models of PTSD are cognitive models that explain PTSD in terms of memory processing. The dual representation theory (Brewin et al., 1996; Brewin, 2001) proposes that in PTSD the experience of trauma gives rise to both consciously and unconsciously held memories, which they termed *verbally accessible memories* (VAM) and *situationally accessible memories* (SAM) respectively.

VAM are narratives that are expressible in words, are integrated with autobiographical memory, and can be voluntarily accessed. SAM are memories of a sensory nature that are involuntarily triggered by cues relating to the original traumatic episode. For example, a war veteran may be able to verbally recount the trauma in a therapeutic session (an example of VAM), but the experience of a 'flashback' would be a separate and involuntary experience brought about by hearing a noise or seeing an object that is associated with the trauma (SAM). Because the SAM system is unconscious and non-verbal, these memories are difficult to communicate to others and not necessarily included in one's autobiographical memory, making them hard to deliberately suppress.

Dual representation theory is consistent with clinical observations of PTSD patients (Brewin, 2001) and is also supported by evidence from neuroimaging studies. These studies have shown that flashbacks are associated with increased activation in sensory and motor areas of the brain, and decreased activation in the parahippocampal gyrus, a region important for conscious memory retrieval (Brewin, 2018). This is consistent with the proposal of two separate systems, with flashbacks being particularly associated with the SAM system.

Along with the dual representation model, another prominent, and related, cognitive model of PTSD is that proposed by Ehlers and Clark (2000). While this model recognises that many individuals will experience PTSD symptoms in the period immediately after a traumatic experience, it also takes account of the fact that not all will go on to develop PTSD. Ehlers and Clark propose that PTSD symptoms become persistent when an individual processes trauma in a maladaptive way, which can induce a strong sense of current threat. For example, if the individual overgeneralises the threat, thinks that they will never recover, or that their life is significantly changed by the trauma, then they would be more likely to suffer enduring PTSD symptoms.

As with dual representation theory, there is fairly wide-ranging evidence to support the Ehlers and Clark model. For example, in two studies of motor vehicle accident survivors, Steil and Ehlers (2000) found that those showing more negative interpretations of their trauma-related thought intrusions were more likely to develop chronic PTSD symptoms. Andrews et al. (2000) also found that, among victims of violent crime, feelings of anger towards others and shame on the part of the victim both predicted a slower recovery from PTSD. Thus Ehlers and Clark's model puts emphasis on the way that an individual appraises their trauma symptoms, and this may provide a basis for understanding individual differences in PTSD susceptibility and why some individuals may find it harder to forget traumatic memories.

Memory-based treatments for PTSD

The most popular cognitive treatment for PTSD is trauma-focused cognitive behavioural therapy (TF-CBT). Although there are many forms of TF-CBT, what they all have in common is a focus on the emotional processing of the trauma and integration of new corrective information (Bryant, 2019). One example is imagery re-scripting therapy, in which patients are urged to re-assess the storyline associated with an intrusive image as a different and less distressing story. The patient is then encouraged to rehearse the re-scripted story in their imagination so as to progressively adjust the appraisal of that memory. TF-CBT approaches have proved to be very effective for many patients. For example, Duffy and colleagues (2007) demonstrated that this type of treatment was very effective for treating PTSD in victims of terror attacks. There is further evidence for it working with other groups, including victims of violent assault, sexual abuse, and displacement, but it is important to note that it is only effective in around two-thirds of cases (Bryant, 2019). Alternative treatment options are therefore required.

In recent years an alternative approach to the treatment of PTSD has been proposed, involving what is called the 'reconsolidation' of memory. The basic principle underlying reconsolidation is that each time we activate a trace from our long-term memory, it goes through a process of being consolidated once again, during which it becomes as fragile as a memory that has just been formed. This means that the memory becomes momentarily vulnerable to alteration or even to erasure. The potential for reconsolidation interventions for PTSD has generated much excitement, but further research is needed before we can establish that they are effective.

Overall evaluation

In summary, experiencing trauma does not always mean that a person will necessarily develop PTSD. While we often think of memory for traumatic events as being particularly powerful and vivid, in reality such events are sometimes poorly remembered and can be forgotten altogether. The likelihood of developing sustained PTSD symptoms is associated with the way that one interprets their trauma-related thought intrusions (Ehlers and Clark, 2000) and might be explained by deficient memory inhibition (Catarino et al., 2015). There remains much to be understood about PTSD and how best to treat it. It is unclear whether it may be more effective to teach patients to supress retrieval of the trauma, or to interfere with the consolidation and reconsolidation of trauma-related memory (Brewin, 2018). But there is now much support for the idea that PTSD can best be understood as a disorder of memory, so it seems likely that understanding the effects of trauma on memory will be crucial to developing more effective treatments.

LABORATORY STUDIES OF INTENTIONAL RETRIEVAL SUPPRESSION

We have so far in this chapter considered the research on repression and PTSD, which both involve the suppression of unwanted memories in real-life settings. However, laboratory studies have also been carried out in recent years to find out whether human beings are capable of suppressing memories when they make a deliberate effort to do so. Researchers have adopted two main techniques for this purpose, which are known as the 'directed forgetting' procedure and the 'think/no think' procedure.

Directed forgetting

Directed forgetting (DF) was covered in Chapter 8, in connection with mechanisms of cognitive inhibition. However, we will now take another look at DF research, this time focusing on DF as an example of motivated forgetting. In DF studies the participants are required to learn some kind of test material, but are then subsequently given an instruction either to remember the material or to forget it. There are two different methods of investigating DF, and these are known as the 'item method' and the 'list method' respectively.

The *item method* involves the presentation of a series of test items, with an instruction directly following each item to either 'remember' or 'forget' that item. Bjork (1972) developed the item method and used it to demonstrate that 'remember' (R) items are more likely to be retrieved than 'forget' (F) items when the participant is subsequently asked to recall the entire list.

The *list method* also involves the presentation of two or more lists of items, but instead of receiving an instruction after each item, the participant receives the instruction after the presentation of the entire list. At this point they are instructed to either remember or forget that list. There are therefore some lists that are to be remembered and some lists that are to be forgotten, but crucially the participant does not know which instruction will apply until an entire list has been presented. Geiselman et al. (1983) used the list method to demonstrate that, as with the item method, in the final recall test the R items were better recalled than the F items.

Mechanisms underlying item and list directed forgetting

As explained above, it has been found that participants are able to deliberately suppress some items from memory with both the item and list methods. However, whilst the item and list methods may seem to be fairly similar, in fact they differ in an important way, which means that these two procedures probably reflect different kinds of memory suppression.

With the item method, participants are given the R or F instruction immediately after the presentation of each item, so they are able to reduce the amount of processing effort they apply to the F items. It is therefore assumed that with the item method, suppression takes place mainly at the encoding stage, when participants can choose whether or not to rehearse the item and subject it to elaborative processing. So with the item method, suppression of the F items probably reflects the fact that participants can devote more effort to processing the R items in an elaborative way, whilst largely neglecting the processing of the F items.

With the list method, the R/F instruction is not given until the entire list has been presented, and by that time some input processing will already have taken place. Suppression of the F items with the list method is therefore likely to occur mainly at the retrieval stage, by somehow suppressing the retrieval of F items despite the fact that they have been encoded and stored in memory.

In summary then, it is widely assumed that the item method mainly involves suppression at the encoding stage, whereas the list method mostly reflects suppression at the retrieval stage. There is some support for this assumption, as Basden and Basden (1996) reported that, with the list method, the suppression of the F items only occurs when a recall test is employed, whereas the F instruction does not affect performance on a recognition test. In contrast, they found that when the item method is employed the directed forgetting effect is equally strong for both recall and recognition tests. These findings suggest that in the list method the F items are actually processed at the input stage and remain present in the memory store, since they can still be recognised. But the fact that they cannot be recalled suggests that suppression has affected the retrieval of the items rather than their encoding. A recent investigation of the item method by Taylor et al. (2018) confirmed that suppression appeared to take place at the encoding stage, probably involving reduced rehearsal and input processing, but they found no evidence for suppression at the retrieval stage.

Two different theories have been put forward to explain the underlying mechanism of suppression in the list method. The *retrieval inhibition hypothesis* (Anderson, 2009) suggests that the F instruction leads to the activation of an inhibitory mechanism, which temporarily reduces the level of activation of a test item in the memory. The inhibited test items will therefore be difficult to access in a recall test, but in a recognition test the access problem is overcome by the fact that the original test items are actually re-presented. Indeed, it is possible that the re-presentation of the items in the recognition procedure may directly re-activate them. The *context-shift hypothesis* (Sahakyan & Kelley, 2002) offers a rather different explanation for the list method DF effect, based on the principle of context reinstatement. Sahakian and Kelly suggest that the F instruction causes test items to be assigned a specific 'forget' context, a context which is not reinstated at the retrieval stage. These F items will therefore be harder to retrieve because the retrieval context does not match the encoding context, and therefore (in accordance with the principle of transfer-appropriate processing) provides less effective retrieval cueing.

It was initially hypothesised that any inhibitory mechanism contributing to the DF effect would last for a relatively short time, but Hupbach (2018) found that when participants were tested 24 hours after performing a list method DF procedure they still recalled fewer of the F items. Hupbach suggested that this longer term DF effect might reflect a different mechanism from that affecting F items over shorter time periods. Participants in this study were also tested after a 12-hour delay, which was spent either sleeping in the night-time or staying awake in the daytime. Those in the sleep group showed better recall of the first list of items to be presented in the R condition, but sleep and wakefulness had no effect on the recall of F items.

Directed forgetting with realistic material

The early DF studies mostly used word lists as their test material, but subsequent studies have shown that the DF effect also occurs with memories of real-life experiences. For example, Josslyn and Oakes (2005) found that participants showed poorer recall of their own diary entries which had been subjected to an F instruction rather than an R instruction. Participants were required to record the events of their lives in a diary for two weeks, and were then instructed to forget the events of one week but to remember the events of the other. This was essentially a list method design, as the DF instruction was given some time after the events and their associated diary entries had been completed.

Another demonstration of DF with fairly complex and life-like test material was reported by Delaney et al. (2009), who found that DF occurs with lists of meaningful sentences. The sentences used by Delaney et al. each provided information about one of two people, named Tom and Alex. After all of the sentences had been presented, participants were instructed to forget the information about Tom, but to remember the information about Alex. A subsequent recall test showed that participants did indeed recall more information about Alex. However, this DF effect was only found when the sentences were unrelated to one another. When the sentences were related to one another so as to form a continuous narrative, the DF effect disappeared, probably because one sentence was able to cue the retrieval of another sentence.

The studies described so far have involved direct instructions to remember or forget test items, and it has been demonstrated that people do indeed have the ability to regulate their memories in this way. It is therefore likely that in real life individuals will use this ability to avoid recalling unpleasant and unwanted memories, but without requiring an instruction from an external source. For example, Sedikides and Green (2000) reported that people tend to have better recall of favourable feedback about themselves than they have for unfavourable feedback. Their study involved presenting participants with a personality questionnaire, for which they were subsequently provided with a set of fake results listing both good and bad aspects of their personality. When the participants were later tested on their recall of their personality test results, they tended to recall more of the positive qualities and fewer of the negative ones. However, this only occurred when they were recalling their own questionnaire data, and not for their recall of the data from a different person's results. This suggests that participants were suppressing memories for the more unfavourable qualities attributed to them, presumably because they did not like this kind of feedback very much. The design of this experiment was essentially a form of item method procedure, since participants would perceive the positive or negative aspect of each item as it was presented. The suppression of unfavourable items is therefore likely to have occurred at the encoding stage. Sedikides and Green suggested that participants were failing to fully encode the less favourable items, a process they refer to as 'the mnemic neglect effect' (as mentioned in the first section of this chapter).

DF mechanisms and brain function

Individuals with frontal lobe lesions have been found to produce a significantly reduced DF effect compared with normal controls (Conway & Fthenaki, 2003). The frontal lobes are known to be involved in central executive function and working memory, so their apparent involvement in DF is consistent with the subsequent finding that individuals with a high working memory capacity show a particularly strong DF effect (Aslan et al., 2010b). These findings support the view that directed forgetting probably involves effortful processing being carried out by the central executive.

A number of studies have reported that individuals suffering from depression do not show the usual DF effect when tested on distressing or emotionally negative items. Using the item method, Xie et al. (2018) showed that depression-prone individuals were unable to suppress their memory for emotionally negative test items, though they were able to suppress emotionally neutral items. Using EEG equipment to measure the event-related potential (ERP), they found that their participants produced an abnormal ERP response following both the presentation of the word and the presentation of the cue to forget the word. Xie et al. speculated that the presentation of an emotionally negative word may have caused depression-prone participants to focus undue attention on that word, thus carrying out extra processing which would make the word harder to suppress when instructed to do so. The fact that depression-prone individuals experience difficulties in suppressing negative items may underlie the well-established finding that depressed individuals are prone to rumination, and have difficulty in excluding unwanted thoughts and memories.

The think/no-think paradigm

Much recent research on memory suppression has used an experimental technique known as the think/no-think paradigm (Anderson & Green, 2001). This paradigm has been used mostly (but not exclusively) to assess motivated forgetting of neutral information. We will work through the various stages involved:

1. Participants learn a list of word pairs consisting of a cue word and a target word (e.g. *Ordeal-Roach*; *Steam-Train*).
2. Participants are presented with the cues studied earlier (e.g. *Ordeal*; *Steam*) and their task is either to recall the associated words (e.g. *Roach*; *Train*) (respond condition) or to prevent the associated words coming to mind (suppress condition). Note that some cues are not presented during this second stage (baseline condition).
3. At this stage, there are two different testing conditions. In the same-probe condition, the original cue words are presented (e.g. *Ordeal*) and participants must recall the target words corresponding to these cues (e.g. *Roach*). In the independent-probe condition, participants are presented with *novel* (not presented previously) category cues (e.g. *Roach* cued with *Insect-r*).

What would we expect to find if people are able to suppress unwanted memories? First, people should have lower recall for items in the suppress condition than in the respond condition. Second, recall should also be lower in the suppress condition than in the baseline condition.

Anderson and Huddleston (2012) carried out a meta-analysis (systematic review) of 47 experiments using the think/no-think paradigm. With respect to the first prediction, overall recall for items in the suppress condition was approximately 18% lower than for items in the respond condition. This finding is hard to interpret – it might reflect *positive* effects of responding on retrieval or *negative* effects of suppressing (or both). However, the additional finding that recall was significantly lower in the suppress condition than in the baseline condition reveals a negative impact of suppression on recall. Note, however, that suppression attempts were often unsuccessful. For example, 82% of the items were recalled in the suppression condition using the same-probe test.

At this point, it is important to consider the strategies individuals use to produce the successful (or unsuccessful) suppression of unwanted memories. One frequently used strategy is direct suppression – this involves focusing on the cue word and blocking out the associated target word. Another common strategy is thought substitution: each cue word is associated with a different, non-target word. Direct suppression and thought substitution are comparably effective in reducing recall in the suppress condition (e.g. Anderson & Hanslmayr, 2014).

Wang et al. (2019) wondered whether suppressing memories has indirect effects *outside* the think/no-think paradigm in which suppression occurred. They made use of this paradigm with the Remote Associates Test, in which individuals have to find a word relevant to three different cues (e.g. PALM is relevant to the words DATE, OASIS, AND OIL). Wang et al.'s key finding was that participants performed worse on the Remote Associates Test when the answer corresponded to a suppressed word on the think/no-think paradigm. Thus, suppression can have an unconscious, indirect influence on subsequent thoughts on an apparently totally independent task.

Note that suppression is not always effective in producing motivated forgetting. Consider the 'white bear effect' (Wegner et al., 1987). Most individuals instructed *not* to think about a specific item (e.g. a white bear) using thought suppression report paradoxically that they find it hard to avoid thinking about the prohibited item. This effect is not necessarily inconsistent with the effectiveness of thought suppression within the think/no-think paradigm. With the 'white bear effect', remembering the task goal requires remembering the prohibited item, a feature absent from the think/no-think paradigm.

What mechanisms underlie the suppression effect?

The most popular explanation of the suppression effect is that it depends on inhibitory control (e.g. Anderson & Huddleston, 2012). In essence, it is assumed that people use active inhibitory control processes to inhibit the previously learned responses to the cues. It is further assumed that these control processes involve the dorsolateral prefrontal cortex and other frontal areas. Finally, it is assumed that this prefrontal activation causes reduced activation in the hippocampus and associated areas centrally involved in learning and long-term memory.

There is accumulating evidence that inhibitory control plays a major role in the suppression effect. Anderson et al. (2016) compared patterns of brain activation either when individuals attempted to suppress memories or when they attempted retrieval. There was greater dorsolateral prefrontal activation but less hippocampal activation in the former condition. Additional evidence was reported by Smith et al. (2018). They focused on co-ordination between the frontal areas associated with inhibitory control in each brain hemisphere. Those individuals having the greatest co-ordination exhibited the most effective memory suppression. There is more on the brain mechanisms involved in the next section.

Emotion regulation

Most of us spend much time engaged in emotion regulation, which is defined as 'the activation of a goal to modify which emotion one has, when one has the emotion, or how one experiences or expresses the emotion' (Ghafur et al., 2018, p. 31). In essence, emotion regulation occurs when we *override* our immediate emotional response to a situation. Emotion regulation is mostly motivated by the attempt to downregulate (reduce) negative emotional states and to upregulate (increase) positive emotional states.

What are the main emotion-regulation strategies? We can distinguish between *cognitive* strategies involving thinking about emotion-causing stimuli and *behavioural* strategies. Cognitive strategies include distraction (disengaging attention from emotional processing) and reappraisal (elaborating emotional information and then changing its meaning). For example, people often use reappraisal when watching a violent movie: the violence and blood are re-interpreted as having been carefully stage-managed rather than being genuine. Behavioural strategies involve physical action (e.g. avoiding emotion-causing stimuli). Hemenover and Harbke (2019) found individuals preferring cognitive engagement strategies (e.g. reappraisal; distraction) had greater psychological well-being than those preferring behavioural avoidance strategies (e.g. passive disengagement; venting by crying, screaming).

Do emotion-regulation strategies involve motivated forgetting? Superficially, the answer is 'no'. Historically, most research has focused on emotion-regulation processes occurring very shortly after an individual has been exposed to an emotionally arousing event (Eysenck & Keane, 2020). However, emotion regulation can also involve retrospective memory processes designed to upregulate positive emotions and downregulate negative ones. Such processes constitute mnemonic emotion regulation (Nørby, 2019).

Memory suppression and emotional regulation

Only recently has research focused on memory processes in emotion regulation. This is surprising because any impact of past emotional events on us (other than our immediate reaction to them) necessarily involves memory. More specifically, memory control is of key significance: 'Because many emotions we experience in daily life stem from recall of emotionally charged memories, the capacity to control whether and when such recall occurs must be a central emotion-regulation mechanism' (Engen & Anderson, 2018, p. 992).

As we saw earlier, direct suppression and thought substitution are two major processes used to inhibit retrieval of unwanted (but emotionally neutral) memories using the think/no-think paradigm. Accordingly, we start our discussion of emotion regulation by considering a study by Noreen and MacLeod (2014) using this paradigm with positive and negative autobiographical memories. Direct suppression was effective at inhibiting retrieval on an immediate memory test. However, it was not effective at a memory test three to four months later, suggesting that suppression has limited long-term effects. However, other research indicates that suppression sometimes inhibits memories over long periods of time (Nörby, 2019).

Gagnepain et al. (2017) used the think/no-think paradigm to investigate the effects of direct suppression on retrieval of aversive pictures. Suppression was effective in inhibiting retrieval of these pictures and also in reducing participants' emotional responses to them. Gagnepain et al. also shed light on the underlying mechanisms. Activation of a top-down fronto-parietal inhibitory network during suppression downregulated (reduced) activation in the hippocampus (involved in memory) and in the amygdala (involved in emotional responses). In sum, direct suppression reduced retrieval of aversive pictures and emotional responsiveness because activation of a top-down inhibitory system caused downregulation of brain areas involved in memory and emotion.

Hertel et al. (2018) used the think/no-think procedure to investigate the problem of rumination (i.e. dwelling on the same thought or memory for an excessive period of time) which commonly occurs in depressed individuals and tends to exacerbate their depression. Hertel et al. found that individuals who were prone to rumination failed to suppress unwanted memories in the think/no-think task, whereas non-ruminators did succeed in the memory suppression task. Indirect tests of memory retrieval were used in this study in order to achieve some resemblance to a real-life situation, since a person suffering from unwanted intrusive memories would be unlikely to make a deliberate effort to retrieve their unpleasant memories. From these findings Hertel et al. concluded that the treatment of rumination and depression in real-life patients was unlikely to work if it depended on the patient making a deliberate attempt to suppress unwanted and disturbing memories. The authors suggested that a more promising approach would involve thought substitution, for example rehearsing and strengthening other rival responses to those cues which had previously triggered the retrieval of a traumatic memory.

Emotion-regulation strategies: reappraisal

Which emotion-regulation strategy is of most theoretical importance in terms of the involvement of motivated forgetting? Engen and Anderson (2018) argued that we should focus on an emotion-regulation strategy using direct suppression and thought substitution. They hypothesised that distraction and problem solving often involve thought substitution. However, reappraisal involves direct suppression of the dominant interpretation of a given emotional event followed by its replacement with a different interpretation. Thus, thought substitution produces a new memory incorporating the information generated during the reinterpretation process, and this new memory is subsequently retrieved.

There are other reasons why reappraisal is of particular interest and importance. It is one of the most commonly used strategies and is often more effective than other strategies. Nevertheless, individuals often fail to use reappraisal to downregulate or reduce negative emotions. Suri et al. (2015) found that people used reappraisal only 16% of the time with very unpleasant pictures because it is a cognitively demanding strategy.

How can we demonstrate significant commonalities among direct suppression, thought substitution, and reappraisal? Engen and Anderson (2018) focused on the neural networks associated with these three strategies as revealed by functional neuroimaging. There were three main findings:

1. Reappraisal was associated with activation in various areas within both hemispheres (e.g. mid-frontal gyrus; inferior frontal gyrus; pre-supplementary motor area; dorsal anterior cingulate cortex).
2. Of major theoretical importance, all the main brain areas associated with the reappraisal network also formed part of the networks associated with direct suppression and thought substitution.
3. The above overlaps with the reappraisal network were greater in the *left* hemisphere for thought substitution but in the *right* hemisphere for direct suppression. These findings strengthen support for the notion that direct suppression and thought substitution probably involve different processes.

In sum, the effectiveness of reappraisal as an emotion-regulation strategy occurs in part because it involves using both direct suppression and thought substitution. However, there are two limitations in the existing evidence. First, it is entirely possible that reappraisal involves processes additional to suppression and thought substitution. Second, it is assumed theoretically that there are sequential processes involving first suppression and then thought substitution. However, there is little direct evidence as yet for this temporal sequence.

Worry: individual differences

We have seen how memory control (closely linked to attentional or cognitive control) influences the effectiveness of emotion regulation. We can obtain additional relevant evidence by considering individual differences in control and emotion regulation. Here we focus specifically on individuals having high trait anxiety (a personality dimension relating to the experience of anxiety). Of central importance, trait anxiety correlates highly with susceptibility to worry (Eysenck & van Berkum, 1992). Perhaps unsurprisingly, high-anxious individuals exhibit rapid initiation of worry but slow termination (e.g. Berenbaum et al., 2018).

Why do high-anxious individuals (and high worriers) find it hard to stop themselves worrying? According to attentional control theory (Eysenck et al., 2007), individuals high in trait anxiety have impaired executive functions (especially inhibitory control), an assumption that has received much behavioural and neuroimaging support. It seems reasonable to predict that this impaired inhibitory control contributes to the slow termination of worry in high-anxious individuals. Eysenck et al. (in preparation) developed this assumption. They assumed there is a vicious circle: high-anxious individuals are more likely than low-anxious ones to start worrying because they are hypervigilant for threat-related information. The worry process requires processing capacity (Hayes et al., 2008); this, combined with their inefficient inhibitory control mechanism, makes it hard for high-anxious individuals to terminate worry.

Marzi et al. (2014) studied memory suppression of negative emotional scenes using the think/no-think paradigm. Individuals low in trait anxiety exhibited memory suppression for such scenes. In contrast, high-anxious individuals did not exhibit memory suppression, and their difficulties in controlling memory retrieval were especially great with negative rather than positive or neutral scenes.

It is of relevance to the above theoretical approach to consider what happens when individuals imagine future threatening events. First, worry is mostly concerned with thoughts relating to future potential threatening events. Second, the brain networks involved in imagining future events overlap considerably with those involved in remembering past events (Benoit & Schacter, 2015). Benoit et al. (2016) discovered that suppression of future fears reduced apprehensiveness concerning those fears. However, this reduction was significantly less for high-anxious than low-anxious individuals.

Evaluation

It is indisputable that the ability to control our access to (and termination of) negative emotionally charged memories (and imagining of future threats) is of major importance with respect to emotion regulation. Research indicates that high trait-anxious individuals are generally less successful than low-anxious ones in their attempts to suppress such memories and threats because they have inefficient control mechanisms (including memory control). Inefficient memory control in high-anxious individuals plays a role in maintaining (or increasing) their experienced anxiety.

What are the limitations of theory and research on motivated forgetting and emotion regulation? First, the focus on a single emotion-regulation strategy (i.e. reappraisal) means that we have limited knowledge of the processes involved in most other strategies. Second, it seems reasonable to assume that the processes and brain areas associated with memory control overlap substantially with those associated with other forms of inhibitory control. As yet, however, there is only limited relevant research. Third, we know that reappraisal involves processes (direct suppression; thought substitution) involved in motivated forgetting. However, the extent to which reappraisal alters the memory traces associated with negative emotional events remains unclear.

Future directions

There is reasonable consensus from research using various different paradigms that neutral and emotional memories can be suppressed through the use of what is variously described as memory control, inhibitory control, use of the central executive, and working memory capacity. It is currently unclear whether these processes are essentially identical with each other or whether there are significant differences among them. For example, there is the question of how generally applicable each memory process is. Memory control may be more limited in scope than inhibitory control, which in turn may be more limited than use of the central executive. A related issue is whether suppression needs to be accompanied by thought substitution to produce long-term motivated forgetting. Another area that requires further research concerns the length of time over which suppression is effective. So far most research has focused on the short-term effects of suppression, and relatively little is known concerning whether or not its effects are long-lasting. These are all important questions, which as yet remain unanswered. We hope that some of them will be resolved in time for the next edition of this book.

Further Reading

Anderson, M. C. (2020). Motivated forgetting. In A. D. Baddeley, M. W. Eysenck, and M. C. Anderson (eds), *Memory* (3rd edn). Abingdon: Psychology Press.

REFERENCES

Abel, M., & Bäuml, K.-H. T. (2014). The roles of delay and retroactive interference in retrieval-induced forgetting. *Memory & Cognition*, 42, 141–150.

Abel, M., & Bäuml, K.-H. T. (2017). Testing the context-change account of list-method directed forgetting: The role of retention interval. *Journal of Memory and Language*, 92, 170–182.

Abel, M., & Bäuml, K.-H. T. (2019). List-method directed forgetting after prolonged retention interval: Further challenges to contemporary accounts. *Journal of Memory and Language*, 106, 18–28.

Abramowitz, J. S., Tolin, D. F., & Street, G. P. (2001). Paradoxical effects of thought suppression: A meta-analysis of controlled studies. *Clinical Psychology Review*, 21(5), 683–703. doi: http://dx.doi.org/10.1016/S0272-7358(00)00057-X

Addis, D. R., & Schacter, D. L. (2008). Constructive episodic simulation: Temporal distance and detail of past and future events modulate hippocampal engagement. *Hippocampus*, 18, 227–237. doi: 10.1002/hipo.20405

Addis, D. R., Wong, A. T., & Schacter, D. L. (2007). Remembering the past and imagining the future: Common and distinct neural substrates during event construction and elaboration. *Neuropsychologia*, 45, 1363–1377.

Akhtar, S., Justice, L. V., Knott, L., Kibowski, F., & Conway, M. A. (2018a). The 'common sense' memory system and its implications. *International Journal of Evidence & Proof*, 22, 289–304.

Akhtar, S., Justice, L. V., Morrison, C. M., & Conway, M. A. (2018b). Fictional first memories. *Psychological Science*, 1–8. doi: 10.1177/0956797618778831

Albiński, R., Sedek, G., & Kliegel, M. (2012). Differences in target monitoring in a prospective memory task. *Journal of Cognitive Psychology*, 24(8), 916–928. doi: https://doi.org/10.1080/20445911.2012.717923

Albright, T. D. (2017). Why eyewitnesses fail. *Proceedings of the National Academy of Sciences*, 114(30), 7758–7764.

Alexander, E. (2012). *Proof of Heaven*. London: Piatkus.

Alexievich, S. (1985/2017). *The Unwomanly Face of War* (R. Pevear & L. Volokhonsky, trans.). London: Penguin.

Allen, J. J., Iacono, W. G., Laravuso, J. J., & Dunn, L. A. (1995). An event-related potential investigation of posthypnotic recognition amnesia. *Journal of Abnormal Psychology*, 104(3), 421–430. doi: http://dx.doi.org/10.1037/0021-843X.104.3.421

Allen, J. J. B., Law, H., & Laravuso, J. J. (1996). Items for assessing posthypnotic recognition amnesia with the HGSHS: A and the SHSS: C. *International Journal of Clinical and Experimental Hypnosis*, 44(1), 52–65. doi: http://dx.doi.org/10.1080/00207149608416067

Altmann, E. M., & Schunn, C.D. (2012). Decay versus interference: A new look at an old interaction. *Psychological Science*, 23, 1435–1437.

Alvarez, A., Zola-Morgan, S., & Squire, L. (1995). Damage limited to the hippocampal region produces long-lasting memory impairment in monkeys. *Journal of Neuroscience*, 15(5), 3796–3807.

American Psychiatric Association. (1980). *Diagnostic and Statistical Manual of Mental Disorders* (3rd edn). Washington, DC: Author.

American Psychiatric Association (2013). *Diagnostic and Statistical Manual of Mental Disorders* (5th edn). Arlington, VA: American Psychiatric Publishing.

Anderson, M. C. (2003). Rethinking interference theory: Executive control and the mechanisms of forgetting. *Journal of Memory and Language*, 49, 415–445.

Anderson, M. C. (2009). Motivated forgetting. In A. Baddeley, M. W. Eysenck, and M. C. Anderson (eds), *Memory*. Hove: Psychology Press.

Anderson, M. C., Bjork, E. L., & Bjork, R. A. (2000). Retrieval-induced forgetting: Evidence for a recall-specific mechanism. *Psychonomic Bulletin & Review*, 7, 522–530.

Anderson, M. C., Bjork, R. A., & Bjork, E.L. (1994). Remembering can cause forgetting: Retrieval dynamics in long-term memory. *Journal of Experimental Psychology: Learning, Memory, and Cognition*, 20, 1063–1087.

Anderson, M. C., Bunce, J. G., & Barbas, H. (2016). Prefrontal-hippocampal pathways underlying inhibitory control over memory. *Neurobiology of Learning and Memory*, 134, 145–161.

Anderson, M. C., & Green, C. (2001). Suppressing unwanted memories by executive control. *Nature*, 410, 366–369.

Anderson, M. C., & Hanslmayr, S. (2014). Neural mechanisms of motivated forgetting. *Trends in Cognitive Sciences*, 18, 279–292. doi: https://doi.org/10.1016/j.tics.2014.03.002

Anderson, M. C., & Huddleston, E. (2012). Towards a cognitive and neurobiological model of motivated forgetting. *Nebraska Symposium on Motivation*, 58, 53–120.

Anderson, M. C., & Levy, B. J. (2007). Theoretical issues in inhibition: Insights from research on human memory. In A. S. Benjamin (ed.), *Successful Remembering and Successful Forgetting: A Festschrift in Honor of Robert A. Bjork* (pp. 107–132). New York: Psychology Press.

Anderson, M. C., & Levy, B. J. (2009). Suppressing unwanted memories. *Current Directions in Psychological Science*, 18(4), 189–194(186). doi: http://dx.doi.org/10.1111/j.1467-8721.2009.01634.x

Anderson, M. C., & Spellman, B. A. (1995). On the status of inhibitory mechanisms in cognition: Memory retrieval as a model case. *Psychological Review*, 102, 68–100.

Anderson, S. A., & Conway, M.A. (1993). Investigating the structure of autobiographical memories. *Journal of Experimental Psychology: Learning, Memory, and Cognition*, 19, 1178–1196.

Andrews, B., Brewin, C., Rose, S., & Kirk, M. (2000). Predicting PTSD symptoms in victims of violent crime: The role of shame, anger, and childhood abuse. *Journal of Abnormal Psychology*, 109(1), 69–73.

Armstrong, T., Zaid, D. H., & Olatunji, B. O. (2011). Attentional control in OCD and GAD: Specificity and associations with core cognitive symptoms. *Behavior Research and Therapy*, 49, 756–762.

Aslan, A., & Bäuml, K.-H. T. (2010). Retrieval-induced forgetting in young children. *Psychonomic Bulletin & Review*, 17, 704–709.

Aslan, A., & Bäuml, K.-H. T. (2012). Retrieval-induced forgetting in old and very old age. *Psychology and Aging*, 27, 1027–1032.

Aslan, A., & Bäuml, K.-H. T. (2013). Listwise directed forgetting is present in young-old adults, but is absent in old-old adults. *Psychology and Aging*, 28, 213–218.

Aslan, A., Bäuml, K.-H. T., & Pastötter, B. (2007). No inhibitory deficit in older adults' episodic memory. *Psychological Science*, 18, 72–78.

Aslan, A., Staudigl, T., Samenieh, A., & Bäuml, K.-H. T. (2010a). Directed forgetting in young children: Evidence for a production deficiency. *Psychonomic Bulletin & Review*, *17*, 784–789.

Aslan, A., Zellner, B. H., & Bäuml K.-H. T. (2010b). Working memory capacity predicts listwise directed forgetting in adults and children. *Memory*, 18, 442–450.

Azevedo, F. A. C., Carvalho, L. R. B., Grinberg, L. T., Farfel, J. M., Ferretti, R. E. L., Leite, R. E. P., et al. (2009). Equal numbers of neuronal and non-neuronal cells make the human brain an isometrically scaled-up primate brain. *Journal of Comparative Neurology*, 513, 532–541.

Baddeley, A., Eysenck, M. W., & Anderson, M. C. (2015). *Memory*. New York: Psychology Press.

Badre, D., & Wagner, A. D. (2007). Left ventrolateral prefrontal cortex and the cognitive control of memory. *Neuropsychologia*, 45, 2883–2901.

Bahar-Fuchs, A., Clare, L., & Woods, B. (2013). Cognitive training and cognitive rehabilitation for mild to moderate Alzheimer's disease and vascular dementia. *Cochrane Database of Systematic Reviews*, 6.

Ball, B. H., Brewer, G. A., Loft, S., & Bowden, V. (2015). Uncovering continuous and transient monitoring profiles in event-based prospective memory. *Psychonomic Bulletin & Review*, 22(2), 492–499. doi: https://doi.org/10.3758/s13423-014-0700-8

Ballhausen, N., Schnitzspahn, K. M., Horn, S. S., & Kliegel, M. (2017). The interplay of intention maintenance and cue monitoring in younger and older adults' prospective memory. *Memory & Cognition*, 45(7), 1113–1125. doi: https://doi.org/10.3758/s13421-017-0720-5

Banister, H., & Zangwill, O. L. (1941a). Experimentally induced olfactory paramnesia. *British Journal of Psychology*, 32, 155–175.

Banister, H., & Zangwill, O. L. (1941b). Experimentally induced visual paramnesias. *British Journal of Psychology*, 32, 30–51.

Barber, T. X. (1969). *Hypnosis: A scientific approach*. New York: Van Nostrand Reinhold.

Barber, T. X., & Calverley, D. S. (1966). Toward a theory of "hypnotic" behavior: Experimental analyses of suggested amnesia. *Journal of Abnormal Psychology*, 71(2), 95–107. doi: http://dx.doi.org/10.1037/h0023096

Barense, M. D., Gaffan, D., & Graham, K. S. (2007). The human medial temporal lobe processes online representations of complex objects. *Neuropsychologia*, 45(13), 2963–2974.

Barner, C., Seibold, M., Born, J., & Diekelmann, S. (2017). Consolidation of prospective memory: Effects of sleep on completed and reinstated intentions. *Frontiers in Psychology*, 7, 1–18. doi: https://doi.org/10.3389/fpsyg.2016.02025.

Barnier, A. J. (2002). Posthypnotic amnesia for autobiographical episodes: A laboratory model of functional amnesia? *Psychological Science*, 13(3), 232–237. doi: http://dx.doi.org/10.1111/1467-9280.00443

Barnier, A. J., Bryant, R. A., & Briscoe, S. (2001). Posthypnotic amnesia for material learned before or during hypnosis: Explicit and implicit memory effects. *International Journal of Clinical & Experimental Hypnosis*, 49(4), 286–304. doi: http://dx.doi.org/10.1080/0020714 0108410079

Barnier, A. J., Conway, M. A., Mayoh, L., & Speyer, J. (2007). Directed forgetting of autobiographical memories. *Journal of Experimental Psychology: General*, 136(2), 301–322.

Barnier, A. J., Hung, L., & Conway, M. A. (2004). Retrieval-induced forgetting of emotional and unemotional autobiographical memories. *Emotion & Cognition*, 18, 457–477.

Barnier, A. J., & McConkey, K. M. (1998). Post-hypnotic suggestion, amnesia, and hypnotisability. *Australian Journal of Clinical & Experimental Hypnosis*, 26, 10–18.

Barr, R., Brito, N., & Simcock, G. (2013). Revisiting the effect of reminders on infants' media memories: Does the encoding format matter? *Developmental Psychology*, 49, 2112–2119.

Barr, R., Rovee-Collier, C., & Learmonth, A. E. (2011). Potentiation in young infants: The origin of the prior knowledge effect? *Memory & Cognition*, 39, 625–636.

Barr, R., Walker, J., Gross, J., & Hayne, H. (2014). Age-related changes in spreading activation during infancy. *Child Development*, 85, 549–563.

Barsalou, L. W. (1983). Ad hoc categories. *Memory & Cognition*, 11, 211–227.

Barsalou, L. W. (1988). The content and organization of autobiographical memories. In U. Neisser and E. Wonograd (eds), *Remembering Reconsidered: Ecological and traditional approaches to the study of memory* (pp. 193–243). Cambridge: Cambridge University Press.

Basden, B. H., & Basden, D. R. (1996). Directed forgetting: Further comparisons of the item and list methods. *Memory*, 4, 633–653.

Basden, B. H., Basden, D. R., Coe, W. C., Decker, S., & Crutcher, K. (1994). Retrieval inhibition in directed forgetting and posthypnotic amnesia. *International Journal of Clinical & Experimental Hypnosis*, 42, 184–203. doi: http://dx.doi.org/10.1080/00207149408409351

Bassok, D., Fitzpatrick, M., Greenberg, E., & Loeb, S. (2016). Within- and between-sector quality differences in early childhood education and care, *Child Development*, 87, 1627–1645, 10.1111/cdev.12551

Bates, B. L. (1992). The effect of demands for honesty on the efficacy of the Carleton Skills Training Program. *International Journal of Clinical & Experimental Hypnosis*, 40, 88–102. doi: http://dx.doi.org/10.1080/00207149208409650

Bates, B. L., Miller, R. J., Cross, H. J., & Brigham, T. A. (1988). Modifying hypnotic suggestibility with the Carleton Skills Training Program. *Journal of Personality and Social Psychology*, 55(1), 120–127. doi: http://dx.doi.org/10.1037/0022-3514.55.1.120

Bauer, P. J. (2015). A complementary processes account of the development of childhood amnesia and a personal past. *Psychological Review*, 122, 204–231.

Bäuml, K.-H. T., & Aslan, A. (2004). Part-list cuing as instructed retrieval inhibition. *Memory & Cognition*, 32, 610–617.

Bäuml, K.-H. T., Hanslmayr, S., Pastötter, B., & Klimesch, W. (2008). Oscillatory correlates of intentional updating in episodic memory. *NeuroImage*, 41, 596–604.

Bäuml, K.-H. T., & Kliegl, O. (2013). The critical role of retrieval processes in release from proactive interference. *Journal of Memory and Language*, 68, 39–53.

Bäuml, K.-H. T., & Kliegl, O. (2017). Retrieval-induced remembering and forgetting. In J. T. Wixted (ed.), *Learning and Memory: A comprehensive reference. Vol. 2: Cognitive Psychology of Memory* (2nd edn, pp. 27–51), J. H. Byrne T. (ed.). Oxford: Academic Press.

Bäuml, K.-H. T., Pastötter, B., & Hanslmayr, S. (2010). Binding and inhibition in episodic memory: Cognitive, emotional, and neural processes. *Neuroscience & Biobehavioral Reviews*, 34, 1047–1054.

Bäuml, K.-H. T., & Samenieh, A. (2010). The two faces of memory retrieval. *Psychological Science*, 21, 793–795.

Beadle, J., Tranel, D., Cohen, N. J., & Duff, M. C. (2013). Empathy in hippocampal amnesia. *Frontiers in Psychology*, 4(69). doi: 10.3389/fpsyg.2013.00069.

Bell, B. E., & Loftus, E. F. (1989). Trivial persuasion in the courtroom: The power of (a few) minor details. *Journal of Personality and Social Psychology*, 56, 669–679.

Bell, V., Oakley, D. A., Halligan, P. W., & Deeley, Q. (2011). Dissociation in hysteria and hypnosis: Evidence from cognitive neuroscience. *Journal of Neurology, Neurosurgery, & Psychiatry*, 82(3), 332–339. doi: http://dx.doi.org/10.1016/0028-3932(84)90040-X

Benge, J., Dinh, K. L., Logue, E., Phenis, R., Dasse, M. N., & Scullin, M. K. (2020). The smartphone in the memory clinic: A study of patient and care partner's utilisation habits. *Neuropsychological Rehabilitation*, 30, 101–115. doi: 10.1080/09602011.2018.1459307

Benge, J., & Scullin, M. K. (2020). Commentary on Osiurak and Reynaud: Implications for technological reserve development in advancing age, cognitive impairment, and dementia. *Behavioral and Brain Sciences*.

Benjamin, A. S. (2006). The effects of list-method directed forgetting on recognition memory. *Psychonomic Bulletin & Review*, 13, 831–836.

Benoit, R. G., & Anderson, M. C. (2013) Opposing mechanisms support the voluntary forgetting of unwanted memories. *Neuron*, 76, 450–460.

Benoit, R. G., Davies, D. J., & Anderson, M. C. (2016). Reducing future fears by suppressing the brain mechanisms underlying episodic simulation. *Proceedings of the National Academy of Sciences*, 113, E8492–E8501.

Benoit, R. G., & Schacter, D. L. (2015). Specifying the core network supporting episodic simulation and episodic memory by activation likelihood estimation. *Neuropsychologia*, 75, 450–457.

Berenbaum, H., Chow, P. I., Fiores, L. E., Schoenleber, M., Thompson, R. J., & Most, S. B. (2018). A test of the initiation-termination model of worry. *Journal of Experimental Pathology*, 9, 1–13.

Bergström, Z., Anderson, M. C., Buda, M., Simons, J. S., & Richardson-Klavehn, A. (2013). Intentional retrieval suppression can conceal guilty knowledge in ERP memory detection tests. *Biological Psychology*, 94, 1–11.

Bergström, Z., de Fockert, J. W., & Richardson-Klavehn, A. (2009). ERP and behavioural evidence for direct suppression of unwanted memories. *NeuroImage*, 48, 726–737.

Bernstein, D. M., Scoboria, A., Desjarlais, L., & Soucie, K. (2018). "False memory" is a linguistic convenience. *Psychology of Consciousness: Theory, Research, and Practice*, 5(2), 161.

Berntsen, D. (2012). *Involuntary Memories: An introduction to the unbidden past*. Cambridge: Cambridge University Press.

Bertrand, L. D., Spanos, N. P., & Radtke, H. L. (1990). Contextual effects on priming during hypnotic amnesia. *Journal of Research in Personality*, 24(3), 271–290. doi: http://dx.doi.org/10.1016/0092-6566(90)90021-W

Billingsley, R. L., Smith, M. L., & McAndrews, M. P. (2002). Developmental patterns in priming and familiarity in explicit recollection. *Journal of Experimental Child Psychology*, 82, 251–277.

Bitterman, M. E., & Marcuse, F. L. (1945). Autonomic response in posthypnotic amnesia. *Journal of Experimental Psychology*, 35(3), 248–252. doi: http://dx.doi.org/10.1037/h0053585

Bjork, E. L., & Bjork, R. A. (1996). Continuing influences of to-be-forgotten information. *Consciousness and Cognition*, 5, 176–196.

Bjork, R. A. (1970). Positive forgetting: The noninterference of items intentionally forgotten. *Journal of Verbal Learning and Verbal Behavior*, 9, 255–268.

Bjork, R. A. (1972). Theoretical implications of directed forgetting. In A.W. Melton and E. Martin (eds), *Coding Processes in Human Memory* (pp. 217–235). Washington, D.C.: Winston.

Bjork, R. A. (1978). The updating of human memory. In G. H. Bower (ed.), *The Psychology of Learning and Motivation* (pp. 235–259). New York: Academic.

Bjork, R. A. (1989). Retrieval inhibition as an adaptive mechanism in human memory. In H.L. Roediger and F. I. M. Craik (eds), *Varieties of Memory and Consciousness: Essays in honour of Endel Tulving* (pp. 309–330). Hillsdale, NJ: Erlbaum.

Bjork, R.A., & Bjork, E.L. (1992). A new theory of disuse and an old theory of stimulus fluctuation. In A. F. Healy, S. M. Kosslyn, & R. M. Shiffrin (eds), *From Learning Processes to Cognitive Processes: Essays in honour of William K. Estes* (Vol. 2, pp. 35–67). Hillsdale, NJ: Erlbaum.

Bjorklund, D. F., & Harnishfeger, K. K. (1990). The resources construct in cognitive development: Diverse sources of evidence and a theory of inefficient inhibition. *Developmental Review*, 10, 48–71.

Blank, H., & Launay, C. (2014). How to protect eyewitness memory against the misinformation effect: A meta-analysis of post-warning studies. *Journal of Applied Research in Memory and Cognition*, 3(2), 77–88.

Blank, H., Walther, E., & Isemann, S. D. (2017). The past is a social construction. In R. A. Nash and J. Ost (eds), *False and Distorted Memories* (Current Issues in Memory series) (pp. 55–71). Abingdon: Routledge.

Blank, T. J. (2009). Fieldwork, memory, and the impact of 9/11 on an Eastern Tennessee Klansman: A folklorist's reflection. *Voices*, 35(3/4), 23.

Bluck, S., Alea, N., Habermas, T., & Rubin, D. C. (2005). A tale of three functions: The self-reported uses of autobiographical memory. *Social Cognition*, 23, 91–117.

Bluck, S., & Habermas, T. (2000). The life story schema. *Motivation and Emotion*, 24, 121–147.

Boag, S. (2010). Repression, suppression, and conscious awareness. *Psychoanalytic Psychology*, 27, 164–181.

Bodner, G. E., & Lindsay, D. S. (2003). Remembering and knowing in context. *Journal of Memory and Language*, 48, 563–580.

Boot, W. R., Simons, D. J., Stothart, C., & Stutts, C. (2013). The pervasive problem with placebos in psychology: Why active control groups are not sufficient to rule out placebo effects. *Perspectives on Psychological Science*, 8(4), 445–454.

Bowden, V. K., Smith, R. E., & Loft, S. (2017). Eye movements provide insights into the conscious use of context in prospective memory. *Consciousness and Cognition*, 52, 68–74. doi: https://doi.org/10.1016/j.concog.2017.04.003

Bowen, H. J., Kark, S. M., & Kensinger, E. A. (2017). NEVER forget: Negative emotional valence enhances recapitulation. *Psychonomic Bulletin & Review*, 25, 870–981.

Bower, G. H. (1972). Stimulus-sampling theory of encoding variability. In A. W. Melton and E. Martin (eds), *Coding Processes in Human Memory* (pp. 85–123). Washington, DC: Winston.

Bowers, K. S. (1967). The effect for demands of honesty upon reports of visual and auditory hallucinations. *International Journal of Clinical and Experimental Hypnosis*, 15, 31–36. doi: http://dx.doi.org/10.1080/00207146708407503

Bowers, K. S. (1981). Do the Stanford Scales tap the "classic suggestion effect"? *International Journal of Clinical and Experimental Hypnosis*, 29, 42–53. doi: http://dx.doi.org/10.1080/00207148108409142

Bowers, K. S., & Gilmore, J. B. (1969). Subjective report and credibility: An inquiry involving hypnotic hallucinations. *Journal of Abnormal Psychology*, 74(4), 443–451. doi: http://dx.doi.org/10.1037/h0027745

Bowers, K. S., & Woody, E. Z. (1996). Hypnotic amnesia and the paradox of intentional forgetting. *Journal of Abnormal Psychology*, 105(3), 381–390. doi: http://dx.doi.org/10.1037/0021-843X.105.3.381

Bowers, P. (1982). The classic suggestion effect: Relationships with scales of hypnotizability, effortless experiencing, and imagery vividness. *International Journal of Clinical and Experimental Hypnosis*, 30, 270–279. doi: http://dx.doi.org/10.1080/00207148208407264

Bowers, P., Laurence, J. R., & Hart, D. (1988). The experience of hypnotic suggestions. *International Journal of Clinical and Experimental Hypnosis*, 36, 336–349. doi: http://dx.doi.org/10.1080/00207148808410523

Bowman, C. (1997). *Children's Past Lives: How past life memories can effect your child*. Shaftesbury, Dorset: Element Books Limited.

Bowman, C. (2001). *Return From Heaven*. New York: HarperTorch.

Brandstätter, V., Lengfelder, A., & Gollwitzer, P. M. (2001). Implementation intentions and efficient action initiation. *Journal of Personality and Social Psychology*, 81, 946–960.

Braver, T. S. (2012). The variable nature of cognitive control: A dual mechanisms framework. *Trends in Cognitive Sciences*, 16(2), 106–113.

Breneiser, J. E., & McDaniel, M. A. (2006). Discrepancy processes in prospective memory retrieval. *Psychonomic Bulletin & Review*, 13(5).

Brewer, G. A. (2011). Analyzing response time distributions: Methodological and theoretical suggestions for prospective memory researchers. *Zeitschrift für Psychologie*, 219(2), 117–124. doi: https://doi.org/10.1027/2151-2604/a000056

Brewer, N., & Weber, N. (2008). Eyewitness confidence and latency: Indices of memory processes not just markers of accuracy. *Applied Cognitive Psychology: The Official Journal of the Society for Applied Research in Memory and Cognition*, 22(6), 827–840.

Brewin, C. (2001). A cognitive neuroscience account of posttraumatic stress disorder and its treatment. *Behaviour Research and Therapy*, 39(4), 373–393.

Brewin, C. (2003). *Posttraumatic Stress Disorder: Malady or myth?* New Haven, CT: Yale University Press.

Brewin, C. (2018). Memory and forgetting. *Current Psychiatry Reports*, 20(10), 87–87.

Brewin, C., & Andrews, B. (2017). Creating memories for false autobiographical events in childhood: A systematic review. *Applied Cognitive Psychology*, 31(1), 2–23.

Brewin, C., Dalgleish, T., & Joseph, S. (1996). A dual representation theory of posttraumatic stress disorder. *Psychological Review*, 103(4), 670–686.

Brown, A. S., Caderao, K. C., Fields, L. M., & Marsh, E. J. (2015). Borrowing personal memories. *Applied Cognitive Psychology*, 29, 471–477.

Brown, D. A., Lamb, M. E., Lewis, C. N., Pipe, M. E., Orbach, Y., & Wolfman, M. (2013). The NICHD investigative interview protocol: An analogue study. *Journal of Experimental Psychology: Applied*, 19(4), 367–382. doi: https://doi.org/10.1037/a0035143

Brown, G. D. A., & Lewandowsky, S. (2010). Forgetting in memory models: Arguments against trace decay and consolidation failure. In S. Della Sala (ed.), *Forgetting*. Hove: Psychology Press.

Bruck, M., Melnyk, L., & Ceci, S. J. (2000). Draw it again Sam: The effect of drawing on children's suggestibility and source monitoring ability. *Journal of Experimental Child Psychology*, 77(3), 169–196. https://doi.org/10.1006/jecp.1999.2560

Bryant, R. A. (2019). Post-traumatic stress disorder: A state-of-the-art review of evidence and challenges. *World Psychiatry*, 18(3), 259–269.

Buckner, R., & Carroll, D. (2007). Self-projection and the brain. *TRENDS in Cognitive Science*, 11(2), 49–57.

Buckner, R. L., Andrews-Hanna, J. R., & Schacter, D. L. (2008). The brain's default network: Anatomy, function, and relevance to disease. *Annals of the New York Academy of Sciences*, 1124, 1–38.

Bugg, J. M., & Ball, B. H. (2017). The strategic control of prospective memory monitoring in response to complex and probabilistic contextual cues. *Memory & Cognition*, 45(5), 755–775. doi: https://doi.org/10.3758/s13421-017-0696-1

Bugg, J. M., McDaniel, M. A., Scullin, M. K., & Braver, T. S. (2011). Revealing list-level control in the Stroop task by uncovering its benefits and a cost. *Journal of Experimental Psychology: Human Perception and Performance*, 37(5), 1595–1606.

Bugg J. M., Scullin, M. K., & McDaniel, M. A. (2013). Strengthening encoding via implementation intention formation increases prospective memory commission errors. *Psychonomic Bulletin & Review*, 20, 522–527.

Bugg, J. M., Scullin, M. K., & Rauvola, R. S. (2016). Forgetting no-longer-relevant prospective memory intentions is (sometimes) harder with age but easier with forgetting practice. *Psychology and Aging*, 31(4), 358–369. doi: https://doi.org/10.1037/pag0000087

Bull, R. (2019). Roar or "PEACE": Is it a "tall story?". In R. Bull and I. Blandon-Gitlin (eds), *The Routledge International Handbook of Legal and Investigative Psychology* (p. 20). Abingdon: Routledge.

Burgess, P. W., Dumontheil, I., & Gilbert, S. J. (2007). The gateway hypothesis of rostral prefrontal cortex (area 10) function. *Trends in Cognitive Sciences*, 11(7), 290–298.

Burkard, C., Rochat, L., Van der Linden, A. C. J., Gold, G., & Van der Linden, M. (2014). Is working memory necessary for implementation intentions to enhance prospective memory in older adults with cognitive problems? *Journal of Applied Research in Memory and Cognition*, 3, 37–43.

Calvillo, D. P., & Parong, J. A. (2016). The misinformation effect is unrelated to the DRM effect with and without a DRM warning. *Memory*, 24(3), 324–333.

Canada, K. L., Ngo, C. T., Newcombe, N. S., Geng, F., & Riggins, T. (2019). It's all in the details: Relations between young children's developing pattern separation abilities and hippocampal subfield volumes. *Cerebral Cortex*, 29(8), 3427–3433. doi-org.ezproxy.uow.edu.au/10.1093/cercor/bhy211

Carey, N. (2012). *The Epigenetics Revolution*. London: Icon.

Catarino, A., Küpper, C. S., Werner-Seidler, A., Dalgleish, T., & Anderson, M. C. (2015). Failing to forget: Inhibitory-control deficits compromise memory suppression in posttraumatic stress disorder. *Psychological Science*, 26(5), 604–616.

Cauvin, S., Moulin, C. J., Souchay, C., Kliegel, M., & Schnitzspahn, K. M. (2019). Prospective memory predictions in aging: Increased overconfidence in older adults. *Experimental Aging Research*, 45.

Charlesworth, C. J., Smit, E., Lee, D. S.H., Alramadhan, F., & Odden, M. C. (2015). Polypharmacy among adults aged 65 years and older in the United States: 1988–2010. *Journals of Gerontology Series A: Biological Sciences and Medical Sciences*, 70, 989–995. doi: https://doi.org/10.1093/gerona/glv013.

Chasteen, A. L., Park, D. C., & Schwarz, N. (2001). Implementation intentions and facilitation of prospective memory. *Psychological Science*, 12, 457–461.

Chatterjee, A. (2005). A madness to the methods in cognitive neuroscience? *Journal of Cognitive Neuroscience*, 17(6), 847–849.

Chen, X. J., Wang, Y., Liu, L. L., Cui, J. F., Gan, M. Y., Shum, D. H., & Chan, R. C. (2015). The effect of implementation intention on prospective memory: A systematic and meta-analytic review. *Psychiatry Research*, 226(1), 14–22.

Chrobak, Q. M., & Zaragoza, M. S. (2008). Inventing stories: Forcing witnesses to fabricate entire fictitious events leads to freely reported false memories. *Psychonomic Bulletin & Review*, 15(6), 1190–1195.

Chrobak, Q. M., & Zaragoza, M. S. (2013). When forced fabrications become truth: Causal explanations and false memory development. *Journal of Experimental Psychology: General*, 142(3), 827.

Cialdini, R. B., & Goldstein, N. J. (2004). Social influence: Compliance and conformity. *Annual Review of Psychology*, 55, 591–621.

Ciranni, M. A., & Shimamura, A. P. (1999). Retrieval-induced forgetting in episodic memory. *Journal of Experimental Psychology: Learning, Memory, and Cognition*, 25, 1403–1414.

Clancy, S. A., & McNally, R. J. (2005/2006). Who needs repression? Normal memory processes can explain "forgetting" of childhood sexual abuse. *Scientific Review of Mental Health Practice*, 4, 66–73.

Claparede, E. (1911/1951). Reconnaissance et moitié [Recognition and me-ness]. In D. Rapaport (ed.), *Organization and Pathology of Thought: Selected sources* (pp. 58–75). New York: Columbia University Press.

Clarke, C., Milne, R., & Bull, R. (2011). Interviewing suspects of crime: The impact of PEACE training, supervision and the presence of a legal advisor. *Journal of Investigative Psychology and Offender Profiling*, 8(2), 149–162.

Coe, W. C. (1978). Credibility of post-hypnotic amnesia – a contextualist's view. *International Journal of Clinical and Experimental Hypnosis*, 26, 218–245. doi: http://dx.doi.org/10.1080/00207147808411250

Coe, W. C. (1989). Posthypnotic amnesia: Theory and research. In N. P. Spanos and J. F. Chaves (eds), *Hypnosis: The Cognitive-Behavioral Perspective* (pp. 110–148). Buffalo, NY: Prometheus.

Coe, W. C., Basden, B., Basden, D., & Graham, C. (1976). Posthypnotic amnesia: Suggestions of an active process in dissociative phenomena. *Journal of Abnormal Psychology*, 85(5), 455–458. doi: http://dx.doi.org/10.1037/0021-843X.85.5.455

Cohen, N. J. (1984). Preserved learning capacity in amnesia: Evidence for multiple memory systems. In L. R. Squire and N. Butters (eds), *Neuropsychology of Memory* (pp. 83–103). New York: Guilford Press.

Cohen, N. J., & Eichenbaum, H. (1993). *Memory, Amnesia and the Hippocampal System*. Cambridge, MA: MIT Press.

Cohen, N. J., & Squire, L. R. (1980). Preserved learning and retention of a pattern-analyzing skill in amnesia: Dissociation of knowing how and knowing that. *Science*, 210, 207–210.

Collins, A. M., & Loftus, E. F. (1975). A spreading activation theory of semantic processing. *Psychological Review*, 82, 407–428.

Compo, N. S., & Parker, J. F. (2010). Gaining insight into long-term effects of inviting speculation: Does recantation help? *Applied Cognitive Psychology*, 24(7), 969–990.

Cona, G., Scarpazza, C., Sartori, G., Moscovitch, M., & Bisiacchi, P. S. (2015). Neural bases of prospective memory: A meta-analysis and the "Attention to Delayed Intention" (AtoDI) model. *Neuroscience and Biobehavioral Reviews*, 52, 21–37. doi: http://dx.doi.org/10.1016/j. neubiorev.2015.02.007.

Conway, M. A. (1996). Autobiographical memories and autobiographical knowledge. In D. C. Rubin (ed.), *Remembering Our Past: Studies in autobiographical memory* (pp. 67–93). Cambridge: Cambridge University Press.

Conway, M. A. (2005). Memory and the self. *Journal of Memory and Language*, 53, 594–628.

Conway, M. A. (2009). Episodic memories. *Neuropsychologia*, 47, 2305–13.

Conway, M. A., & Bekerian, D. A. (1987). Organization in autobiographical memory. *Memory & Cognition*, 15, 119–132.

Conway, M. A., & Fthenaki, A. (2003). Disruption of inhibitory control of memory following lesions to the frontal and temporal lobes. *Cortex*, 39, 667–686.

Conway, M. A., Harries, K., Noyes, J., Racsmany, M., & Frankish, C. R. (2000). The disruption and dissolution of directed forgetting: Inhibitory control of memory. *Journal of Memory & Language*, 43, 409–430.

Conway, M. A., & Loveday, C. (2015). Remembering, imagining, & personal meanings. *Consciousness and Cognition*, 33, 574–581.

Conway, M. A., Loveday, C., & Cole, S. N. (2016). The remembering-imagining system. *Memory Studies*, 9, 256–265.

Conway, M. A., & Pleydell-Pearce, C. W. (2000) The construction of autobiographical memories in the self-memory system. *Psychological Review*, 107, 261–288.

Conway, M. A., Justice, L. V., & D'Argembeau, A. (2019). The self-memory system revisited: Past, present, and future. In J. H. Mace (ed.), *The Organization and Structure of Autobiographical Memory* (pp. 28–51). New York: Oxford University Press.

Conway, M. A., Singer, J. A., & Tagini, A. (2004). The self and autobiographical memory: Correspondence and coherence. *Social Cognition*, 22, 495–537.

Cooper, L. M. (1966). Spontaneous and suggested posthypnotic source amnesia. *International Journal of of Clinical and Experimental Hypnosis*, 14(2), 180–193. doi: http://dx.doi.org/10.1080/ 00207146608412960

Cooper, L. M. (1979). Hypnotic amnesia. In E. Fromm and R. E. Shor (eds), *Hypnosis: Developments in research and new perspectives* (pp. 305–350). Chicago, IL: Aldine.

Corkin, S. (2002). What's new with the amnesic patient HM? *Nature Reviews Neuroscience*, 3, 153–160.

Corkin, S., Amaral, D. G., Gonzalez, R. G., Johnson, K. A., & Hyman, B. (1997). H. M.'s medial temporal lobe lesion: Findings from magnetic resonance imaging. *Journal of Neuroscience*, 17, 3964–3979.

Croft, K. E., Duff, M. C., Kovach, C., Anderson, S. W., Adolphs, R., & Tranel, D. (2010). Destestable or marvelous? Neuroanatomical correlates of character judgments. *Neuropsychologia*, 48, 1789–1801.

Crombag, H. F., Wagenaar, W. A., & Van Koppen, P. J. (1996). Crashing memories and the problem of 'source monitoring'. *Applied Cognitive Psychology*, 10(2), 95–104.

Crowder, R. G. (1996). The trouble with prospective memory: A provocation. In M. Brandimonte, G. O. Einstein and M. A. McDaniel (eds), *Prospective Memory: Theory and applications* (pp. 143–148). Hillsdale, NJ: Erlbaum.

Crozier, W. E., & Strange, D. (2019). Correcting the misinformation effect. *Applied Cognitive Psychology*, *33*(4), 585–595.

Crystal, J., & Smith, A. (2014). Binding of episodic memories in the rat. *Current Biology*, 24(24), 2957–2961.

Cui, X., Jeter, C. B., Yang, D., Montague, P. R., & Eagleman, D. M. (2007). Vividness of mental imagery: Individual variability can be measured objectively. *Vision Research*, 47(4), 474–478.

Curot, J., Busigny, T., Valton, L., Denuelle, M., Vignal, J.-P., Maillard, L., et al. (2017). Memory scrutinized through electrical brain stimulation: A review of 80 years of experiential phenomena. *Neuroscience and Biobehavioral Reviews*, 78, 161–177.

Dahl, J. J., Kingo, O. S., & Krojgaard, P. (2015). The magic shrinking machine revisited: The presence of props at recall facilitates memory in 3-year-olds. *Developmental Psychology*, 51, 1704–1716.

Dalton, A. L., & Daneman, M. (2006). Social suggestibility to central and peripheral misinformation. *Memory*, 14(4), 486–501.

Damaser, E., Whitehouse, W. G., Orne, M. T., Orne, E. C., & Dinges, D. F. (2010). Behavioral persistence in carrying out a posthypnotic suggestion beyond the hypnotic context: A consideration of the role of perceived demand characteristics. *International Journal of Clinical & Experimental Hypnosis*, 58(1), 1–20. doi: http://dx.doi.org/10.1080/0020714090331620

Dando, C. J. (2013). Drawing to remember: External support of older adults' eyewitness performance. *PloSOne*, 8, e69937. doi: 10.1371/journal.pone.0069937

Dando, C. J., Gabbert, F., & Hope, L. (2020). Supporting older eyewitnesses' episodic memory: The Self-Administered Interview and Sketch Reinstatement of Context. Manuscript submitted for publication.

Dando, C. J., & Milne, R. (2018). The Cognitive Interview. In R. N. Kocsis (ed.), *Applied Criminal Psychology: A guide to forensic behavioural sciences.* Springfield, IL: Charles. C. Thomas.

Dando, C. J., Wilcock, R., Behnkle, C., & Milne, R. (2011). Modifying the Cognitive Interview: Countenancing forensic application by enhancing practicability. *Psychology, Crime, & Law*, 17, 491–511.

Dando, C. J., Wilcock, R., & Milne, R. (2008). Victims and witnesses of crime: Police officers' perceptions of interviewing practices. *Legal and Criminological Psychology*, 13, 59–70.

Dando, C. J., Wilcock, R., & Milne, R. (2009a). The Cognitive Interview: The efficacy of a modified mental reinstatement of context procedure for frontline police investigators. *Applied Cognitive Psychology*, 23, 138–147.

Dando, C. J., Wilcock, R., & Milne, R. (2009b). Novice police officers' application of the Cognitive Interview procedure. *Psychology, Crime, & Law*, 15, 679–696.

Davachi, L. (2006) Item, context and relational episodic encoding in humans. *Current Opinion in Neurobiolology*, 16, 693–700.

Davachi, L., & Preston, A. R. (2014) The medial temporal lobe and memory. In M. S. Gazzaniga and G. R. Mangun (eds), *The Cognitive Neurosciences* (5th edn, pp. 539–546). Cambridge, MA: MIT Press.

David, D., Brown, R., Pojoga, C., & David, A. (2000). The impact of posthypnotic amnesia and directed forgetting on implicit and explicit memory: New insights from a modified process dissociation procedure. *International Journal of Clinical & Experimental Hypnosis*, 48(3), 267–289. doi: http://dx.doi.org/10.1080/00207140008415246

Davidson, T. M., & Bowers, K. S. (1991). Selective hypnotic amnesia: Is it a successful attempt to forget or an unsuccessful attempt to remember? *Journal of Abnormal Psychology*, 100, 133–143. doi: http://dx.doi.org/10.1037/0021-843X.100.2.133

Davidson, P., Drouin, H., Kwan, D., Moscovitch, M., & Rosenbaum, R. (2012). Memory as social glue: Close interpersonal relationships in amnesic patients. *Fronteirs in Psychology*, 3, 1–9. https://doi.org/10.3389/fpsyg.2012.00531

Davis, D., & Loftus, E. F. (2017). Internal and external sources of misinformation in adult witness memory. In *The Handbook of Eyewitness Psychology* (Vol. I, pp. 195–238). New York: Psychology Press. doi: https://doi.org/10.4324/9781315086309

Davis, N., Gross, J., & Hayne, H. (2008). Defining the boundary of childhood amnesia. *Memory*, 16, 465–474.

Delaney, P., Nghiem, K., & Waldum, E. (2009). The selective directed forgetting effect: Can people forget only part of a text? *Quarterly Journal of Experimental Psychology*, 62, 1542– 1550.

Deutsch, M., & Gerard, H. B. (1955). A study of normative and informational influences upon individual judgment. *Journal of Abnormal and Social Psychology*, 51, 629–636.

Devitt, A. L., & Schacter, D. L. (2016). False memories with age: Neural and cognitive underpinnings. *Neuropsychologia*, 91, 346–359.

Diana, R. A., Yonelinas, A. P., & Ranganath, C. (2008). High-resolution multi-voxel pattern analysis of category selectivity in the medial temporal lobes. *Hippocampus*, 18, 536–541.

Dias, B. G., & Ressler, K. J. (2014). Parental olfactory experience influences behavior and neural structure in subsequent generations. *Nature Neuroscience*, 17, 89–96.

Diekelmann, S., Wilhelm, I., Wagner, U., & Born, J. (2013). Sleep improves prospective remembering facilitating spontaneous-associative retrieval processes. *PLoS One*, 8(10), 1–10. doi: https://doi.org/10.1371/journal.pone.0077621.

Dismukes, R. K. (2012). Prospective memory in workplace and everyday situations. *Current Directions in Psychological Science*, 21(4), 215–220.

Ditta, A. S., & Storm, B. C. (2018). A consideration of the seven sins of memory in the context of creative cognition. *Creativity Research Journal*, 30, 402–417.

Divis, K. M., & Benjamin, A. S. (2014). Retrieval speeds context fluctuation: Why semantic generation enhances later learning, but hinders prior learning. *Memory & Cognition*, 42, 1049–1062.

Dodson, C. S., Powers, E., & Lytell, M. (2015). Aging, confidence, and misinformation: Recalling information with the cognitive interview. *Psychology and Aging*, 30(1), 46.

Dorfman, J., & Kihlstrom, J. F. (1994, November). Semantic priming in posthypnotic amnesia. Paper presented at the Psychonomic Society, St Louis.

Dorfman, J., Kihlstrom, J. F., Cork, R. C., & Misiaszek, J. (1995). Priming and recognition in ECT-induced amnesia. *Psychonomic Bulletin & Review*, 2(2), 244–248. doi: http://dx.doi.org/10.3758/BF03210964

Drivdahl, S. B., & Zaragoza, M. S. (2001). The role of perceptual elaboration and individual differences in the creation of false memories for suggested events. *Applied Cognitive Psychology: The Official Journal of the Society for Applied Research in Memory and Cognition*, 15(3), 265–281.

Dudokovic, N. M., Marsh, E. J., & Tversky, B. (2004). Telling a story or telling it straight: The effects of entertaining versus accurate retellings on memory. *Applied Cognitive Psychology*, 18, 125–143.

Dudycha, G. J., & Dudycha, M. M. (1933a). Adolescents' memories of preschool experiences. *Journal of Genetic Psychology: General*, 42, 468–480.

Dudycha, G. J., & Dudycha, M. M. (1933b). Some factors and characteristics of childhood memories. *Child Development*, 4, 265–278.

Duff, M. C., & Brown-Schmidt, S. (2012). The hippocampus and the flexible use and processing of language. *Frontiers in Human Neuroscience*, 6. doi: 10.3389/fnhum.2012.00069

Duff, M. C., Hengst, J., Tranel, D., & Cohen, N. J. (2006). Development of shared information in communication despite hippocampal amnesia. *Nature Neuroscience*, 9(1), 140–146.

Duff, M. C., Hengst, J., Tranel, D., & Cohen, N. J. (2007). Talking across time: Using reported speech as a communicative resource in amnesia. *Aphasiology*, 21(6, 7, 8), 702–716.

Duff, M. C., Hengst, J., Tranel, D., & Cohen, N. J. (2009). Hippocampal amnesia disrupts verbal play and the creative use of language in social interaction. *Aphasiology*, 23(7), 926–939.

Duff, M. C., Kurczek, J., Rubin, R., Cohen, N. J., & Tranel, D. (2013). Hippocampal amnesia impairs creative thinking. *Hippocampus*, 23(12), 1143–1149.

Duffy, M., Gillespie, K., & Clark, D. (2007). Post-traumatic stress disorder in the context of terrorism and other civil conflict in Northern Ireland: Randomised controlled trial. *BMJ*, 334(7604), 1147–1153.

Dunsmoor, J. E., Martin, A., & LaBar, K. S. (2012). Role of conceptual knowledge in learning and retention of conditioned fear. *Biological Psychology*, 89, 300–305.

Dyer, W.W., & Garnes, D. (2015). *Memories of Heaven*. London: Hay House.

Earhard, M. (1967). Cued recall and free recall as a function of the number of items per cue. *Journal of Verbal Learning and Verbal Behaviour*, 6, 257–263.

Ebbinghaus, H. (1885). *Über das Gedächtnis: Untersuchugen zur experimentellen psychologie*. Leipzig: Dunker & Humbolt.

Ece, B., Demiray, B., & Gulgoz, S. (2019). Consistency of adults' earliest memories across two years. *Memory*, 27, 28–37.

Echterhoff, G., & Higgins, E. T. (2018). Shared reality: Construct and mechanisms. *Current Opinion in Psychology*, 23, iv–vii.

Ecker, U. K., Lewandowsky, S., & Tang, D. T. (2010). Explicit warnings reduce but do not eliminate the continued influence of misinformation. *Memory & Cognition*, 38(8), 1087–1100.

Ehlers, A., & Clark, D. M. (2000). A cognitive model of posttraumatic stress disorder. *Behaviour Research and Therapy*, 38(4), 319–345.

Eich, E. (1985). Context, memory, and integrated item/context imagery. *Journal of Experimental Psychology: Learning, Memory, and Cognition*, 11, 764–770.

Eich, E. (1989). Theoretical issues in state dependent memory. In H. L. Roediger and F. I. M. Craik (eds), *Varieties of Memory and Consciousness: Essays in honour of Endel Tulving* (pp. 331–354). Hillsdale, NJ: Erlbaum.

Eichenbaum, H., & Cohen, N. J. (2001). *From Conditioning to Conscious Recollection: Memory systems of the brain*. New York: Oxford University Press.

Eichenbaum, H., & Cohen, N. J. (2014) Can we reconcile the declarative memory and spatial navigation views on hippocampal function? *Neuron*, 83, 764–770.

Eichenbaum, H., Yonelinas, A., & Ranganath, C. (2007). The medial temporal lobe and recognition memory. *Annu Rev Neurosci*, 20, 123–152.

Einstein, G. O., & McDaniel, M. A. (1990). Normal aging and prospective memory. *Journal of Experimental Psychology: Learning, Memory, and Cognition*, 16(4), 717–726.

Einstein, G. O., McDaniel, M. A., Manzi, M., Cochran, B., & Baker, M. (2000). Prospective memory and aging: Forgetting intentions over short delays. *Psychology and Aging*, 15(4), 671–683.

Einstein, G. O., McDaniel, M. A., Thomas, R., Mayfield, S., Shank, H., Morrisette, N., & Breneiser, J. (2005). Multiple processes in prospective memory retrieval: Factors determining monitoring versus spontaneous retrieval. *Journal of Experimental Psychology: General*, 134(3), 327–342. doi: https://doi.org/10.1037/0096-3445.134.3.327

Eisen, M. L., Winograd, E., & Qin, J. (2002). Individual differences in adults' suggestibility and memory performance. In M. L. Eisen, J. A. Quas and G. S. Goodman (eds), *Memory and Suggestibility in the Forensic Interview* (LEA Series in Personality and Clinical Psychology) (pp. 205–233). Mahwah, NJ: Erlbaum.

El Haj, M., Gallouj, K., & Antoine, P. (2017). Google calendar enhances prospective memory in Alzheimer's disease: A case report. *Journal of Alzheimer's Disease*, 57(1), 285–291.

Engelhard, I. M., McNally, R. J., & van Schie, K. (2019). Retrieving and modifying traumatic memories: Recent research relevant to three controversies. *Current Directions in Psychological Science*, 28, 91–96.

Engen, H. G., & Anderson, M. C. (2018). Memory control: A fundamental mechanism of emotion regulation. *Trends in Cognitive Sciences*, 22, 982–995.

Ennis, C., & Pugh, O. (2017). *Epigenetics: A graphic guide*. London: Icon.

Erdelyi, M. H. (2001). Defence processes can be conscious or unconscious. *American Psychologist*, 56, 761–762.

Erdelyi, M. H. (2006). The unified theory of repression. *Behavioral and Brain Sciences*, 29, 499–551.

Erdelyi, M. H., & Becker, J. (1974). Hypermnesia for pictures: Incremental memory for pictures but not words in multiple recall trials. *Cognitive Psychology*, 6, 159–171.

Eschen, A., Freeman, J., Dietrich, T., Martin, M., Ellis, J., Martin, E., & Kliegel, M. (2007). Motor brain regions are involved in the encoding of delayed intentions: A fMRI study. *International Journal of Psychophysiology*, 64(3), 259–268.

Esposito, M. J., Occhionero, M., & Cicogna, P. (2015). Sleep deprivation and time-based prospective memory. *Sleep*, 38(11), 1823–1826. doi: https://doi.org/10.5665/sleep.5172

Estes, W. K. (1955). Statistical theory of spontaneous recovery and regression. *Psychological Review*, 62, 145–154.

Evans, F. J. (1979). Contextual forgetting: Posthypnotic source amnesia. *Journal of Abnormal Psychology*, 88, 556–563. doi: http://dx.doi.org/10.1037/0021-843X.88.5.556

Evans, F. J., & Kihlstrom, J. F. (1973). Posthypnotic amnesia as disrupted retrieval. *Journal of Abnormal Psychology*, 82(2), 317–323. doi: http://dx.doi.org/10.1037/h0035003

Evans, F. J., & Thorn, W. A. (1966). Two types of posthypnotic amnesia: Recall amnesia and source amnesia. *International Journal of Clinical and Experimental Hypnosis*, 14(2), 162–179. doi: http://dx.doi.org/10.1080/00207146608412959

Eysenck, M. W., Derakshan, N., Santos, R., & Calvo, M. G. (2007). Anxiety and cognitive performance: Attentional control theory. *Emotion*, 7, 336–353.

Eysenck, M. W., & Keane, M. T. (2020). *Cognitive Psychology: A student's handbook* (8th edn). Hove: Psychology Press.

Eysenck, M. W., Moser, J. S., Derakshan, N., & Allen, P. (in preparation). Trait anxiety, processing efficiency and performance effectiveness: A neurocognitive attentional control theory.

Eysenck, M. W., & van Berkum, J. (1992). Trait anxiety, defensiveness, and the structure of worry. *Personality and Individual Differences*, 13, 1285–1290.

Ferguson, S., Friedland, D., & Woodberry, E. (2015). Smartphone technology: Gentle reminders of everyday tasks for those with prospective memory difficulties post-brain injury. *Brain Injury*, 29, 583–591.

Fernandez, A., & Glenberg, A. M. (1985). Changing environmental context does not reliably affect memory. *Memory & Cognition*, 13, 333–345.

Finn, B., & Roediger, H.L. III. (2011). Enhancing retention through reconsolidation: Negative emotional arousal flowing retrieval enhances later recall. *Psychological Science*, 22, 781–786.

Fisher, R. P., & Geiselman, R. E. (1992). *Memory-Enhancing Techniques for Investigative Interviewing: The cognitive interview*. Springfield, IL: Charles C Thomas.

Fisher, R. P., Ross, S. J., & Cahill, B. S. (2017). Interviewing witnesses and victims. In P. A. Granhag (ed.), *Forensic Psychology in Context: Nordic and international approaches* (pp. 56–74). Cullompton: Willan.

Fivush, R. (2007). Maternal reminiscing style and children's developing understanding of self and emotion. *Clinical Social Work Journal*, 35, 37–46.

Fivush, R., Habermas, T., Waters, T. E. A., & Zaman, W. (2011). The making of autobiographical memory: Intersections of culture, narratives and identity. *International Journal of Psychology*, 46, 321–345.

Fivush, R., Haden, C. A., & Reese, E. (2006). Elaborating on elaborations: Role of maternal reminiscing style in cognitive and socioemotional development. *Child Development*, 77, 1568–1588.

Foley, M. A., Johnson, M. K., & Raye, C. L. (1983). Age-related changes in confusion between memories for speech and memories for thought. *Child Development*, 54, 51–60.

Foster, E. R., McDaniel, M. A., Repovš, G., & Hershey, T. (2009). Prospective memory in Parkinson disease across laboratory and self-reported everyday performance. *Neuropsychology*, 23(3), 347–358. doi: https://doi.org/10.1037/a0014692

Foster, J. L., Huthwaite, T., Yesberg, J. A., Garry, M., & Loftus, E. F. (2012). Repetition, not number of sources, increases both susceptibility to misinformation and confidence in the accuracy of eyewitnesses. *Acta Psychologica*, 139(2), 320–326.

Fraley, R. C., Roisman, G. I., & Haltigan, J. D. (2013). The legacy of early experiences in development: Formalizing alternative models of how early experiences are carried forward over time. *Developmental Psychobiology*, 49, 109–126.

French, L., Garry, M., & Mori, K. (2008). You say tomato? Collaborative remembering leads to more false memories for intimate couples than for strangers. *Memory*, 16(3), 262–273.

Frenda, S. J., Nichols, R. M., & Loftus, E. F. (2011). Current issues and advances in misinformation research. *Current Directions in Psychological Science*, 20(1), 20–23.

Freud, S. (1914/1957). The history of the psychoanalytic movement. In J. Strachey (ed.), *The Standard Edition of the Complete Psychological Works of Sigmund Freud*. London: Hogarth.

Freud, S. (1915/1963). Repression. In J. Strachey (ed.), *Standard Edition of the Collected Works of Sigmund Freud* (Vol. 14). London: Hogarth.

Freud, S. (1920/1935). *A General Introduction to Psycho-analysis* (J. Riviere, trans.). Garden City, NY: Garden City Publishing Company, Inc.

Gabbert, F., Hope, L., & Fisher, R. P. (2009). Protecting eyewitness evidence: Examining the efficacy of a self-administered interview tool. *Law and Human Behavior*, 33(4), 298–307.

Gabbert, F., Hope, L., Fisher, R. P., & Jamieson, K. (2012). Protecting against misleading post-event information with a self-administered interview. *Applied Cognitive Psychology*, 26(4), 568–575.

Gabbert, F., Memon, A., & Allan, K. (2003). Memory conformity: Can eyewitnesses influence each other's memories for an event? *Applied Cognitive Psychology: The Official Journal of the Society for Applied Research in Memory and Cognition*, 17(5), 533–543.

Gabrieli, J. D., Cohen, N. J., & Corkin, S. (1988). The impaired learning of semantic knowledge following bilateral medial temporal-lobe resection. Special Issue: Single-Case Studies in Amnesia: Theoretical Advances. *Brain and Cognition*, 7, 157–177.

Gagnepain, P., Hulbert, J., & Anderson, M. C. (2017). Parallel regulation of memory and emotion supports the suppression of intrusive memories. *Journal of Neuroscience*, 37, 6423–6441.

Garcia-Bajos, E., Migueles, M., & Anderson, M. C. (2009). Script knowledge modulates retrieval-induced forgetting for eyewitness events. *Memory*, 17, 92–103.

Gardiner, J. M., & Richardson-Klavehn, A. (2000). Remembering and knowing. In E. Tulving and F. I. M. Craik (eds), *The Oxford Handbook of Memory* (pp. 229–244). Oxford: Oxford University Press.

Garret, B. (2011). *Convicting the Innocent: Where criminal prosecutions go wrong*. Cambridge, MA: Harvard University Press.

Gauld, A. (1992). *A History of Hypnotism*. Cambridge: Cambridge University Press.

Geiselman, R. E., Bjork, R. A., & Fishman, D. (1983). Disrupted retrieval in directed forgetting: A link with posthypnotic amnesia. *Journal of Experimental Psychology: General*, 112, 58–72.

Geraerts, E. (2012). Cognitive underpinnings of recovered memories of childhood abuse. True and false recovered memories: Toward a reconciliation of the debate. *Nebraska Symposium on Motivation*, 58, 175–191.

Geraerts, E., Schooler, J. W., Merckelbach, H., Jelicic, M., Hunter, B. J. A., & Ambadar, Z. (2007). Corroborating continuous and discontinuous memories of childhood sexual abuse. *Psychological Science*, 18, 564–568.

Ghafur, R. D., Suri, G., & Gross, J. J. (2018). Emotion regulation choice: The role of orienting attention and action readiness. *Current Opinion in Behavioral Sciences*, 19, 31–35.

Ghetti, S., Edelstein, R. S., Goodman, G. S., Cordòn, I. M., Quas, J. A., Alexander, K. W., Redlich, A.D. & Jones, D.P. (2006). What can subjective forgetting tell us about memory for childhood trauma? *Memory & Cognition*, 34(5), 1011–1025.

Gilbert, S. J. (2015). Strategic offloading of delayed intentions into the external environment. *Quarterly Journal of Experimental Psychology*, 68(5), 971–992.

Gilboa, A., Claude, A., Stuss, D., Melo, B., Miller, S., & Moscovitch, M. (2006). Mechanisms of spontaneous confabulations: A strategic retrieval account. *Brain*, 129, 1399–1414.

Godden, D. R., & Baddeley, A. D. (1975). Context-dependent memory in two natural environments: On land and under water. *British Journal of Psychology*, 66, 325–331.

Golding, J. M., & MacLeod, C. M. (eds) (1998). *Intentional Forgetting: Interdisciplinary approaches*. Mahwah, NJ: Erlbaum.

Gollwitzer, P. M. (1999). Implementation intentions: Strong effects of simple plans. *American Psychologist*, 54, 493–503.

Goodman, G. S., Quas, J. A., Goldfarb, D., Gonzalves, L., & Gonzalez, A. (2019). Trauma and long-term memory for childhood events: Impact matters. *Child Development Perspectives*, 13, 3–9.

Graham, K. R., & Patton, A. (1968). Retroactive inhibition, hypnosis, and hypnotic amnesia. *International Journal of Clinical & Experimental Hypnosis*, 16(1), 68–74. doi: http://dx.doi.org/10.1080/00207146808407535

Granhag, P. A., Strömwall, L., & Billings, F. J. (2003). "I'll never forget the sinking ferry": How social influence makes false memories surface. In M. Vanderhallen, G. Vervaeke, P. J. van Koppen and J. Goethals (eds), *Much Ado About Crime: Chapters on psychology and law* (pp. 129–140). Brussels: Uitgeverij Politeia.

Greenspoon, J., & Ranyard, R. (1957). Stimulus conditions and retroactive inhibition. *Journal of Experimental Psychology*, 53, 55–59.

Greyson, B. (1983). The near-death experience scale: Construction, reliability, and validity. *Journal of Nervous and Mental Disease*, 171, 369–375.

Gross, J., & Hayne, H. (1999). Drawing facilitates children's verbal reports after long delays. *Journal of Experimental Psychology: Applied*, 5, 265–283.

Gross, J., Hayne, H., & Poole, A. (2006). The use of drawing in interviews with children: A potential pitfall. In J. R. Marrow (ed.), *Focus on Child Psychology Research* (pp. 119–144). New York: Nova Publishers.

Gross, J., Jack, F., Davis, N., & Hayne, H. (2013). Do children remember the birth of a sibling? Implications for the study of childhood amnesia. *Memory*, 21, 336–346.

Gross, S. R., Jacoby, K., Matheson, D. J., Montgomery, N., & Patil, S. (2005). Exonerations in the United States 1989 through 2003. *Journal of Criminal Law and Criminology*, 95, 523–553.

Grundgeiger, T., Sanderson, P., MacDougall, H. G., & Venkatesh, B. (2010). Interruption management in the intensive care unit: Predicting resumption times and assessing distributed support. *Journal of Experimental Psychology: Applied*, 16(4), 317–334. doi: https://doi.org/10.1037/a0021912

Gruzelier, J. (2005). Altered states of consciousness and hypnosis in the twenty-first century. *Contemporary Hypnosis*, 22(6), 1–7. doi: http://dx.doi.org/10.1002/ch.14

Gupta, R., Duff, M.C., Denburg, N.L., Cohen, N.J., Bechara, A., & Tranel, D. (2009). Declarative memory is critical for sustained advantageous complex decision-making. *Neuropsychologia*, 47(7), 1686–1693.

Gurney, D. J., Ellis, L. R., & Vardon-Hynard, E. (2016). The saliency of gestural misinformation in the perception of a violent crime. *Psychology, Crime & Law*, 22(7), 651–665.

Guynn, M. J. (2003). A two-process model of strategic monitoring in event-based prospective memory: Activation/retrieval mode and checking. *International Journal of Psychology*, 38(4), 245–256.

Guynn, M. J., & McDaniel, M. A. (2007). Target preexposure eliminates the effect of distraction on event-based prospective memory. *Psychonomic Bulletin & Review*, 14(3), 484–488.

Hafting, T., Fyhn, M., Molden, S., Moser, M.-B., & Moser, E. I. (2005) Microstructure of a spatial map in the entorhinal cortex. *Nature*, 436, 801–806.

Halligan, P. W., & Oakley, D. A. (2013). Hypnosis and cognitive neuroscience: Bridging the gap. *Cortex*, 49(2), 359–364. doi: http://dx.doi.org/10.1016/j.cortex.2012.12.002

Halligan, S. L., Michael, T., Clark, D. M., & Ehlers, A. (2003). Posttraumatic stress disorder following assault: The role of cognitive processing, trauma memory, and appraisals. *Journal of Consulting and Clinical Psychology*, 71, 419–431.

Hannula, D., & Duff, M. C. (eds.) (2017). *The Hippocampus from Cells to Systems: Structure, connectivity, and functional contributions to memory and flexible cognition*. Springer International Publishing: Switzerland.

Hannula, D. E., & Ranganath, C. (2009). The eyes have it: Hippocampal activity predicts expression of memory in eye movements. *Neuron*, 63(5), 592–599.

Hannula, D. E., Tranel, D., & Cohen, N. J. (2006). The long and the short of it: Relational memory impairments in amnesia, even at short lags. *Journal of Neuroscience*, 26(32), 8352–8359.

Hanslmayr, S., Staudigl, T., Aslan, A., & Bäuml, K.-H. T. (2010). Theta oscillations predict the detrimental effects of memory retrieval. *Cognitive, Affective, and Behavioral Neuroscience*, 10, 329–338.

Hanslmayr, S., Volberg, G., Wimber, M., Oehler, N., Staudigl, T., Hartmann, T., et al. (2012). Prefrontally driven down-regulation of neural synchrony mediates goal-directed forgetting. *Journal of Neuroscience*, 32, 14742–14751.

Haque, S., & Conway, M. A. (2001). Probing the process of autobiographical memory retrieval. *European Journal of Cognitive Psychology*, 13, 529–547.

Hardt, O., Nader, K., & Nadel, L. (2013). Decay happens: The role of active forgetting in memory. *Trends in Cognitive Sciences*, 17, 111–120.

Harnishfeger, K. K., & Pope, R. S. (1996). Intending to forget: The development of cognitive inhibition in directed forgetting. *Journal of Experimental Child Psychology*, 62, 292–315.

Harris, A. J., & Hahn, U. (2009). Bayesian rationality in evaluating multiple testimonies: Incorporating the role of coherence. *Journal of Experimental Psychology: Learning, Memory, and Cognition*, 35(5), 1366.

Harris, J. E., & Wilkins, A. J. (1982). Remembering to do things: A theoretical framework and an illustrative experiment. *Human Learning*, 1(2), 123–136.

Harrison, T. L., Mullet, H. G., Whiffen, K. N., Ousterhout, H., & Einstein, G. O. (2014). Prospective memory: Effects of divided attention on spontaneous retrieval. *Memory & Cognition*, 42(2), 212–224. doi: https://doi.org/10.3758/s13421-013-0357-y

Hartshorn, K., Rovee-Collier, C., Gerhardstein, P. C., Bhatt, R. S., Wondoloski, T. L., Klein, P., et al. (1998). Ontogeny of long-term memory over the first year-and-a-half of life. *Developmental Psychobiology*, 32, 69–89.

Hartwig, J., Schnitzspahn, K. M., Kliegel, M., Velichkovsky, B. M., & Helmert, J. R. (2013). I see you remembering: What eye movements can reveal about process characterists of prospective memory. *International Journal of Psychophysiology*, 88, 193–199. doi: https://doi.org/10.1016/j.ijpsycho.2013.03.020.

Hasher, L., & Zacks, R. T. (1988). Working memory, comprehension, and aging: A review and a new view. In G.H. Bower (ed.), *The Psychology of Learning and Motivation*, 22 (pp. 193–225). Orlando, FL: Academic.

Hassabis, D., Kumaran, D., Vann, S. D., & Maguire, E. A. (2007). Patients with hippocampal amnesia cannot imagine new experiences. *Proceedings of the National Academy of Sciences of the United States of America*, 104(5), 1726–1731.

Hayes, S., Hirsch, C., & Mathews, A. (2008). Restriction of working memory capacity during worry. *Journal of Abnormal Psychology*, 117, 712–717.

Hayne, H. (2004). Infant memory development: Implications for childhood amnesia. *Developmental Review*, 24, 33–73.

Hayne, H. (2006). Age-related changes in infant memory retrieval: Implications for knowledge acquisition. In Y. Munakata and M. H. Johnson (eds), *Processes of Change in Brain and Cognitive Development* (Attention and Performance series XXI) (pp. 209–231). New York: Oxford University Press.

Hayne, H., Garry, M., & Loftus, E. F. (2006). On the continuing lack of scientific evidence for repression. *Behavioral and Brain Sciences*, 29, 521–522.

Hayne, H., & Gross, J. (2015). 24-month-olds use conceptual similarity to solve new problems after a delay. *International Journal of Behavioral Development*, 39, 339–345.

Hayne, H., & Gross, J. (2017). Memory by association: Integrating memories prolongs retention by two-year-olds. *Infant Behavior and Development*, 46, 7–13. doi:10.1016/j.infbeh.2016.11.004

Hayne, H., & Herbert, J. (2004). Verbal cues facilitate memory retrieval during infancy. *Journal of Experimental Child Psychology*, 89, 127–139.

Hayne, H., & Herbert, J. (in press). Infant memory. In J. Lockman and C. Tamis-LeMonda (eds), *The Cambridge Handbook of Infant Development*. Cambridge: Cambridge University Press.

Hayne, H., & Jack, F. (2011). Childhood amnesia. *Wiley Interdisciplinary Reviews in Cognitive Science*, 2, 136–145.

Hefer, C., Cohen, A.-L., Jaudas, A., & Dreisbach, G. (2017). The flexible engagement of monitoring processes in non-focal and focal prospective memory tasks with salient cues. *Acta Psychologica*, 179, 42–53. doi: https://doi.org/10.1016/j.actpsy.2017.06.008

Hemenover, S. H., & Harbke, C. R. (2019). Individual differences in negative affect repair style. *Cognition & Emotion*, 43, 517–533.

Henri, V., & Henri, C. (1895). On our earliest recollections of childhood. *Psychological Review*, 2, 215–216.

Herbert, J. S. (2011). The effect of language cues on infants' representational flexibility in a deferred imitation task. *Infant Behavior and Development*, 34, 632–635.

Herbert, J. S., & Hayne, H. (2000). The ontogeny of long-term retention during the second year of life. *Developmental Science*, 3, 50–56.

Hering, A., Rendell, P. G., Rose, N. S., Schnitzspahn, K. M., & Kliegel, M. (2014). Prospective memory training in older adults and its relevance for successful aging. *Psychological Research*, 78, 892–904.

Hertel, P.T., Maydon, A., Ogilvie, A., & Mor, N. (2018). Ruminators (unlike others) fail to show suppression-induced forgetting on indirect tests of memory. *Clinical Psychological Science*, 6, 872–881.

Hessen-Kayfitz, J. K., & Scoboria, A. (2012). False memory is in the details: Photographic details predict memory formation. *Applied Cognitive Psychology*, 26, 333–341.

Hicks, J. L., & Starns, J. J. (2004). Retrieval-induced forgetting occurs in tests of item recognition. *Psychonomic Bulletin & Review*, 11, 125–130.

Hilgard, E. R. (1965). *Hypnotic Susceptibility*. New York: Harcourt, Brace, & World.

Hilgard, E. R. (1973). The domain of hypnosis, with some comments on alternative paradigms. *American Psychologist*, 28, 972–982. doi: http://dx.doi.org/10.1016/j.beproc.2011.04.006

Hilgard, E. R., & Cooper, L. M. (1965). Spontaneous and suggested posthypnotic amnesia. *International Journal of Clinical & Experimental Hypnosis*, 13, 261–273. doi: https://doi.org/10.1080/00207146508412948

Hilgard, E. R., & Hommel, L. S. (1961). Selective amnesia for events within hypnosis in relation to repression. *Journal of Personality*, 29, 205–216. doi: http://dx.doi.org/10.1111/j.1467-6494.1961.tb01656.x

Hirsch, C. R., & Mathews, A. (2012). A cognitive model of pathological worry. *Behaviour Research and Therapy*, 50, 636–646.

Hirst, W., & Echterhoff, G. (2012). Remembering in conversations: The social sharing and reshaping of memories. *Annual Review of Psychology*, 63, 55–79.

Hirst, W., & Manier, D. (2008). Towards a psychology of collective memory. *Memory*, 16(3), 183–200.

Holliday, R. (2006). Epigenetics: A historical overview. *Epigenetics*, 1(2), 76–80.

Holliday, R. E., & Albon, A. J. (2004). Minimising misinformation effects in young children with cognitive interview mnemonics. *Applied Cognitive Psychology: The Official Journal of the Society for Applied Research in Memory and Cognition*, 18(3), 263–281.

Holliday, R. E., Humphries, J. E., Milne, R., Memon, A., Houlder, L., Lyons, A., & Bull, R. (2012). Reducing misinformation effects in older adults with cognitive interview mnemonics. *Psychology and Aging*, 27(4), 1191.

Hope, L., Gabbert, F., & Fisher, R. P. (2011). From laboratory to the street: Capturing witness memory using the Self-Administered Interview. *Legal and Criminological Psychology*, 16(2), 211–226.

Hope, L., Ost, J., Gabbert, F., Healey, S., & Lenton, E. (2008). "With a little help from my friends...": The role of co-witness relationship in susceptibility to misinformation. *Acta Psychologica*, 127(2), 476–484.

Howard, M. L., & Coe, W. C. (1980). The effects of context and subjects' perceived control in breaching posthypnotic amnesia. *Journal of Personality*, 48(3), 342–359. doi: http://dx.doi.org/10.1111/j.1467-6494.1980.tb00838.x

Howe, M. L. (2011). *The Nature of Early Memory: An Adaptive Theory of the Genesis and Development of Memory*. New York: Oxford University Press.

Howe, M. L. (2013). Memory lessons from the courtroom: Reflections on being a memory expert on the witness stand. *Memory*, 21(5), 576–583. doi: https://doi.org/10.1080/09658211.2012.725735

Howe, M. L., & Courage, M. L. (1993). On resolving the enigma of infantile amnesia. *Psychological Bulletin*, 113, 305–326.

Howe, M. L., & Courage, M. L. (1997). The emergence and early development of autobiographical memory. *Psychological Review*, 104, 499–523.

Howe, M. L., Knott, L. M., & Conway, M. A. (2018). *Memory and Miscarriages of Justice*. Abingdon: Routledge.

Howe, P.D., & Leiserowitz, A. (2013). Who remembers a hot summer or a cold winter? The asymmetric effects of beliefs about global warming on perceptions of local conditions in the U.S. *Global Environmental Change*, 23, 1488–1500.

Huesmann, L. R., Gruder, C. L., & Dorst, G. (1987). A process model of posthypnotic amnesia. *Cognitive Psychology*, 19(1), 33–62. doi: http://dx.doi.org/10.1016/0010-0285(87)90003-X

Huff, M. J., Weinsheimer, C. C., & Bodner, G. E. (2016). Reducing the misinformation effect through initial testing: Take two tests and recall me in the morning? *Applied Cognitive Psychology*, 30(1), 61–69.

Hull, C. L. (1933). *Hypnosis and Suggestibility: An Experimental Approach*. New York: Appleton.

Hupbach, A. (2018). Long-term effects of directed forgetting. *Memory*, 26, 321–329.

Hyman Jr, I. E., Husband, T. H., & Billings, F. J. (1995). False memories of childhood experiences. *Applied Cognitive Psychology*, 9(3), 181–197.

Hyman Jr, I. E., & Loftus, E. F. (2001). False childhood memories and eyewitness memory errors. In M. Eisen, J. Quas and G.S. Goodman (eds), *Memory and Suggestibility in the Forensic Interview* (LEA Series in Personality and Clinical Psychology) (pp. 63–84). Mahwah, NJ: Erlbaum.

Ihle, A., Albiński, R., Gurynowicz, K., & Kliegel, M. (2018). Four-week strategy-based training to enhance prospective memory in older adults: Targeting intention retention is more beneficial than targeting intention formation. *Gerontology*, 64(3), 257–265.

Imuta, K., Scarf, D., & Hayne, H. (2013). The effect of verbal reminders on memory reactivation in 2-, 3-, and 4-year-old children. *Developmental Psychology*, 49, 1056–1065.

Insel, K. C., Einstein, G. O., Morrow, D. G., Koerner, K. M., & Hepworth, J. T. (2016). Multifaceted prospective memory intervention to improve medication adherence. *Journal of the American Geriatrics Society*, 64(3), 561–568.

Jack, F., & Hayne, H. (2007). Eliciting adults' earliest memories: Does it matter how we ask the question? *Memory*, 15, 647–663.

Jack, F., MacDonald, S., Reese, E., & Hayne, H. (2009). Maternal reminiscing style during early childhood predicts the age of adolescents' earliest memories. *Child Development*, 80, 496–505.

Jack, F., Simcock, G., & Hayne, H. (2012). Magic memories: Young children's verbal recall after a 6-year delay. *Child Development*, 83, 159–172.

Jack, F., Zydervelt, S., & Zajac, R. (2014). Are co-witnesses special? Comparing the influence of co-witness and interviewer misinformation on eyewitness reports. *Memory*, 22(3), 243–255.

Jäger, T., & Kliegel, M. (2008). Time-based and event-based prospective memory across adulthood: Underlying mechanisms and differential costs on the ongoing task. *Journal of General Psychology*, 135(1), 4–22.

James, W. (1890). *The Principles of Psychology* (Vol. 1). New York: Holt.

James, W. (1890/1980). *Principles of Psychology*. Cambridge, MA: Harvard University Press.

James, W. (1902/1985). *The Varieties of Religious Experience: A Study in Human Nature*. Cambridge, MA: Harvard University Press.

Jamieson, M., Cullen, B., McGee-Lennon, M., Brewster, S., & Evans, J. J. (2014). The efficacy of cognitive prosthetic technology for people with memory impairments: A systematic review and meta-analysis. *Neuropsychological Rehabilitation*, 24(3–4), 419–444.

Jang, Y., & Huber, D. E. (2008). Context retrieval and context change in free recall: Recalling from long-term memory drives list isolation. *Journal of Experimental Psychology: Learning Memory and Cognition*, 34, 112–127.

Jarosz, A. F., Colflesh, G. J. H., & Wiley, J. (2012). Uncorking the muse: Alcohol intoxication facilitates creative problem. *Consciousness and Cognition*, 21, 487–493.

Johansson, M., Aslan, A., Bäuml, K.-H., Gäbel, A., & Mecklinger, A. (2007). When remembering causes forgetting: Electrophysiological correlates of retrieval-induced forgetting. *Cerebral Cortex*, 17, 1335–1341.

Johnson, M. K., Hastroudi, S., & Lindsay, D. S. (1993). Source monitoring. *Psychological Bulletin*, 114(1), 328.

Jones, E. J. H., & Herbert, J. S. (2006). Exploring memory in infancy: Deferred imitation and the development of declarative memory. *Infant and Child Development*, 15, 195–205.

Jones, K. A., Crozier, W. E., & Strange, D. (2018). Objectivity is a myth for you but not for me or police: A bias blind spot for viewing and remembering criminal events. *Psychology, Public Policy, and Law*, 24(2), 259.

Jonker, T. R., Seli, P., & MacLeod, C. M. (2013). Putting retrieval-induced forgetting in context: An inhibition-free, context-based account. *Psychological Review*, 120, 852–872.

Jonker, T. R., Seli, P., & MacLeod, C. M. (2015). Retrieval-induced forgetting and context. *Current Directions in Psychological Science*, 24, 273–278.

Josselyn S. A., & Frankland, P. W. (2012). Infantile amnesia: A neurogenic hypothesis. *Learning & Memory*, 19(9), 423–433. doi: 10.1101/lm.021311.110

Josslyn, S. L., & Oakes, M. A. (2005). Directed forgetting in autobiographical events. *Memory & Cognition*, 33, 577–587.

Kallio, S., & Revonsuo, A. (2003). Hypnotic phenomena and altered states of consciousness: A multilevel framework of description and explanation. *Contemporary Hypnosis*, 20, 111–164. doi: http://dx.doi.org/10.1002/ch.273

Kassin, S. M. (2014). False confessions: Causes, consequences, and implications for reform. *Policy Insights from the Behavioral and Brain Sciences*, 1(1), 112–121.

Kensington, E. A., Ullman, M. T., & Corkin, S. (2001). Bilateral medial temporal lobe damage does not affect lexical or grammatical processing: Evidence from the amnesic patient H.M. *Hippocampus*, 11(4), 347–360.

Kidder, D. P., Park, D. C., Hertzog, C., & Morrell, R. W. (1997). Prospective memory and aging: The effects of working memory and prospective memory task load. *Aging, Neuropsychology, and Cognition*, 4(2), 93–112. doi: https://doi.org/10.1080/13825589708256639

Kihlstrom, J. F. (1978). Context and cognition in posthypnotic amnesia. *International Journal of Clinical & Experimental Hypnosis*, 26(4), 246–267. doi: http://dx.doi.org/10.1080/00207147 808411251

Kihlstrom, J. F. (1979). Hypnosis and psychopathology: Retrospect and prospect. *Journal of Abnormal Psychology*, 88(5), 459–473. doi: http://dx.doi.org/10.1037/0021-843X.88.5.459

Kihlstrom, J. F. (1980). Posthypnotic amnesia for recently learned material: Interactions with 'episodic' and 'semantic' memory. *Cognitive Psychology*, 12, 227–251. doi: http://dx.doi.org/10.1016/0010-0285(80)90010-9

Kihlstrom, J. F. (1983). Instructed forgetting: Hypnotic and nonhypnotic. *Journal of Experimental Psychology: General*, 112(1), 73–79. doi: http://dx.doi.org/10.1037/0096-3445.112.1.73

Kihlstrom, J. F. (1985). Posthypnotic amnesia and the dissociation of memory. In G. H. Bower (ed.), *Psychology of Learning and Motivation* (Vol. 19, pp. 131–178). New York: Academic.

Kihlstrom, J. F. (1986). Strong inferences about hypnosis. *Behavioral & Brain Sciences*, 9(3), 474–475. doi: http://dx.doi.org/10.1017/S0140525X00046616

Kihlstrom, J. F. (1992). Hypnosis: A sesquicentennial essay. *International Journal of Clinical & Experimental Hypnosis*, 40(4), 301–314. doi: http://dx.doi.org/10.1080/00207149208409663

Kihlstrom, J. F. (1994). One hundred years of hysteria. In S. J. Lynn and J. W. Rhue (eds), *Dissociation: Clinical and Theoretical Perspectives* (pp. 365–394). New York: Guilford.

Kihlstrom, J. F. (1995). Memory and consciousness: An appreciation of Claparede and Recognition et Moiite. *Consciousness & Cognition: An International Journal*, 4(4), 379–386. doi: http://dx.doi.org/10.1006/ccog.1995.1045

Kihlstrom, J. F. (2002a). Demand characteristics in the laboratory and the clinic: Conversations and collaborations with subjects and patients. *Prevention & Treatment* [Special issue honoring Martin T. Orne], 5(1), Article_36c. doi: http://dx.doi.org/10.1037/1522-3736.5.1.536c

Kihlstrom, J. F. (2002b). Mesmer, the Franklin Commission, and hypnosis: A counterfactual essay. *International Journal of Clinical & Experimental Hypnosis*, 50(4), 408–419. doi: http://dx.doi.org/10.1080/00207140208410114

Kihlstrom, J. F. (2003). The fox, the hedgehog, and hypnosis. *International Journal of Clinical & Experimental Hypnosis*, 51(2), 166–189. doi: http://dx.doi.org/10.1076/iceh.51.2.166.14611

Kihlstrom, J. F. (2004). Clark L. Hull, hypnotist [Review of Hypnosis and Suggestibility: An Experimental Approach by C.L. Hull]. *Contemporary Psychology*, 49, 141–144. doi: http://dx.doi.org/10.1037/004274

Kihlstrom, J. F. (2005a). Dissociative disorders. *Annual Review of Clinical Psychology*, 1, 227–253. doi: http://dx.doi.org/10.1146/annurev.clinpsy.1.102803.143925

Kihlstrom, J. F. (2005b). Is hypnosis an altered state of consciousness or what? *Contemporary Hypnosis*, 22, 34–38. doi: http://dx.doi.org/10.1002/ch.20

Kihlstrom, J. F. (2008). The domain of hypnosis, revisited. In M. Nash and A. Barnier (eds), *Oxford Handbook of Hypnosis: Theory, research and practice* (pp. 21–52). Oxford: Oxford University Press.

Kihlstrom, J. F. (2013). Neuro-hypnotism: Hypnosis and neuroscience. *Cortex*, 49(2), 365–374. doi: http://dx.doi.org/10.1016/j.cortex.2012.05.016

Kihlstrom, J. F. (2018). Hypnosis as an altered state of consciousness. *Journal of Consciousness Studies*, 25(11–12), 53–72.

Kihlstrom, J. F. (2019a). Finding implicit memory in posthypnotic amnesia. In R. J. Sternberg (ed.), *My Biggest Research Mistake: Adventures and misadventures in psychological research* (pp. 34–37). Thousand Oaks, CA: SAGE.

Kihlstrom, J. F. (2019b). Recognition in posthypnotic amnesia, revisited. MS in preparation.

Kihlstrom, J. F. (2020). Varieties of recollective experience. *Neuropsychologia*, 137. https://doi.org/10.1016/j.neuropsychologia.2019.107295.

Kihlstrom, J. F., & Barnhardt, T. M. (1993). The self-regulation of memory: For better and for worse, with and without hypnosis. In D. M. Wegner and J. W. Pennebaker (eds), *Handbook of Mental Control* (pp. 88–125). Englewood Cliffs, NJ: Prentice Hall.

Kihlstrom, J. F., Brenneman, H. A., Pistole, D. D., & Shor, R. E. (1985). Hypnosis as a retrieval cue in posthypnotic amnesia. *Journal of Abnormal Psychology*, 94(3), 264–271. doi: http://dx.doi.org/10.1037/0021-843X.94.3.264

Kihlstrom, J. F., Dorfman, J., & Park, L. (2017). Conscious and unconscious memory. In S. Schneider and M. Velmans (eds), *Blackwell Companion to Consciousness* (2nd edn, pp. 562–575). Oxford: Wiley.

Kihlstrom, J. F., Easton, R. D., & Shor, R. E. (1983). Spontaneous recovery of memory during posthypnotic amnesia. *International Journal of Clinical & Experimental Hypnosis*, 31(4), 309–323. doi: http://dx.doi.org/10.1080/00207148308406625

Kihlstrom, J. F., & Evans, F. J. (1976). Recovery of memory after posthypnotic amnesia. *Journal of Abnormal Psychology*, 85(6), 564–569. doi: http://dx.doi.org/10.1037/0021-843X.85.6.564

Kihlstrom, J. F., & Evans, F. J. (1977). Residual effect of suggestions for posthypnotic amnesia: A reexamination. *Journal of Abnormal Psychology*, 86(4), 327–333. doi: http://dx.doi.org/10.1037/0021-843X.86.4.327

Kihlstrom, J. F., & Evans, F. J. (1978). Generic recall during posthypnotic amnesia. *Bulletin of the Psychonomic Society*, 12(1), 57–60. doi: http://dx.doi.org/10.3758/BF03329624

Kihlstrom, J. F., & Evans, F. J. (1979). Memory retrieval processes in posthypnotic amnesia. In J. F. Kihlstrom and F. J. Evans (eds), *Functional Disorders of Memory* (pp. 179–218). Hillsdale, NJ: Erlbaum.

Kihlstrom, J. F., Evans, F. J., Orne, E. C., & Orne, M. T. (1980). Attempting to breach posthypnotic amnesia. *Journal of Abnormal Psychology*, 89(5), 603–616. doi: http://dx.doi.org/10.1037/0021-843X.89.5.603

Kihlstrom, J. F., & Harackiewicz, J. M. (1982). The earliest recollection: A new survey. *Journal of Personality*, 50, 134–180.

Kihlstrom, J. F., & McGlynn, S. M. (1991). Experimental research in clinical psychology. In M. Hersen, A. E. Kazdin and A. S. Bellack (eds), *Clinical Psychology Handbook* (2nd edn, pp. 239–257). New York: Pergamon.

Kihlstrom, J. F., & Register, P. A. (1984). Optimal scoring of amnesia on the Harvard Group Scale of Hypnotic Susceptibility, Form A. *International Journal of Clinical & Experimental Hypnosis*, 32(1), 51–57. doi: http://dx.doi.org/10.1080/00207148408416000

Kihlstrom, J. F., & Shor, R. E. (1978). Recall and recognition during posthypnotic amnesia. *International Journal of Clinical & Experimental Hypnosis*, 26(4), 330–349. doi: http://dx.doi.org/10.1080/00207147808411257

Kihlstrom, J. F., & Twersky, M. (1978). Relationship of posthypnotic amnesia to waking memory performance. *International Journal of Clinical & Experimental Hypnosis*, 26(4), 292–306. doi: http://dx.doi.org/10.1080/00207147808411254

Kihlstrom, J. F., & Wilson, L. (1984). Temporal organization of recall during posthypnotic amnesia. *Journal of Abnormal Psychology*, 93(2), 200–208. doi: http://dx.doi.org/10.1037/0021-843X.93.2.200

Kihlstrom, J. F., & Wilson, L. (1988). Rejoinder to Spanos, Bertrand, and Perlini. *Journal of Abnormal Psychology*, 97(3), 381–383. doi: https://doi.org/10.1037/h0092432

Kimmel, S. E., Chen, Z., Price, M., Parker, C. S., Metlay, J. P., Christie, J. D., et al. (2007). The influence of patient adherence on anticoagulation control with warfarin: Results from the International Normalized Ratio Adherence and Genetics (IN-RANGE) Study. *Archives of Internal Medicine*, 167(3), 229–235.

King, M., Devitt, M., Letterman, M., Seaton, M., & Sprowls, D. (1998). *Interviewer-driven versus eyewitness-driven interviews: Implications for legal officials.* American Psychology – Law Society Biennial Conference, Redondo Beach, CA, 5–7 March 1998.

Kingo, O. S., Bohn, A., & Krojgaard, P. (2013). Warm-up questions on early childhood memories affect the reported age of earliest memories in late adolescence. *Memory*, 21, 280–284.

Kingo, O. S., Staugaard, S. R., & Krojgaard, P. (2014). Three-year-olds' memory for a person met only once at the age of 12 months: Very long-term memory revealed by a late manifesting novelty preference. *Consciousness and Cognition*, 24, 49–56.

Kinnunen, T., Zamansky, H. S., & Block, M. L. (1994). Is the hypnotized subject lying? *Journal of Abnormal Psychology*, 103(2), 184–191. doi: http://dx.doi.org/10.1037/0021-843X.103.2.184

Klein, S. B. (2001). A self to remember: A cognitive neuropsychological perspective on how self creates memory and memory creates self. In C. Sedikides and M. B. Brewer (eds), *Individual Self, Relational Self, Collective Self* (pp. 25–46). New York: Psychology Press.

Klein, S. B., & Gangi, C. E. (2010). The multiplicity of self: Neuropsychological evidence and its implications for the self as a construct in psychological research. *Annals of the New York Academy of Sciences*, 1191, 1–15.

Kliegel, M., Jäger, T., & Phillips, L. H. (2008). Adult age differences in event-based prospective memory: A meta-analysis on the role of focal versus nonfocal cues. *Psychology and Aging*, 23(1), 203–208. doi: https://doi.org/10.1037/0882-7974.23.1.203

Kliegel, M., McDaniel, M. A., & Einstein, G. O. (2000). Plan formation, retention, and execution in prospective memory: A new approach and age-related effects. *Memory & Cognition*, 28(6), 1041–1049.

Klooster, N., & Duff, M. C. (2015). Remote semantic memory is impoverished in hippocampal amnesia. *Neuropsychologia*, 79(Part A), 42–52.

Kohler, W. (1947). *Gestalt Psychology: An introduction to new concepts in modern psychology.* New York: Liveright.

Köhnken, G., Milne, R., Memon, A., & Bull, R. (1999). The cognitive interview: A meta-analysis. *Psychology, Crime and Law*, 5(1–2), 3–27.

Koriat, A., & Goldsmith, M. (1996). Monitoring and control processes in the strategic regulation of memory accuracy. *Psychological Review*, 103(3), 490.

Koriat, A., Goldsmith, M., & Pansky, A. (2000). Toward a psychology of memory accuracy. *Annual Review of Psychology*, 51(1), 481–537.

Koslov, S. R., Mukerji, A., Hedgpeth, K. R., & Lewis-Peacock, J. A. (2019). Cognitive flexibility improves memory for delayed intentions. *eNeuro*, *6*(6). doi: 10.1523/ENEURO.0250-19.2019

Koster, E. H. W., De Lissnyder, E., Derakshan, N., & De Raedt, R. (2011). Understanding depressive rumination from a cognitive science perspective: The impaired disengagement hypothesis. *Clinical Psychology Review*, 31(1), 138–145.

Krauss, R. M., & Chiu, C.-Y. (1998). Language and social behavior. In D. T. Gilbert, S. T. Fiske and G. Lindzey (eds), *The Handbook of Social Psychology* (pp. 41–88). New York: McGraw-Hill.

Kris, E. (1952/1975). *Selected Papers of Ernst Kris*. New Haven, CT: Yale University Press.

Kuhlmann, B. G., & Rummel, J. (2014). Context-specific prospective-memory processing: Evidence for flexible attention allocation adjustments after intention encoding. *Memory & Cognition*, 42(6), 943–949. doi: https://doi.org/10.3758/s13421-014-0405-2

Kumaran, D., Banino, A., Blundell, C., Hassabis, D., & Dayan, P. (2016). Computations underlying social hierarchy learning: Distinct neural mechanisms for updating and representing self-relevant information. *Neuron*, 92(5), 1135–1147.

Kurczek, J., Wechsler, E., Ahuja, S., Jensen, U., Cohen, N., Tranel, D., & Duff, M. C. (2015). Differential contributions of hippocampus and medial prefrontal cortex to self-projection and self-referential processing. *Neuropsychologia*, 73, 116–126.

Kvavilashvili, L., Cockburn, J., & Kornbrot, D. E. (2013). Prospective memory and ageing paradox with event-based tasks: A study of young, young-old, and old-old participants. *Quarterly Journal of Experimental Psychology*, 66(5), 864–875.

LaBar, K. S., & Cabeza, R. (2006). Cognitive neuroscience of emotional memory. *Nature Reviews Neuroscience*, 7, 54–64.

Lamb, M. E., Brown, D. A., Hershkowitz, I., Orbach, Y., & Esplin, P. W. (2018). *Tell Me What Happened: Questioning Children About Abuse*. Oxford: Wiley.

Landry, M., & Raz, A. (2015). Hypnosis and imaging of the living human brain. *American Journal of Clinical Hypnosis*, 57, 285–313. doi: http://dx.doi.org/10.1080/00029157.2014.978496

Lashley, K. (1950). In search of the engram. *Society of Experimental Biology Symposium*, 4, 454–482.

Lassiter, G., & Meissner, C. A. (2010). *Police Interrogations and False Confessions: Current research, practice, and policy recommendations*. Washington, DC: American Psychological Association.

Laurence, J.-R., & Perry, C. (1988). *Hypnosis, Will, and Memory: A psycho-legal history*. New York: Guilford.

Lawson, M., Rodriquez-Steen, L., & London, K. (2018). A systematic review of the reliability of children's event reports after discussing experiences with a naïve, knowledgeable, or misled parent. *Developmental Review*, 49, 62–79.

Lee, J. H, & McDaniel, M. A. (2013). Discrepancy-plus-search processes in prospective memory retrieval. *Memory & Cognition*, *41*(3), 443–451. doi: https://doi.org/10.3758/s13421-012-0273-6

Lee, J. H., Shelton, J. T., Scullin, M. K., & McDaniel, M. A. (2016). An implementation intention strategy can improve prospective memory in older adults with very mild Alzheimer's disease. *British Journal of Clinical Psychology*, 55(2), 154–166. doi: https://doi.org/10.1111/bjc.12084

Lehman, M., & Malmberg, K. J. (2009). A global theory of remembering and forgetting from multiple lists. *Journal of Experimental Psychology: Learning, Memory, and Cognition*, 35(4), 970–988.

Leichtman, M. D., Steiner, K. L., Camilleri, K. A., Pillemer, D. B., & Thomsen, D. K. (2019). What happened in kindergarten? Mother-child conversations about life story chapters. *Memory*, 27, 49–62.

Leviston, Z., Walker, I., & Morwinski, S. (2013). Your opinion on climate change might not be as common as you think. *Nature Climate Change*, 3, 334–337.

Lewis, S.J., Arseneault, L., Caspi, A., Fisher, H. L., Matthews, T., Moffitt, T. E., et al. (2019). The epidemiology of trauma and post-traumatic stress disorder in a representative cohort of young people in England and Wales. *The Lancet Psychiatry*, 6(3), 247–256.

Lewis-Peacock, J. A., Cohen, J. D., & Norman, K. A. (2016). Neural evidence of the strategic choice between working memory and episodic memory in prospective remembering. *Neuropsychologia*, 93, 280–288. doi: https://doi.org/10.1016/j.neuropsychologia.2016.11.006

Li., S., Callaghan, B. L., & Richardson, R. (2014). Infantile amnesia: Forgotten but not gone. *Learning & Memory*, 21, 135–139.

Lieberman, J., Lavoie, G., & Brisson, A. (1978). Suggested amnesia and order of recall as a function of hypnotic susceptibility and learning conditions in chronic schizophrenic patients. *International Journal of Clinical & Experimental Hypnosis*, 26(4), 268–280. doi: http://dx.doi.org/10.1080/00207147808411252

Lief, H., & Fetkewicz, J. (1995). Retractors of false memories: The evolution of pseudo- memories. *Journal of Psychiatry & Law*, 23, 411–436.

Lindsay, D. S., Allen, B. P., Chan, J. C., & Dahl, L. C. (2004). Eyewitness suggestibility and source similarity: Intrusions of details from one event into memory reports of another event. *Journal of Memory and Language*, 50(1), 96–111.

Lindsay, D. S., & Hyman Jr, I. E. (2017). Commentary on Brewin and Andrews. *Applied Cognitive Psychology*, 31(1), 37–39.

Lindsay, D. S., & Read, J. D. (1994). Psychotherapy and memories of childhood sexual abuse: A cognitive perspective. *Applied Cognitive Psychology*, 8(4), 281–338.

Lockhart, R. S., Craik, F. I. M., & Jacoby, L. L. (1976). Depth of processing, recognition, and recall. In J. Brown (ed.), *Recall and Recognition* (pp. 75–102). New York: Wiley.

Loft, S., Bowden, V. K., Ball, B. H., & Brewer, G. A. (2014). Fitting an ex-Gaussian function to examine costs in event-based prospective memory: Evidence for a continuous monitoring profile. *Acta Psychologica*, 152, 177–182.

Loftus, E. F. (1993). The reality of repressed memories. *American Psychologist*, 48(5), 518.

Loftus, E. F. (2005). Planting misinformation in the human mind: A 30-year investigation of the malleability of memory. *Learning & Memory*, 12(4), 361–366.

Loftus, E. F. (2019). Eyewitness testimony. *Applied Cognitive Psychology*, 33(4), 498–503.

Loftus, E.F., Garry, M., & Hayne, H. (2008). Repressed and recovered memory. In S. T. Fiske & E. Borgida (eds), *Psychological Science in Court: Beyond common knowledge* (pp. 177–194). Boston, MA: Blackwell.

Loftus, E.F., & Loftus, G.R. (1980). On the permanence of stored information in the human brain. *American Psychologist*, 35, 409–420.

Loftus, E. F., & Pickrell, J. E. (1995). The formation of false memories. *Psychiatric Annals*, 25(12), 720–725.

Lourenço, J. S., Hill, J. H., & Maylor, E. A. (2015). Too easy? The influence of task demands conveyed tacitly on prospective memory. *Frontiers in Human Neuroscience*, 9, 242.

MacDonald, S., Uesiliana, K., & Hayne, H. (2000). Cross-cultural and gender differences in childhood amnesia. *Memory*, 8, 365–376.

MacKay, D., & Goldstein, R. (2016). Creativity, comprehension, conversation, and the hippocampal region: New data and theory. *AIMS Neuroscience*, 3(1), 105–140.

MacLeod, M. D., & Macrae, C. N. (2001). Gone but not forgotten: The transient nature of retrieval-induced forgetting. *Psychological Science*, 12, 148–152.

Macrae, C. N., Bodenhausen, G. V., Milne, A. B., & Ford, R. L. (1997). In the regulation of recollection: The intentional forgetting of sterotypical memories. *Journal of Personality and Social Psychology*, 72, 709–719.

Madison, P. (1956). Freud's repression concept: A survey and attempted clarification. *International Journal of Psychoanalysis*, 37, 75–81.

Madore, K., Addis, D., & Schacter, D. (2015). Creativity and memory: Effects of an episodic-specificity induction on divergent thinking. *Psychological Science*, 26(9), 1461–1468.

Mandler, G. (1980). Recognizing: The judgment of previous occurrence. *Psychological Review*, 87(3), 252–271. doi: http://dx.doi.org/10.1037/0033-295X.87.3.252

Markus, H. & Nurius, P. (1986). Possible selves. *American Psychologist*, 41, 954–969.

Marsh, E. J., & Arnold, K.M. (2018). Retelling experiences and writing essays: How storytelling reflects and changes memory. In E. J. Marsh & K. M. Arnold (eds), *Representations in Mind and World: Essays inspired by Barbara Tversky* (pp. 137–155). New York: Routledge.

Marsh, R. L., Hancock, T. W., & Hicks, J. L. (2002a). The demands of an ongoing activity influence the success of event-based prospective memory. *Psychonomic Bulletin & Review*, 9(3), 604–610.

Marsh, R. L., & Hicks, J. L. (1998). Event-based prospective memory and executive control of working memory. *Journal of Experimental Psychology: Learning, Memory, and Cognition*, 24(2), 336–349.

Marsh, R. L., Hicks, J. L., & Cook, G. I. (2006). Task interference from prospective memories covaries with contextual associations of fulfilling them. *Memory & Cognition*, 34(5), 1037–1045.

Marsh, R. L., Hicks, J. L., Hancock, D. W., & Munsayac, K. (2002b). Investigating the output monitoring component of event-based prospective memory performance. *Memory & Cognition*, 30(2), 302–311.

Marzi, T., Regina, A., & Righi, S. (2014). Emotions shape memory suppression in trait anxiety. *Frontiers in Psychology*, 4, 1–10.

Mattison, M., Dando, C. J., & Ormerod, T. C. (2015). Drawing to remember: Supporting child witnesses and victims with Autistic Spectrum Disorder to give 'Best Evidence'. *Journal of Autism and Developmental Disorders*, 15. doi:10.1007/s10803-014-2335-2.

Mattison, M., Dando, C. J., & Ormerod, T. C. (2018). Drawing the answers: How sketch reinstatement supports free and probed recall by child witnesses with ASD. *Autism*, 22, 181–194.

Mazzoni, G., Laurence, J.-R., & Heap, M. (2014). Hypnosis and memory: Two hundred years of adventures and still going! *Psychology of Consciousness: Theory, Research, & Practice*, 1(2), 153–167. doi: http://dx.doi.org/10.1037/cns0000016

McAdams, D. P. (2001). The psychology of life stories. *Review of General Psychology*, 5, 100–122.

McBride, D. M., Beckner, J. K., & Abney, D. H. (2011). Effects of delay of prospective memory cues in an ongoing task on prospective memory task performance. *Memory & Cognition*, 39(7), 1222–1231. doi: https://doi.org/10.3758/s13421-011-0105-0

McClelland, J. L., McNaughton, B. L., & O'Reilly, R. C. (1995). Why there are complementary learning systems in the hippocampus and neocortex. Insights from the successes and failures of connectionist models of learning and memory. *Psychological Review*, 102(3), 419–457.

McConkey, K. M., & Sheehan, P. W. (1981). The impact of videotape playback of hypnotic events on posthypnotic amnesia. *Journal of Abnormal Psychology*, 90(1), 46–54. doi: http://dx.doi.org/10.1037/0021-843X.90.1.46

McConkey, K. M., Sheehan, P. W., & Cross, D. G. (1980). Post-hypnotic amnesia: Seeing is not remembering. *British Journal of Social & Clinical Psychology*, 19(1), 99–107. doi: http://dx.doi.org/10.1111/j.2044-8260.1980.tb00934.x

McDaniel, M. A., & Einstein, G. O. (2007). *Prospective Memory: An overview and synthesis of an emerging field*. Thousand Oaks, CA: SAGE.

McDaniel, M. A., Einstein, G. O., Stout, A. C., & Morgan, Z. (2003). Aging and maintaining intentions over delays: Do it or lose it. *Psychology and Aging*, 18(4), 823–835. doi: https://doi.org/10.1037/0882-7974.18.4.823.

McDaniel, M. A., & Fisher, R. P. (1991). Tests and test feedback as learning sources. *Contemporary Educational Psychology*, 16, 192–201.

McDaniel, M. A., Umanath, S., Einstein, G. O., & Waldum, E. R. (2015). Dual pathways to prospective remembering. *Frontiers in Human Neuroscience*, 9, 1–12.

McDonald, A., Haslam, C., Yates, P., Gurr, B., Leeder, G., & Sayers, A. (2011). Google calendar: A new memory aid to compensate for prospective memory deficits following acquired brain injury. *Neuropsychological Rehabilitation*, 21(6), 784–807.

McGeoch, J. A. (1932). Forgetting and the law of disuse. *Psychological Review*, 39, 352–370.

McGorrery, P. (2017). A further critique of brain fingerprinting: The possibility of propranolol usage by offenders. *Alternative Law Journal*, 42, 216–220.

McNally, R. J. (2003). Progress and controversy in the study of posttraumatic stress disorder. *Annual Review of Psychology*, 54(1), 229–252.

McNally, R. J. (2012). Searching for repressed memory. In R. F. Belli (ed.), *Nebraska Symposium on Motivation, Volume 58. True and false recovered memories: Toward a reconciliation of the debate* (pp. 121–147). New York: Springer.

McNally, R. J. (2017). Repressed memories. In V. Zeigler-Hill and T. K. Shackelford (eds), *Encyclopedia of Personality and Individual Differences*. New York: Springer.

McNally, R. J., & Geraerts, E. (2009). A new solution to the recovered memory debate. *Perspectives on Psychological Science*, 4, 126–134.

McNally, R. J., Lasko, N. B., Clancy, S. A., Macklin, M. L., Pitman, R. K., & Orr, S. P. (2004). Psychophysiological responding during script-driven imagery in people reporting abduction by space aliens. *Psychological Science*, 15, 493–497.

McNeill, D. (1992). *Hand and Mind: What gestures reveal about thought*. Chicago, IL: University of Chicago Press.

Meacham, J. A. (1982). A note on remembering to execute planned actions. *Journal of Applied Developmental Psychology*, 3(2), 121–133.

Meade, M. L., & Roediger, H. L. (2002). Explorations in the social contagion of memory. *Memory & Cognition*, 30(7), 995–1009. doi: https://doi.org/10.3758/BF03194318

Meier, B., & Zimmermann, T. D. (2015). Loads and loads and loads: The influence of prospective load, retrospective load, and ongoing task load in prospective memory. *Frontiers in Human Neuroscience*, 9. doi: https://doi.org/10.3389/fnhum.2015.00322

Melhuish, E. (2011). Preschool matters, *Science*, 333, 299–300.

Memon, A., Meissner, C. A., & Fraser, J. (2010). The Cognitive Interview: A meta-analytic review and study space analysis of the past 25 years. *Psychology, Public Policy, and Law*, 16(4), 340.

Mendelsohn, A., Chalamish, Y., Solomonovich, A., & Dudai, Y. (2008). Mesmerizing memories: Brain substrates of episodic memory suppression in posthypnotic amnesia. *Neuron*, 57(1), 159–170. doi: http://dx.doi.org/10.1016/j.neuron.2007.11.022

Miles, C. (1895). A study of individual psychology. *American Journal of Psychology*, 6, 534–558.

Milne, B., & Powell, M. (2010). Investigative interviewing. In J. Brown and E. Campbell (eds), *The Cambridge Handbook of Forensic Psychology* (p. 208). Cambridge: Cambridge University Press.

Milne, B., Griffiths, A., Clarke, C., & Dando, C. J. (2019). The cognitive interview: A tiered approach in the real world. In J. J. Dickinson, N. Schreiber Compo, R. N. Carol, B. L. Schwartz and M. R. McCauley (eds), *Evidence-based Investigative Interviewing* (pp. 56–73). Abingdon: Routledge.

Milner, B. (1966). Amnesia following operation on the temporal lobes. In C. W. M. Whitty and O. L. Zangwill (eds), *Amnesia*. London: Butterworth.

Milner, B., Corkin, S., & Teuber, H.-L. (1968). Further analysis of the hippocampal amnesic syndrome: 14-year follow-up study of H.M. *Neuropsychologia*, 6, 215–234.

Milner, B., & Klein, D. (2016). Loss of recent memory after bilateral hippocampal lesions: Memory and memories – looking back and looking forward. *Journal of Neurology, Neurosurgery, and Psychiatry*, 87, 230.

Milner, B., Squire, L. R., & Kandel, E. R. (1998). Cognitive neuroscience and the study of memory. *Neuron*, 20, 445–468.

Mirandola, C., Toffalini, E., Grassano, M., Cornoldi, C., & Melinder, A. (2014). Inferential false memories of events: Negative consequences protect from distortions when the events are free from further elaboration. *Memory*, 22(5), 451–461.

Mitchell, K. J., & Johnson, M. K., (2000). Source monitoring: Attributing mental experiences. In E. Tulving & F. I. M. Craik (eds) *The Oxford Handbook of Memory* (pp. 179–195). New York: Oxford University Press.

Mitchell, K. J., Johnson, M. K., & Mather, M. (2003). Source monitoring and suggestibility to misinformation: Adult age-related differences. *Applied Cognitive Psychology: The Official Journal of the Society for Applied Research in Memory and Cognition*, 17(1), 107–119.

Mitchell, K. J., & Zaragoza, M. S. (1996). Repeated exposure to suggestion and false memory: The role of contextual variability. *Journal of Memory and Language*, 35(2), 246–260.

Momennejad, I., & Haynes, J. D. (2013). Encoding of prospective tasks in the human prefrontal cortex under varying task loads. *Journal of Neuroscience*, 33(44), 17342–17349.

Moody, R. A. (1975). *Life After Life*. Covington, GA: Mocking Bird Books.

Morgan, K., & Hayne, H. (2007). Nonspecific verbal cues alleviate forgetting by young children. *Developmental Science*, 10, 727–733.

Morgan, K., & Hayne, H. (2011). Age-related changes in visual recognition memory during infancy and early childhood. *Developmental Psychobiology*, 53, 157–165.

Morris, C.D., Bransford, J.D., & Franks, J.J. (1977). Levels of processing versus transfer appropriate processing. *Journal of Verbal Learning and Verbal Behaviour*, 16, 519–533.

Morris, G., & Baker-Ward, L. (2007). Fragile but real: Children's capacity to use newly acquired words to convey preverbal memories. *Child Development*, 78, 448–458.

Morris, G., Baker-Ward, L., & Bauer, P. J. (2010). What remains of that day: The survival of children's autobiographical memories over time. *Applied Cognitive Psychology*, 24, 527–544.

Morris, R.G., Garrud, P., Rawlins, J.N., & O'Keefe, J. (1982). Place navigation impaired in rats with hippocampal lesions. *Nature*, 297, 681–683.

Morrison, C. M., & Conway, M. A. (2010). First words and first memories. *Cognition*, 116, 23–32.

Moscovitch, M. (1992). Memory and working with memory: A component process model based on modules and central systems. *Journal of Cognitive Neuroscience*, 4, 257–267.

Moscovitch, M., Cabeza, R., Winocur, G., & Nadel, L. (2016). Episodic memory and beyond: The hippocampus and neocortex in transformation. *Annual Review of Psychology*, 67, 105–134.

Moser, E. I., Kropff, E., & Moser M. B. (2008) Place cells, grid cells, and the brain's spatial representation system. *Neuroscience*, 31(1), 69.

Mudd, K., & Govern, J. M. (2004). Conformity to misinformation and time delay negatively affect eyewitness confidence and accuracy. *North American Journal of Psychology*, 6(2).

Mullen, M. K. (1994). Earliest recollections of childhood: A demographic analysis. *Cognition*, 52, 55–79.

Müller, G. E., & Pilzecker, A. (1900). Experimentelle beiträge zur lehre vom gedächtnis. *Zeitschrift für Psychologie, Ergänzungsband*, 1, 1–300.

Muller, R. U., Kubie, J. L., & Ranck, J. B. Jr (1987). Spatial firing patterns of hippocampal complex spike cells in a fixed environment. *Journal of Neuroscience*, 7, 1935–1950.

Nader, K., Schafe, G., & Ledoux, J. E. (2000). The labile nature of the consolidation theory. *Nature Neuroscience Reviews*, 1, 216–219.

Nash, R. A., & Ost, J. (eds) (2016). *False and Distorted Memories*. Hove: Psychology Press.

Nash, R. A., Wade, K. A., Garry, M., Loftus, E. F., & Ost, J. (2017). Misrepresentations and flawed logic about the prevalence of false memories. *Applied Cognitive Psychology*, 31(1), 31–33.

Nelson, C. A. (2000). Neural plasticity and human development: The role of early experience sculpting memory systems. *Developmental Science*, 3, 115–130.

Nelson, K., & Fivush, R. (2004). The emergence of autobiographical memory: A social cultural developmental theory. *Psychological Review*, 111, 486–511.

Newcombe, N., & Fox, N. A., (1994). Infantile amnesia: Through the glass darkly. *Child Development*, 65, 31–40.

Newcombe, N., Lloyd, M. E., & Ratliff, K. R. (2007). Development of episodic and autobiographical memory: A cognitive neuroscience perspective. In R. V. Kail (ed.) *Advances in Child Development and Behaviour, Volume 35: Advances in child development and behaviour* (pp. 37–85). San Diego, CA: Elsevier.

Nørby, S. (2015). Why forget? On the adaptive value of memory loss. *Perspectives on Psychological Science*, 10, 551–578.

Nørby, S. (2018) Forgetting and emotion regulation in mental health, anxiety and depression. *Memory*, 26, 342–363.

Nørby, S. (2019). Mnemonic emotion regulation: A three-process model. *Cognition & Emotion*, 33, 959–975.

Noreen, S., & MacLeod, M. D. (2014). To think or not to think, that is the question: Individual differences in suppression and rebound effects in autobiographical memory. *Acta Psychologica*, 145, 84–97.

Nori, R., Palmiero, M., Bocchi, A., & Piccardi, L. (2018). The enhanced cognitive interview: Could individual differences in visuo-spatial working memory explain differences in recalling an event? *Psychology, Crime & Law*, 24(10), 998–1015.

Norman, D. A., & Bobrow, D. G. (1979). Descriptions: An intermediate stage in memory retrieval. *Cognitive Psychology*, 11(1), 107–123.

Oakley, D. A. (1999). Hypnosis and conversion hysteria: A unifying model. *Cognitive Neuropsychiatry*, 4(3), 243–265. doi: https://doi.org/10.1080/135468099395954

Oakley, D. A., & Halligan, P. W. (2013). Hypnotic suggestion: Opportunities for cognitive neuroscience. *Nature Reviews Neuroscience*, 14, 565–576. doi: http://dx.doi.org/10.1038/nrn3538

Ogle, C. M., Rubin, D. C., Berntsen, D., & Siegler, I. C. (2013). The frequency and impact of exposure to potentially traumatic events over the life course. *Clinical Psychological Science*, 1(4), 426–434.

O'Keefe, J., & Burgess, N. (1996). Geometric determinants of the place fields of hippocampal neurons. *Nature,* 381, 425–428.

O'Keefe, J., & Dostrovsky, J. (1971). The hippocampus as a spatial map: Preliminary evidence from unit activity in the freely-moving rat. *Brain Research*, 34(1), 171–175.

O'Keefe, J., & Nadel, L. (1978). *The Hippocampus as a Cognitive Map*. New York: Oxford University Press.

Olson, I. R., & Newcombe, N. S. (2014). Binding together the elements of episodes: Relational memory and the developmental trajectory of the hippocampus. In P. J. Bauer and R. Fivush (eds), *The Wiley-Blackwell Handbook on the Development of Children's Memory* (pp. 285–308). Chichester: Wiley-Blackwell.

Olson, I. R., Page, K., Moore, K. S., Chatterjee, A., & Verfaellie, M. (2006). Working memory for conjunctions relies on the medial temporal lobe. *Journal of Neuroscience*, 26(17), 4596–4601.

Öngür, D., Cullen, T., Wolf, D., Rohan, M., Barreira, P., Zalesak, M., & Heckers, S. (2006). The neural basis of relational memory deficits in schizophrenia. *Archives of General Psychiatry*, 63(4), 356–365. doi: 10.1001/archpsyc.63.4.356

Orne, M. T. (1962). On the social psychology of the psychological experiment: With particular reference to demand characteristics and their implications. *American Psychologist*, 17, 776–783. doi: http://dx.doi.org/10.1037/h0043424

Orne, M. T. (1966). On the mechanisms of posthypnotic amnesia. *International Journal of Clinical and Experimental Hypnosis*, 14(2), 121–134. doi: http://dx.doi.org/10.1080/00207146608412955

Ortega, A., Gómez-Ariza, C. J., Román, P., & Bajo, M. T. (2012). Memory inhibition, aging, and the executive deficit hypothesis. *Journal of Experimental Psychology: Learning, Memory, and Cognition*, 38, 178–86.

Ost, J. (2017). Adults' retractions of childhood sexual abuse allegations: High-stakes and the (in)validation of recollection. *Memory*, 25, 900–909.

Ost, J., Foster, S., Costall, A., & Bull, R. (2005). False reports of childhood events in appropriate interviews. *Memory*, 13(7), 700–710.

Ost, J., Hogbin, I., & Granhag, P. A. (2006). Altering false reports via confederate influence. *Social Influence*, 1(2), 105–116.

Ost, J., Vrij, A., Costall, A., & Bull, R. (2002). Crashing memories and reality monitoring: Distinguishing between perceptions, imaginations and 'false memories'. *Applied Cognitive Psychology: The Official Journal of the Society for Applied Research in Memory and Cognition*, 16(2), 125–134.

Otgaar, H., Howe, M. L., Merckelbach, H., & Muris, P. (2018). Who is the better eyewitness? Sometimes adults but at other times children. *Current Directions in Psychological Science*, 27(5), 378–385. doi: https://doi.org/10.1177/0963721418770998

Otgaar, H., Howe, M. L., Patihis, L., Merchelbach, H., Lynn, S. J., Lilienfeld, S., & Loftus, E. (2019). The return of the repressed: The persistent and problematic forgotten trauma. *Perspectives on Psychological Science*, 14(6), 1072–1095.

Otgaar, H., Merckelbach, H., Jelicic, M., & Smeets, T. (2017). The potential for false memories is bigger than what Brewin and Andrews suggest. *Applied Cognitive Psychology*, 31(1), 24–25.

Packard, M. G., & Goodman, J. (2012). Emotional arousal and multiple memory systems in the mammalian brain. *Front. Behav. Neurosci.*, 6, 14. doi: 10.3389/fnbeh.2012.00014

Pajón, L., & Walsh, D. (2017). Examining the effects of violence and personality on eyewitness memory. *Psychiatry, Psychology and Law*, 24(6), 923–935.

Palombo, D. J., Hayes, S. M., Reid, A. G., & Verfaellie, M. (2019). Hippocampal contributions to value-based learning: Converging evidence from fMRI and amnesia. *Cognitive, Affective, & Behavioral Neuroscience*, 19(3), 523–536.

Parker, E.S., Cahill, L., & McGaugh, J.L. (2006). A case of unusual autobiographical remembering. *Neurocase*, 12, 35–49.

Pastötter, B., & Bäuml, K.-H. T. (2007). The crucial role of postcue encoding in directed forgetting and context-dependent forgetting. *Journal of Experimental Psychology: Learning, Memory, and Cognition*, 33, 977–982.

Pastötter, B., & Bäuml, K.-H. T. (2010). Amount of postcue encoding predicts amount of directed forgetting. *Journal of Experimental Psychology: Learning, Memory, and Cognition*, 36, 54–65.

Pastötter, B., Kliegl, O., & Bäuml, K.-H. T. (2016). List-method directed forgetting: Evidence for the reset-of-encoding hypothesis employing item-recognition testing. *Memory*, 24, 63–74.

Paterson, H. M., Eijkemans, H., & Kemp, R. I. (2015). Investigating the impact of delayed administration on the efficacy of the Self-Administered Interview. *Psychiatry, Psychology and Law*, 22(2), 307–317.

Paterson, H. M., & Kemp, R. I. (2006). Comparing methods of encountering post-event information: The power of co-witness suggestion. *Applied Cognitive Psychology: The Official Journal of the Society for Applied Research in Memory and Cognition*, 20(8), 1083–1099.

Patihis, L., Ho, L. Y., Tingen, I. W., Lilienfeld, S. O., & Loftus, E. F. (2014). Erratum: Are the "memory wars" over? A scientist-practitioner gap in beliefs about repressed memory. *Psychological Science*, 25, 519–530. doi: 10.1177/0956797613510718

Patihis, L., & Pendergrast, M. (2019). Reports of recovered memories of abuse in therapy in a large age-representative U.S. national sample: Therapy type and decade comparisons. *Clinical Psychological Science*, 7, 3–21.

Paulo, R. M., Albuquerque, P. B., & Bull, R. (2019). Witnesses' verbal evaluation of certainty and uncertainty during investigative interviews: Relationship with report accuracy. *Journal of Police and Criminal Psychology*, 34, 1–10.

Peira, N., Ziaei, M., & Persson, J. (2016). Age differences in brain systems supporting transient and sustained processes involved in prospective memory and working memory. *NeuroImage*, 125, 745–755. doi: https://doi.org/10.1016/j.neuroimage.2015.10.075

Penfield, W. (1958). Some mechanisms of consciousness discovered during electrical stimulation of the brain. *Proceedings of the National Academy of Sciences*, 44, 51–66.

Penfield, W., & Perot, P. (1963). The brain's record of auditory and visual experience: A final summary and discussion, *Brain*, 86, 595–696.

Perfect, T. J., & Lindsay, D. S. (eds) (2014) *The SAGE Handbook of Applied Memory*. London: SAGE.

Peterson, C. (1999). Children's memory for medical emergencies: 2 years later. *Developmental Psychology*, 35, 1493–1506.

Peterson, C., & Bell, M. (1996). Children's memory for traumatic injury. *Child Development*, 67, 3045–3070.

Peterson, C., Grant, V. V., & Boland, L. D. (2005). Childhood amnesia in children and adolescents: Their earliest memories. *Memory*, 13, 622–637.

Peterson, C., Hallett, D., & Compton-Gillingham, C. (2018). Childhood amnesia in children: A prospective study across eight years. *Child Development*, 89, e520–e534.

Peterson, C., Morris, G., Baker-Ward, L., & Flynn, S. (2014). Predicting which childhood memories persist: Contributions of memory characteristics. *Developmental Psychology*, 50, 439–448.

Peterson, C., & Rideout, R. (1998). Memory for medical emergencies experienced by 1- and 2-year-olds. *Developmental Psychology*, 34, 1059–1072.

Peterson, C., & Whalen, N. (2001). Five years later: Children's memory for medical emergencies. *Applied Cognitive Psychology*, 15, 7–24.

Pettinati, H. M., Evans, F. J., Orne, E. C., & Orne, M. T. (1981). Restricted use of success cues in retrieval during posthypnotic amnesia. *Journal of Abnormal Psychology*, 90(4), 345–353. doi: http://dx.doi.org/10.1037/0021-843X.90.4.345

Pew Research Center (2018). Millennials stand out for their technology use. Accessed 28 May 2019 at: www.pewresearch.org/fact-tank/2018/05/02/millennials-stand-out-for-theirtechnology-use-but-older-generations-also-embrace-digital-life/

Pezdek, K., Lam, S. T., & Sperry, K. (2009). Forced confabulation more strongly influences event memory if suggestions are other-generated than self-generated. *Legal and Criminological Psychology*, 14(2), 241–252.

Pezdek, K., Sperry, K., & Owens, S. M. (2007). Interviewing witnesses: The effect of forced confabulation on event memory. *Law and Human Behavior*, 31(5), 463–478.

Piai, V., Anderson, K., Lin, J., Dewar, C., Parvizi, J., Dronkers, N., & Knight, R. (2016). Direct brain recordings reveal hippocampal rhythm underpinnings of language processing. *Proceedings of the National Academy of Sciences*, 113(40), 11366–11371.

Pillemer, D. B. (1998). What is remembered about early childhood events? *Clinical Psychology Review*, 18, 895–913.

Pillemer, D. B. (2003). Directive functions of autobiographical memory: The guiding power of the specific episode. *Memory*, 11, 193–202.

Polczyk, R., Wesołowska, B., Gabarczyk, A., Minakowska, I., Supska, M., & Bomba, E. (2004). Age differences in interrogative suggestibility: A comparison between young and older adults. *Applied Cognitive Psychology*, 18(8), 1097–1107.

Poldrack, R. (2006). Can cognitive processes be inferred from neuroimaging data? *Trends in Cognitive Sciences*, 10(2), 59–63.

Poldrack, R. A., & Packard, M. G. (2003). Competition among multiple memory systems: Converging evidence from animal and human brain studies. *Neuropsychologia*, 41, 245–251

Poldrack, R. A., & Rodriguez, P. (2004). How do memory systems interact? Evidence from human classification learning. *Neurobiology of Learning and Memory*, 82(3), 324–332. doi: https://doi.org/10.1016/j.nlm.2004.05.003

Poole, D. A., & Lindsay, S. D. (2001). Children's eyewitness reports after exposure to misinformation from parents. *Journal of Experimental Psychology: Applied*, 7, 27–50.

Poole, D. A., & Lindsay, S. D. (2002). Reducing child witnesses' false reports of misinformation from parents. *Journal of Experimental Child Psychology*, 81(2), 117–140. doi: https://doi.org/10.1006/jecp.2001.2648

Pope, H. G., & Hudson, J. I. (1995). Can memories of childhood sexual abuse be repressed? *Psychological Medicine*, 25, 121–126.

Pope, H. G., Oliva, P. S., & Hudson, J. I. (1999). Repressed memories: The scientific status. In D. L. Faigman, D. H. Kaye, M. J. Saks and J. Sanders (eds), *Modern Scientific Testimony: The Law and Science of Expert Testimony* (Vol. 1, pp. 115–155). St Paul, MN: West Publishing.

Porter, S., Yuille, J. C., & Lehman, D. R. (1999). The nature of real, implanted, and fabricated memories for emotional childhood events: Implications for the recovered memory debate. *Law and Human Behavior*, *23*(5), 517–537.

Prebble, S. C., Addis, D. R., & Tippet, L. J. (2013). Autobiographical memory and sense of self. *Psychological Bulletin*, 139, 815–840.

Principe, G. F., & Schindewolf, E. (2012). Natural conversations as a source of false memories in children: Implications for the testimony of young witnesses. *Developmental Review*, 32(3), 205–223. doi: https://doi.org/10.1016/j.dr.2012.06.003

Putnam, A. L., Sungkhasettee, V. W., & Roediger III, H. L. (2017). When misinformation improves memory: The effects of recollecting change. *Psychological Science*, 28(1), 36–46.

Raaijmakers, J. G. W., & Jakab, E. (2012). Retrieval-induced forgetting without competition: Testing the retrieval specificity assumption of the inhibition theory. *Memory & Cognition*, 40, 19–27.

Raaijmakers, J. G. W., & Shiffrin, R. M. (1981). Search of associative memory. *Psychological Review*, 88, 93–134.

Rabbitt, P. (1996). Why are studies of "prospective memory" planless? In M. Brandimonte, G. O. Einstein and M. A. McDaniel (eds), *Prospective Memory: Theory and applications* (pp. 239–248). Hillsdale, NJ: Erlbaum.

Race, E., Keane, M. M., and Verfaellie, M. (2013). Losing sight of the future: Impaired semantic prospection following medial temporal lobe lesions. *Hippocampus*, 23, 268–277.

Rajaram, S., & Pereira-Pasarin, L. P. (2010). Collaborative memory: Cognitive research and theory. *Perspectives on Psychological Science*, 5(6), 649–663.

Raphael, K., Cloitre, M., & Dohrenwend, B. P. (1991). Problems of recall and misclassification with checklist methods of measuring stressful life events. *Health Psychology*, 10(1), 62–74.

Ranganath, C., & D'Esposito, M. (2001). Medial temporal lobe activity associated with active maintenance of novel information. *Neuron*, 31(5), 865–873.

Rasch, B., & Born, J. (2013). About sleep's role in memory. *Physiological Reviews*, 93(2), 681–766. doi: https://doi.org/10.1152/physrev.00032.2012

Ratcliff, R., Clark, S. E., & Shiffrin, R. M. (1990). List-strength effect: I. Data and discussion. *Journal of Experimental Psychology: Learning, Memory, and Cognition*, 16, 163–178.

Raymaekers, L., Smeets, T., Peters, M. J. V., Orgaar, H., & Merckelbach, H. (2012). The classification of recovered memories: A cautionary note. *Consciousness and Cognition*, 21, 1640–1643.

Reese, E., Haden, C. A., Baker-Ward, L., Bauer, P., Fivush, R., & Ornstein, P. A. (2011). Coherence of personal narratives across the lifespan: A multidimensional model and coding method. *Journal of Cognition and Development*, 12, 424–462.

Reese, E., Hayne, H., & MacDonald, S. (2008). Looking back to the future: Māori and Pakeha mother–child birth stories. *Child Development*, 79, 114–125.

Reese, E., Jack, F., & White, N. (2010). Origins of adolescents' autobiographical memories. *Cognitive Development*, 25, 352–367.

Reese, E., & Robertson, S-J. (2019). Origins of adolescents' earliest memories. *Memory*, 27, 79–91.

Reyher, J., & Smyth, L. (1971). Suggestibility during the execution of a posthypnotic suggestion. *Journal of Abnormal Psychology*, 78(3), 258–265. doi: http://dx.doi.org/10.1037/h0031802

Ribot, T. (1882). *Diseases of Memory: An Essay in Positive Psychology* (W. H. Smith, trans.). New York: Appleton.

Richards, B. A., & Frankland, P. W. (2017). The persistence and transience of memory. *Neuron*, 94, 1071–1084.

Richardson, R., & Hayne, H. (2007). You can't take it with you: The translation of memory across development. *Current Directions in Psychological Science*, 16, 223–227.

Rickard, T. C., & Pan, S. C. (2018). A dual memory theory of the testing effect. *Psychonomic Bulletin & Review*, 25, 847–869.

Righarts, S., Jack, F., Zajac, R., & Hayne, H. (2015). Young children's responses to cross-examination style questioning: The effects of delay and subsequent questioning. *Psychology, Crime and Law*, 21(3), 274–296. doi: https://doi.org/10.1080/1068316X.2014.951650

Rigon, A., Schwarb, H., Klooster, N., Cohen, N. J., & Duff, M. C. (2019). Spatial relational memory in individuals with traumatic brain injury. *Journal of Clinical and Experimental Neuropsychology*. doi: 10.1080/13803395.2019.1659755

Ritchey, M., Libby, L., & Ranganath, C. (2015). Cortico-hippocampal systems involved in memory and cognition: The PMAT framework. *Progress in Brain Research*, 219, 45–64.

Roebers, C. M., & McConkey, K. M. (2003). Mental reinstatement of the misinformation context and the misinformation effect in children and adults. *Applied Cognitive Psychology: The Official Journal of the Society for Applied Research in Memory and Cognition*, 17(4), 477–493.

Roediger, H. L. (1996). Prospective memory and episodic memory. In M. Brandimonte, G. O. Einstein and M. A. McDaniel (eds), *Prospective Memory: Theory and applications* (pp. 149–155). Hillsdale, NJ: Erlbaum.

Roediger, H. L., & Bergman, E. T. (1998). The controversy over recovered memories. *Psychology, Public Policy, and Law*, 4, 1091–1109.

Roediger, H. L., & Geraci, L. (2007). Aging and the misinformation effect: A neuropsychological analysis. *Journal of Experimental Psychology: Learning, Memory, and Cognition*, 33(2), 321.

Roediger, H. L., & Karpicke, J. D. (2006). Test-enhanced learning: Taking memory tests improves long-term retention. *Psychological Science*, 17, 249–255.

Roediger, H. L., & Neely, J. H. (1982). Retrieval blocks in episodic and semantic memory. *Canadian Journal of Psychology*, 36, 213–242.

Román, P., Soriano, M. F., Gómez-Ariza, C. J., & Bajo, M. T. (2009). Retrieval-induced forgetting and executive control. *Psychological Science*, 20, 1053–1058.

Rorden, C., & Karnath, H. (2004). Using human brain lesions to infer functions: A relic from a past era in the fMRI age? *Nature Reviews Neuroscience*, 5(10), 813–819.

Rose, N. S., Rendell, P. G., Hering, A., Kliegel, M., Bidelman, G. M., & Craik, F. I. (2015). Cognitive and neural plasticity in older adults' prospective memory following training with the Virtual Week computer game. *Frontiers in Human Neuroscience*, 9, 592.

Rosenbaum, R. S., Kohler, S., Schacter, D., Moscovitch, M., Westmacott, R., Black, S., Gao, R., & Tulving, E. (2005). The case of K.C.: Contributions of a memory-impaired person to memory theory. *Neuropsychologia*, 43(7), 989–1021.

Rovee-Collier, C., & Cuevas, K. (2009). Multiple memory systems are unnecessary to account for infant memory development: An ecological model. *Developmental Psychology*, 45, 160–174.

Rovee-Collier, C., & Hayne, H. (2000). Memory in infancy and early childhood. In E. Tulving and F. Craik (eds), *The Oxford Handbook of Memory* (pp. 267–282). New York: Oxford University Press.

Rovee-Collier, C., Hayne, H., & Colombo, M. (2001). *The Development of Implicit and Explicit Memory*. Amsterdam: John Benjamins Publishing Co.

Rubin, D. C., & Wenzel, A. (1996). One hundred years of forgetting: A quantitative description of retention. *Psychological Review*, 103, 734–760.

Rubin, R., Brown-Schmidt, S., Duff, M.C., Tranel, D., & Cohen, N.J. (2011). How do I remember that I know you know that I know? *Psychological Science*, 22(12), 1574–1582.

Rubin, R., & Cohen, N. (2017). Memory, relational representations, and the long reach of the hippocampus. In D. Hannula and M. C. Duff (eds.), *The Hippocampus from Cells to Systems: Structure, connectivity, and functional contributions to memory and flexible cognition* (pp. 337–368). Springer International Publishing. Switzerland.

Rubin, R., Watson, P., Duff, M. C., & Cohen, N. J. (2014). The role of the hippocampus in flexible cognition and social behavior. *Frontiers in Human Neuroscience*, 8. doi: 10.3389/fnhum.2014.00742.

Rummel, J., & Meiser, T. (2013). The role of metacognition in prospective memory: Anticipated task demands influence attention allocation strategies. *Consciousness and Cognition*, 22(3), 931–943.

Rundus, D. (1973). Negative effects of using list items as recall cues. *Journal of Verbal Learning and Verbal Behavior*, 12, 43–50.

Rupprecht, J., & Bäuml, K.-H. T. (2016). Retrieval-induced forgetting in item recognition: Retrieval specificity revisited. *Journal of Memory and Language*, 86, 97–118.

Rupprecht, J., & Bäuml, K.-H. T. (2017). Retrieval-induced versus context-induced forgetting: Can restudy preceded by context change simulate retrieval-induced forgetting? *Journal of Memory and Language*, 93, 259–275.

Ryan, J. D., Althoff, R. R., Whitlow, S., & Cohen, N. J. (2000). Amnesia is a deficit in relational memory. *Psychological Science*, 11(6), 454–461.

Sabom, M. B. (1982). *Recollections of Death*. London: Corgi.

Sahakyan, L., & Delaney, P. F. (2003). Can encoding differences explain the benefits of directed forgetting in the list-method paradigm? *Journal of Memory and Language*, 48, 195–206.

Sahakyan, L., Delaney, P. F., Foster, N. L., & Abushanab, B. (2013). List-method directed forgetting in cognitive and clinical research: A theoretical and methodological review. *Psychology of Learning and Motivation*, 59, 131–189.

Sahakyan, L., Delaney, P. F., & Waldum, E. R. (2008). Intentional forgetting is easier after two 'shots' than one. *Journal of Experimental Psychology: Learning, Memory, and Cognition*, 34, 408–414.

Sahakyan, L., & Kelley, C. M. (2002). A contextual change account of the directed forgetting effect. *Journal of Experimental Psychology: Learning, Memory, and Cognition*, 28, 1064–1072.

Salmon, K., Yao, J., Berntsen, O., & Pipe, M. E. (2007). Does providing props during preparation help children to remember a novel event? *Journal of Experimental Child Psychology*, 97, 99–116.

Santangelo, V., Cavallina, C., Colucci, P., Santori, A., Macri, S., McGaugh, J. L., & Campolongo, P. (2018). Enhanced brain activity associated with memory access in highly superior autobiographical memory. *Proceedings of the National Academy of Sciences*, 115, 7795–7800.

Santiago, P. N., Ursano, R. J., Gray, C. L., Pynoos, R. S., Spiegel, D., Lewis-Fernandez, R., Friedman, M. J., & Fullerton, C. S. (2013). A systematic review of PTSD prevalence and trajectories in DSM-5 defined trauma exposed populations: Intentional and non-intentional traumatic events. *PloS One*, 8(4), e59236.

Sarbin, T. R. (2002). Dialogical components in theory-building: Contributions of Hilgard, Orne and Spanos. *Contemporary Hypnosis*, 19(4), 190–197. doi: http://dx.doi.org/10.1002/ch.257

Sartori, P. (2006). The incidence and phenomenology of near-death experiences. *Network Review*, 90, 23–25.

Schacter, D. L. (1987). Implicit memory: History and current status. *Journal of Experimental Psychology: Learning, Memory, and Cognition*, 13, 501–518. doi: http://dx.doi.org/10.1037/0278-7393.13.3.501

Schacter, D. (2012). Adaptive constructive processes and the future of memory. *American Psycholologist*, 67, 603–613. doi: 10.1037/a0029869

Schacter, D. L. (1995). Memory distortion: History and current status. In D. L. Schacter, J. T. Coyle, G. D. Fischback, M. M. Mesulam & L. E. Sullivan (eds), *Memory Distortion: How minds, brains, and societies reconstruct the past* (pp. 1–43). Cambridge, MA: Harvard University Press.

Schank, R. C. (1982). *Dynamic Memory*. New York: Cambridge University Press.

Schapiro, A. C., Turk-Browne, N. B., Botvinick, M. M., & Norman, K. A. (2017). Complementary learning systems within the hippocampus: A neural network modelling approach to reconciling episodic memory with statistical learning. *Philosophical Transactions of the Royal Society B*, 372(1711).

Schare, M. L., Lisman, S. A., & Spear, N. E. (1984). The effects of mood variation on state-dependent retention. *Cognitive Therapy and Research*, 8, 387–408.

Schilling, C. J., Storm, B. C., & Anderson, M. C. (2014). Examining the costs and benefits of inhibition in memory retrieval. *Cognition*, 133, 358–370.

Schnyer, D. M., & Allen, J. J. (1995). Attention related electroencephalographic and event-related potential predictors of responsiveness to suggested posthypnotic amnesia. *International Journal of Clinical & Experimental Hypnosis*, 43(3), 295–315. doi: http://dx.doi.org/10.1080/00207149508409972

Schuyler, B. A., & Coe, W. C. (1989). More on volitional experiences and breaching posthypnotic amnesia. *International Journal of Clinical and Experimental Hypnosis*, 37(4), 320–331. doi: http://dx.doi.org/10.1080/00207148908414486

Schwarb, H., Johnson, C. L., Daugherty, A. M., Hillman, C. H., Kramer, A. F., Cohen, N. J., & Barbey, A. K. (2017). Aerobic fitness, hippocampal viscoelasticity, and relational memory performance. *Neuroimage*, 153, 179–188.

Scoboria, A., Wade, K. A., Lindsay, D. S., Azad, T., Strange, D., Ost, J., & Hyman, I. E. (2017). A mega-analysis of memory reports from eight peer-reviewed false memory implantation studies. *Memory*, 25, 146–163.

Scoville, W. B. (1968). Amnesia after bilateral medial temporal-lobe excision: Introduction to case H. M. *Neuropsychologia*, 6, 211–213.

Scoville, W. B., & Milner, B. (1957). Loss of recent memory after bilateral hippocampal lesions. *Journal of Neurology, Neurosurgery & Psychiatry*, 20, 11–21.

Scullin, M. K., & Bliwise, D. L. (2015). Sleep, cognition, and normal aging: Integrating a half century of multidisciplinary research. *Perspectives on Psychological Science*, 10(1), 97–137.

Scullin, M. K., Bugg, J. M., & McDaniel, M. A. (2012). Whoops, I did it again: Commission errors in prospective memory. *Psychology and Aging*, 27(1), 46–53. doi: https://doi.org/10.1037/a0026112

Scullin, M. K., Gao, C., Fillmore, P., Roberts, R. L., Pruett, N., & Bliwise, D. L. (2019). REM sleep mediates age-related decline in prospective memory consolidation. *SLEEP*, 42, zsz055.

Scullin, M. K., Kurinec, C., & Nguyen, K. (2017). The effects of implementation intention strategies on prospective memory cue encoding. *Journal of Cognitive Psychology*, 29, 929–938.

Scullin, M. K. & McDaniel, M. A. (2010). Remembering to execute a goal: Sleep on it! *Psychological Science*, 21(7), 1028–1035.

Scullin, M. K., McDaniel, M. A., Dasse, M. N., Lee, J. H., Kurinec, C. A., Tami, C., & Krueger, M. L. (2018). Thought probes during prospective memory encoding: Evidence for perfunctory processes. *PloS One*, 13(6), e0198646.

Scullin, M. K., McDaniel, M. A., & Einstein, G. O. (2010a). Control of cost in prospective memory: Evidence for spontaneous retrieval processes. *Journal of Experimental Psychology: Learning, Memory, and Cognition*, 36(1), 190–203. doi: https://doi.org/10.1037/a0017732

Scullin, M. K., McDaniel, M. A., & Shelton, J. T. (2013). The Dynamic Multiprocess Framework: Evidence from prospective memory with contextual variability. *Cognitive Psychology*, 67(1–2), 55–71. doi: https://doi.org/10.1016/j.cogpsych.2013.07.001

Scullin, M. K., McDaniel, M. A., Shelton, J. T., & Lee, J. H. (2010b). Focal/nonfocal cue effects in prospective memory: Monitoring difficulty or different retrieval processes? *Journal of Experimental Psychology: Learning, Memory, and Cognition*, 36(3), 736–749. doi: https://doi.org/10.1037/a0018971

Sedikides, C., & Green, J. D. (2000). On the self-protective nature of inconsistency/negativity management: Using the person memory paradigm to examine self-referent memory. *Journal of Personality and Social Psychology*, 79, 906–922.

Sedikides, C., & Green, J. D. (2009). Memory as a self-protective mechanism. *Social and Personality Compass*, 3, 1055–1068.

Sego, S. A., Golding, J. M., & Gottlob, L. R. (2006). Directed forgetting in older adults using the item and list methods. *Aging, Neuropsychology, and Cognition*, 13, 95–114.

Shaw, J., & Porter, S. (2015). Constructing rich false memories of committing crime. *Psychological Science*, 26(3), 291–301.

Sheehan, P. W., & Orne, M. T. (1968). Some comments on the nature of posthypnotic behavior. *Journal of Nervous & Mental Disease*, 146(3), 209–220. doi: http://dx.doi.org/10.1097/00005053-196803000-00002

Sheffield, E. G., & Hudson, J. A. (2006). You must remember this: Effects of video and photograph reminders on 18-month-olds' event memory. *Journal of Cognition and Development*, 7, 73–93.

Sheingold, K., & Tenney, Y. J. (1982). Memory for a salient childhood event. In U. Neisser (ed.), *Memory Observed* (pp. 201–212). New York: Freeman.

Shelton, J. T., & Christopher, E. A. (2016). A fresh pair of eyes on prospective memory monitoring. *Memory & Cognition*, 44(6), 837–845. doi: https://doi.org/10.3758/s13421-016-0601-3

Shelton, J. T., Lee, J. H., Scullin, M. K., Rose, N. S., Rendell, P. G., & McDaniel, M. A. (2016). Improving prospective memory in healthy older adults and individuals with very mild Alzheimer's Disease. *Journal of the American Geriatrics Society*, 64(6), 1307–1312. doi: https://doi.org/10.1111/jgs.14134

Shelton, J. T., & Scullin, M. K. (2017). The dynamic interplay between bottom-up and top-down processes supporting prospective remembering. *Current Directions in Psychological Science*, 26, 352–358.

Shelton, J. T., Scullin, M. K., & Hacker, J. (2019). The multiprocess framework: Historical context and the "dynamic" extension. In J. Rummel and M. McDaniel (eds), *Current Issues in Memory: Prospective Memory*. Abingdon: Routledge. doi: https://doi.org/10.4324/9781351000154

Shiffrin, R. M. (1970). Forgetting, trace erosion or retrieval failure? *Science*, *168*, 1601–1603.

Shohamy, D., & Daw, N. (2015). Integrating memories to guide decisions. *Current Opinion in Behavioral Sciences*, 5, 85–90.

Shor, R. E., Pistole, D. D., Easton, R. D., & Kihlstrom, J. F. (1984). Relation of predicted to actual hypnotic responsiveness, with special reference to posthypnotic amnesia. *International Journal of Clinical & Experimental Hypnosis*, 32(4), 376–387. doi: http://dx.doi.org/10.1080/00207148408416029

Shrager, Y., Levy, D. A., Hopkins, R. O., & Squire, L. R. (2008). Working memory and the organization of brain systems. *The Journal of Neuroscience: The Official Journal of the Society for Neuroscience*, 28(18), 4818–4822.

Shroder, T. (1999). *Old Souls.* New York: Simon & Schuster.

Silva, C. E., & Kirsch, I. (1987). Breaching hypnotic amnesia by manipulating expectancy. *Journal of Abnormal Psychology*, 96(4), 325–329. doi: http://dx.doi.org/10.1037/0021-843X.96.4.325

Simcock, G., & Hayne, H. (2002). Breaking the barrier? Children fail to translate their preverbal memories into language. *Psychological Science*, 13, 225–231.

Simcock, G., & Hayne, H. (2003). Age-related changes in verbal and nonverbal recall during early childhood. *Developmental Psychology*, 39, 805–814.

Simons, D. J., & Chabris, C. F. (2011). What people believe about how memory works: A representative survey of the US population. *PLoS One*, 6(8), e22757.

Smith, C. H., Morton, J., & Oakley, D. (1998). An investigation of the "state-dependency" of recall during hypnotic amnesia. *Contemporary Hypnosis*, 15(2), 94–100. doi: http://dx.doi.org/10.1002/ch.120

Smith, C. H., Oakley, D. A., & Morton, J. (2013). Increased response time of primed associates following an "episodic" hypnotic amnesia suggestion: A case of unconscious volition. *Consciousness and Cognition*, 22(4), 13505–11317. doi: http://dx.doi.org/10.1016/j.concog.2013.08.003

Smith, R., Alkozei, A., Bao, J., & Kilgore, W. D. S. (2018). Successful goal-directed memory suppression is associated with increased inter-hemispheric co-ordination between right and left fronto-parietal control networks. *Psychological Reports*, 121, 93–111. doi: https://doi.org/10.1177%2F0033294117723018

Smith, R. E. (2003). The cost of remembering to remember in event-based prospective memory: Investigating the capacity demands of delayed intention performance. *Journal of Experimental Psychology: Learning, Memory, and Cognition*, 29(3), 347–361. doi: https://doi.org/10.1037/0278-7393.29.3.347

Smith, R. E., Hunt, R. R., McVay, J. C., & McConnell, M. D. (2007). The cost of event-based prospective memory: Salient target events. *Journal of Experimental Psychology: Learning, Memory, and Cognition*, 33(4), 734–746. doi: https://doi.org/10.1037/0278-7393.33.4.734

Smith, S. M., Glenberg, A. M., & Bjork, R. A. (1978). Environmental context and human memory. *Memory & Cognition*, 6, 342–353.

Spanos, N. P. (1986). Hypnotic behavior: A social psychological interpretation of amnesia, analgesia, and trance logic. *Behavioral and Brain Sciences*, 9, 449–467. doi: http://dx.doi.org/10.1017/S0140525X00046537

Spanos, N. P., & Barber, T. X. (1968). 'Hypnotic' experiences as inferred from auditory and visual hallucinations. *Journal of Experimental Research in Personality*, 3, 136–150.

Spanos, N. P., Bertrand, L. D., & Perlini, A. H. (1988a). Reduced clustering during hypnotic amnesia for a long word list: Comment on Wilson and Kihlstrom. *Journal of Abnormal Psychology*, 97(3), 378–380. doi: http://dx.doi.org/10.1037/h0092433

Spanos, N. P., & Bodorik, H. L. (1977). Suggested amnesia and disorganized recall in hypnotic and task motivated subjects. *Journal of Abnormal Psychology*, 86(3), 295–305. doi: http://dx.doi.org/10.1037/0021-843X.86.3.295

Spanos, N. P., Gwynn, M. I., Della Malva, C. L., & Bertrand, L. D. (1988b). Social psychological factors in the genesis of posthypnotic source amnesia. *Journal of Abnormal Psychology*, 97(3), 322–329. doi: http://dx.doi.org/10.1037/0021-843X.97.3.322

Spanos, N. P., James, B., & De Groot, H. P. (1990). Detection of simulated hypnotic amnesia. *Journal of Abnormal Psychology*, 99(2), 179–182. doi: http://dx.doi.org/10.1037/0021-843X.99.2.179

Spanos, N. P., Radtke, H. L., & Bertrand, L. D. (1984). Hypnotic amnesia as a strategic enactment: Breaching amnesia in highly susceptible subjects. *Journal of Personality and Social Psychology*, 47(5), 1155–1169. doi: http://dx.doi.org/10.1037/0022-3514.47.5.1155

Spanos, N. P., Radtke, H. L., & Dubreuil, D. L. (1982). Episodic and semantic memory in posthypnotic amnesia: A reevaluation. *Journal of Personality and Social Psychology*, 43(5), 565–573. doi: http://dx.doi.org/10.1037/0022-3514.43.3.565

Spanos, N. P., Stam, H. J., D'Eon, J. L., Pawlak, A. E., & Radtke-Bodorik, H. L. (1980). Effects of social-psychological variables on hypnotic amnesia. *Journal of Personality & Social Psychology*, 39(4), 737–750. doi: http://dx.doi.org/10.1037/0022-3514.39.4.737

Spitzer, B., & Bäuml, K.-H. (2007). Retrieval-induced forgetting in item recognition: Evidence for a reduction in general memory strength. *Journal of Experimental Psychology: Learning, Memory, and Cognition*, 33, 863–875.

Spitzer, B., Hanslmayr, S., Opitz, B., Mecklinger, A., & Bäuml, K.-H. (2009). Oscillatory correlates of retrieval-induced forgetting in recognition memory. *Journal of Cognitive Neuroscience*, 21, 976–990.

Spreng, N. R. (2013). Examining the role of memory in social cognition. *Frontiers in Psychology*, 4, 1–2. https://doi.org/10.3389/fpsyg.2013.00437

Squire, L. R. (1987).*Memory and Brain*. New York: Oxford University Press.

Squire, L. R. (1992a). Declarative and nondeclarative memory: Multiple brain systems supporting learning and memory. *Journal of Cognitive Neuroscience*, 4, 232–243.

Squire, L. R. (1992b). Memory and the hippocampus: A synthesis from findings with rats, monkeys, and humans. *Psychological Review*, 99, 195–231.

Squire, L. R. (2004). Memory systems of the brain: A brief history and current perspective. *Neurobiology of Learning and Memory*, 82, 171–177.

Squire, L. R., & Zola-Morgan, S. (1991). The medial temporal lobe memory system. *Science*, 253, 1380–1386.

Squire, L. R., & Zola-Morgan, S. M. (1996). Structure and function of declarative and nondeclarative memory systems. *Proceedings of the National Academy of Sciences*, 93, 13515–13522.

Staniloiu, A., & Markowitsch, H. J. (2014). Dissociative amnesia. *Lancet Psychiatry*, 1, 226–241. doi: http://dx.doi.org/10.1016/S2215-0366(14)70279-2

Steil, R., & Ehlers, A. (2000). Dysfunctional meaning of posttraumatic intrusions in chronic PTSD. *Behaviour Research and Therapy*, 38(6), 537–558.

Steiner, K. L., Thomsen, D. K., & Pillemer, D. B. (2017). Life story chapters, specific memories, and conceptions of the self. *Applied Cognitive Psychology*, 31, 478–487.

Steinvorth, S., Levine, B., & Corkin, S. (2005). Medial temporal lobe structures are needed to re-experience remote autobiographical memories: Evidence from H.M. and W.R. *Neuropsychologia*, 43, 479–496.

Stern, J. A., Edmonston, W. E., Ulett, G. A., & Levitsky, A. (1963). Electrodermal measures in experimental amnesia. *Journal of Abnormal & Social Psychology*, 67(4), 397–401. doi: http://dx.doi.org/10.1037/h0041527

Stevenson, I. (1990). Phobias in children who claim to remember previous lives. *Journal of Scientific Exploration*, 4(2), 243–254.

Stevenson, I. (1997). *Where Reincarnation and Biology Intersect*. Westport, CT: Praeger.

Storm, B. C., Angello, G., Buchli, D. R., Koppel, R. H., Little, J. L., & Nestojko, J. F. (2015). A review of retrieval-induced forgetting in the contexts of learning, eyewitness memory, social cognition, autobiographical memory, and creative cognition. In B. Ross (ed.), *Psychology of Learning and Motivation* (pp. 141–194). Amsterdam: Elsevier.

Storm, B. C., Bjork, E. L., & Bjork, R. A. (2008). Accelerated relearning after retrieval-induced forgetting: The benefit of being forgotten. *Journal of Experimental Psychology: Learning, Memory, and Cognition*, 34, 230–236.

Storm, B. C., Bjork, E. L., & Bjork, R. A. (2012). On the durability of retrieval-induced forgetting. *Journal of Cognitive Psychology*, 24, 617–629.

Strange, D., & Hayne, H. (2013). The devil is in the detail: Children's recollection of details about their prior experiences. *Memory*, 21, 431–443.

Strange, D., Wade, K., & Hayne, H. (2008). Creating false memories for events that occurred before versus after the offset of childhood amnesia. *Memory*, 16, 475–484.

Struber, N., Struber, D., & Roth, G. (2014). Impact of early adversity on glucocorticoid regulation and later mental disorders. *Neuroscience Biobehavioral Review*, 38, 17–37.

St-Yves, M. (2014). *Investigative Interviewing: The essentials*. Toronto: Carswell, a division of Thomson Reuters Canada Limited.

Suri, G., Whittaker, K., & Gross, J.J. (2015). Launching reappraisal: It's less common than you might think. *Emotion*, 15, 73–77.

Sutherland, R., & Hayne, H. (2001). The effect of postevent information on adults' eyewitness reports. *Applied Cognitive Psychology: The Official Journal of the Society for Applied Research in Memory and Cognition*, 15, 249–263.

Svoboda, E., Richards, B., Yao, C., & Leach, L. (2015). Long-term maintenance of smartphone and PDA use in individuals with moderate to severe memory impairment. *Neuropsychological Rehabilitation*, 25, 353–373.

Sylva, K., Melhuish, E., Sammons, P., Siraj-Blatchford, I., & Taggart, B. (2010). *Early Childhood Matters: Evidence from the Effective Pre-school and Primary Education Project*. Abingdon: Routledge.

Szpitalak, M., & Polczyk, R. (2014). Mental fatigue, mental warm-up, and self-reference as determinants of the misinformation effect. *The Journal of Forensic Psychiatry & Psychology*, 25(2), 135–151.

Szpitalak, M., & Polczyk, R. (2015). Reinforced self-affirmation as a method for reducing the eyewitness misinformation effect. *Psychology, Crime & Law*, 21(10), 911–938.

Szpunar, K. K., Spreng, R. N., & Schacter, D. L. (2014). A taxonomy of prospection: Introducing an organizational framework for future-oriented cognition. *Proceedings of the National Academy of Sciences*, 111(52), 18414–18421.

Taylor, E. (1983). *William James on Exceptional Mental States: Reconstruction of the 1896 Lowell Lectures*. New York: Scribner's.

Taylor, G., Liu, H., & Herbert, J. S. (2016). The role of verbal labels on flexible memory retrieval at 12-months of age. *Infant Behavior and Development*, 45, 11–17.

Taylor, T. L., Cutmore, L., & Pries, L. (2018). Item-method directed forgetting: Effects at retrieval? *Acta Psychologica (Amst.)*, 183, 116–123.

Terhune, D. B., & Brugger, P. (2011). Doing better by getting worse: Posthypnotic amnesia improves random number generation. *PLoS One*, 6(12), e29206. doi: http://dx.doi.org/10.1371/journal. pone.0029206

Tessler, M., & Nelson, K. (1994). Making memories: The influence of joint encoding on later recall by young children. *Consciousness and Cognition: An International Journal*, 3, 307–326.

Thigpen, C. H., & Cleckley, H. (1984). On the incidence of multiple personality disorder. *International Journal of Clinical & Experimental Hypnosis*, 32(2), 63–66. doi: http://dx.doi.org/10.1080/00207148408416004

Thorndyke, E. L. (1914). *The Psychology of Learning*. New York: Teachers College Press.

Thorne, D. E. (1969). Amnesia and hypnosis. *International Journal of Clinical & Experimental Hypnosis*, 17(4), 225–241. doi: http://dx.doi.org/10.1080/00207146908407246

Tinterow, M. M. (ed.) (1970). *Foundations of Hypnosis: From Mesmer to Freud*. Springfield, IL: Charles C. Thomas.

Toglia, M. P., Read, J. D., Ross, D. F., & Lindsay, R. C. L. (2017). *The Handbook of Eyewitness Psychology, Volume I: Memory for events*. Hove: Psychology Press.

Tranel, D., Damasio, H., & Damasio, A. R. (2000). Amnesia caused by herpes simplex encephalitis, infarctions in basal forebrain, and anoxia/ischemia. In F. Boller and J. Grafman (eds.), *Handbook of Neuropsychology* (2nd ed., Vol. 2, pp. 85–110). (L. Cermak, Section Editor). Amsterdam: Elsevier Science.

Travaglia, A., Bisaz, R., Sweet, E. S., Blitzer, R. D., & Alberini, C. M. (2016). Infantile amnesia reflects a developmental critical period for hippocampal learning. *Nature Neuroscience*, 19, 1225–1233.

Tucker, J. B. (2005). *Life Before Life*. London: Piatkus.

Tulving, E. (1974). Cue-dependent forgetting. *American Scientist*, 62, 74–82.

Tulving, E. (1976). Ecphoric processes in recall and recognition. In J. Brown (ed.), *Recall and Recognition* (pp. 352–373). New York: Wiley.

Tulving, E. (1979). Relation between encoding specificity and levels of processing. In L. S. Cermak & F. I. M. Craik (eds), *Levels of Processing in Human Memory*. Hillsdale, NJ: Erlbaum.

Tulving, E. (1984). Precis of elements of episodic memory. *Behavioral and Brain Sciences*, 7(2), 223–238.

Tulving, E. (1985). Memory and consciousness. *Canadian Psychologist*, 26, 1–12. doi: http://dx.doi.org/10.1037/h0080017

Tulving, E. (2002). Episodic memory: From mind to brain. *Annual Review of Psychology*, 53, 1–25.

Tulving, E. (2005). Episodic memory and autonoesis: Uniquely human? In H. S. Terrance and J. Metcalfe (eds), *The Missing Link in Cognition: Origins of self-reflective consciousness* (pp. 3–56). New York: Oxford University Press.

Tulving, E., & Arbuckle, T. Y. (1963). Sources of intratrial interference in immediate recall of paired associates. *Journal of Verbal Learning and Verbal Behaviour*, 1, 321–334.

Tulving, E., & Craik, F. I. (eds) (2005). *The Oxford Handbook of Memory*. Oxford: Oxford University Press.

Tulving, E., & Markowitsch, H. J. (1998). Episodic and declarative memory: Role of the hippocampus. *Hippocampus*, 8, 198–204.

Tulving, E., & Pearlstone, Z. (1966). Availability versus accessibility of information in memory for words. *Journal of Verbal Learning and Verbal Behavior*, 5, 381–391.

Tulving, E., & Thomson, D. M. (1973). Encoding specificity and retrieval processes in episodic memory. *Psychological Review*, 80, 352–373.

Tustin, K., & Hayne, H. (2010). Defining the boundary: Age-related changes in childhood amnesia. *Developmental Psychology*, 46, 1049–1061.

Tustin, K., & Hayne, H. (2019). Recollection improves with age: Children's and adults' accounts of their childhood experiences. *Memory*, 27, 92–102.

Underwood, B. J. (1957). Interference and forgetting. *Psychological Review*, 64, 49–60.

Underwood, B. J., & Postman, L. (1960). Extra-experimental sources of interference in forgetting. *Psychological Review*, 67, 73–95.

Unkelbach, C. (2007). Reversing the truth effect: Learning the interpretation of processing fluency in judgments of truth. *Journal of Experimental Psychology: Learning, Memory, and Cognition*, 33(1), 219.

Unkelbach, C., & Stahl, C. (2009). A multinomial modeling approach to dissociate different components of the truth effect. *Consciousness and Cognition*, 18(1), 22–38.

Unsworth, N. (2017). Examining the dynamics of strategic search from long-term memory. *Journal of Memory and Language*, 93, 135–153.

Usher, J. N., & Neisser, U. (1993). Childhood amnesia and the beginnings of memory for four early life events. *Journal of Experimental Psychology: General*, 122, 155–165.

Van Lommel, P. (2010). *Consciousness Beyond Life: The science of the near-death experience*. New York: HarperCollins.

Verde, M. F. (2013). Retrieval-induced forgetting in recall: Competitor interference revisited. *Journal of Experimental Psychology: Learning, Memory, & Cognition*, 39, 1433–1448.

Wagstaff, G. F. (1977). Posthypnotic amnesia as disrupted retrieval: A role-playing paradigm. *Quarterly Journal of Experimental Psychology*, 29(3), 499–500. doi: http://dx.doi.org/10.1080/14640747708400625

Wagstaff, G. F. (1981). Source amnesia and trance logic: Artifacts in the essence of hypnosis? *Bulletin of the British Society of Experimental and Clinical Hypnosis*, 4, 3–5.

Waldfogel, S. (1948). The frequency and affective character of childhood memories. *Psychological Monographs*, 62, 1–39.

Walser, M., Fischer, R., & Goschke, T. (2012). The failure of deactivating intentions: Aftereffects of completed intentions in repeated prospective memory cue paradigm. *Journal of Experimental Psychology: Learning, Memory, and Cognition*, 38(4), 1030–1044. doi: https://doi.org/10.1037/a0027000

Walser, M., Goschke, T., & Fischer, R. (2014). The difficulty of letting go: Moderators of the deactivation of completed intentions. *Psychological Research*, 78(4), 574–583. doi: https://doi.org/10.1007/s00426-013-0509-5

Walser, M., Goschke, T., Möschl, M., & Fischer, R. (2017). Intention deactivation: Effects of prospective memory task similarity on aftereffects of completed intentions. *Psychological Research*, 81(5), 961–981. doi: https://doi.org/10.1007/s00426-016-0795-9

Wang, E., Paterson, H., & Kemp, R. (2014). The effects of immediate recall on eyewitness accuracy and susceptibility to misinformation. *Psychology, Crime & Law*, 20(7), 619–634.

Wang, J., Cohn, N. J., & Voss, J. (2015). Covert rapid action-memory simulation (CRAMS): A hypothesis of hippocampal-prefrontal interactions for adaptive behavior. *Neurobiology of Learning and Memory*, 117, 22–33.

Wang, Q. (2006a). Earliest recollections of self and others in European American and Taiwanese young adults. *Psychological Science*, 17, 708–714.

Wang, Q. (2006b). Relations of maternal style and child self-concept to autobiographical memories in Chinese, Chinese immigrant, and European American 3-year-olds. *Child Development*, 77, 1794–1809.

Wang, Q., Leichtman, M. D., & Davies, K. I. (2000). Sharing memories and telling stories: American and Chinese mothers and their 3-year-olds. *Memory*, 8, 159–177.

Wang, Q., & Peterson, C. (2014). Your earliest memory may be earlier than you think: Prospective studies of children's dating of earliest childhood memories. *Developmental Psychology*, 50, 1680–1686.

Wang, Q., Peterson, C., Khuu, A., Reid, C. P., Maxwell, K. L., & Vincent, J. M. (2019). Looking at the past through a telescope: Adults postdated their earliest memories. *Memory*, 27, 19–27.

Wang, T. H., Placek, K., & Lewis-Peacock, J. A. (2019a). More is less: Increased processing of unwanted memories facilitates forgetting. *Journal of Neuroscience*, 39(18), 3551–60. doi: https://doi.org/10.1523/JNEUROSCI.2033-18.2019

Wang, Y., Luppi, A., Fawcett, J., & Anderson, M. C. (2019b). Reconsidering unconscious persistence: Suppressing unwanted memories reduces their indirect expression in later thoughts. *Cognition*, 187, 78–94.

Ward, P. (2018). *Lamrck's Revenge: How epigentetics is revolutionizing our understanding of evolition's past and present.* New York: Bloomsbury.

Warren, D. E., Duff, M. C., Tranel, D., & Cohen, N. J. (2011). Observing degradation of visual representations over short intervals when medial temporal lobe is damaged. *Journal of Cognitive Neuroscience*, 23(12), 3862–3873.

Warren, D., Kurczek, J., & Duff, M. C. (2016). What relates newspaper, definite, and clothing? An article describing deficits in convergent problem solving and creativity following hippocampal damage. *Hippocampus*, 26(7), 835–40.

Watkins, M. J., & Gardiner, J. M. (1979). An appreciation of generate–recognize theory of recall. *Journal of Verbal Learning & Verbal Behavior*, 18(6), 687–704. doi: http://dx.doi.org/10.1016/S0022-5371(79)90397-9

Wegner, D. M. (1992). You can't always think what you want: Problems in the suppression of unwanted thoughts. In M. Zanna (ed.), *Advances in Experimental Social Psychology* (pp. 193–225). San Diego, CA: Academic.

Wegner, D. M., Schneider, D. J., Carter, S. R., & White, T. L. (1987). Paradoxical effects of thought suppression. *Journal of Personality and Social Psychology*, 53, 5–13.

Weiss, B. L. (1988). *Many Lives, Many Masters*. London: Piaktus.

Weller, P., Anderson, M. C., Gómez-Ariza, C. J., & Bajo, M. T. (2013). On the status of cue-independence as a criterion for memory inhibition: Evidence against the covert blocking hypothesis. *Journal of Experimental Psychology: Learning, Memory, & Cognition*, 39, 1232–1245.

Wells, C., Morrison, C.M., & Conway, M.A. (2013). Adult recollections of childhood memories: What details can be recalled? *Quarterly Journal of Experimental Psychology*, 67(7), 1249–1261.

Wells, G. L. (1978). Applied eyewitness-testimony research: System variables and estimator variables. *Journal of Personality and Social Psychology*, 36(12), 1546.

Wells, G. L. (1995). Scientific study of witness memory: Implications for public and legal policy. *Psychology, Public Policy, and Law*, 1(4), 726.

Wells, G. L. (2018). Eyewitness identification. In E. Luna (ed.), *Reforming Criminal Justice, Volume 2: Policing* (pp. 259–278). Tempe, AZ: Sandra Day O'Connor College of Law.

Wells, W. R. (1940). The extent and duration of posthypnotic amnesia. *Journal of Psychology*, 9(1), 137–151. doi: http://dx.doi.org/10.1080/00223980.1940.9917682

Wessel, I., Schweig, T., & Huntjens, R. J. C. (2019). Manipulating the reported age in earliest memories. *Memory*, 27, 6–18.

West, R. (2011). The temporal dynamics of prospective memory: A review of the ERP and prospective memory literature. *Neuropsychologia*, 49, 2233–2245. doi: https://doi.org/10.1016/j.neuropsychologia.2010.12.028.

West, R., Bowry, R., & Krompinger, J. (2006). The effects of working memory demands on the neural correlates of prospective memory. *Neuropsychologia*, 44, 197–207. doi: https://doi.org/10.1016/j.neuropsychologia.2005.05.003.

West, R., Carlson, L., & Cohen, A.-L. (2007). Eye movements and prospective memory: What the eyes can tell us about prospective memory. *International Journal of Psychophysiology*, 64(3), 269–277. doi: https://doi.org/10.1016/j.ijpsycho.2006.09.006

West, R., Wymbs, N., Jakubek, K., & Herndon, R.W. (2003). Effects of intention load and background context on prospective remembering: An event-related brain potential study. *Psychophysiology*, 40, 260–276. doi: https://doi.org/10.1111/1469-8986.00028

West, T. A., & Bauer, P. J. (1999). Assumptions of infantile amnesia: Are there differences between early and later memories? *Memory*, 7, 257–278.

Whitehouse, W. G., Orne, E. C., Dinges, D. F., Bates. B. L., Nadon, R., & Orne, M. T. (2005). The cognitive interview: Does it successfully avoid the dangers of forensic hypnosis? *American Journal of Psychology*, 118, 213–234.

Williams, D. M., & Hollan, J. D. (1981). The process of retrieval from very long-term memory. *Cognitive Science*, 5, 87–119.

Williams, L. E., Must, A., Avery, S., Woolard, A., Woodward, N. D., Cohen, N. J., & Heckers, S. (2010). Eye-movement behavior reveals relational memory impairment in schizophrenia. *Biol Pscyhiatry*, 68(7), 617–624.

Williamsen, J. A., Johnson, H. J., & Eriksen, C. W. (1965). Some characteristics of posthypnotic amnesia. *Journal of Abnormal Psychology*, 70, 123–131. doi: http://dx.doi.org/10.1037/h0021934

Wilson, B. A., & Wearing, D. (1995). Prisoner of consciousness: A state of just awakening following herpes simplex encephalitis. In R. Campbell & M. A. Conway (eds), *Broken Memories: Case studies in memory impairment* (pp. 14–30). Cambridge, MA: Blackwell.

Wilson, L., & Kihlstrom, J. F. (1986). Subjective and categorical organization of recall during posthypnotic amnesia. *Journal of Abnormal Psychology*, 95(3), 264–273. doi: http://dx.doi.org/10.1037/0021-843X.95.3.264

Wimber, M., Alink, A., Charest, I., Kriegeskorte, N., & Anderson, M. C. (2015). Retrieval induces adaptive forgetting of competing memories via cortical pattern suppression. *Nature Neuroscience*, 18, 582–589.

Wimber, M., Bäuml, K.-H., Bergström, Z., Markopoulos, G., Heinze, H. J., & Richardson-Klavehn, A. (2008). Neural markers of inhibition in human memory retrieval. *Journal of Neuroscience*, 28, 13419–13427.

Wixted, J. T. (2010). The role of retroactive interference and consolidation in everyday forgetting (pp. 285–312). In S. Della Sala (ed.) *Forgetting*. Hove: Psychology Press.

Wixted, J. T., Mickes, L., Clark, S. E., Gronlund, S. D., & Roediger III, H. L. (2015). Initial eyewitness confidence reliably predicts eyewitness identification accuracy. *American Psychologist*, 70(6), 515.

Woolger, R. J. (1994). *Other Lives, Other Selves*. London: Aquarian.

Wright, D. B. (1993). Misinformation and warnings in eyewitness testimony: A new testing procedure to differentiate explanations. *Memory*, 1(2), 153–166.

Wright, D. B., Self, G., & Justice, C. (2000). Memory conformity: Exploring misinformation effects when presented by another person. *British Journal of Psychology*, 91(2), 189–202.

Wu, Y., & Jobson, L. (2019). Maternal reminiscing and child autobiographical memory elaboration: A meta-analytic review. *Developmental Psychology*, 55(12), 2505–2521. doi: https://psycnet.apa.org/doi/10.1037/dev0000821

Wylie, L. E., Patihis, L., & McCuller, L. L. (2014). Misinformation effect in older versus younger adults: A meta-analysis and review. In M. P. Toglia, D. F. Ross, J. Pozzulo, & E. Pica (eds), *The Elderly Eyewitness in Court* (pp. 52–80). Hove: Psychology Press.

Xie, H., Jiang, D., & Zhang, D. (2018). Individuals with depressive tendencies experience difficulty in forgetting negative material: Two mechanisms revealed by ERP date in the directed forgetting paradigm. *Scientific Reports*, 8(1), 1113. doi: 10.1038/s41598-018-19570-0

Yeates, L. B. (2018a). James Braid (I): Natural philosopher, structured thinker, gentleman scientist, and innovative surgeon. *Australian Journal of Clinical Hypnotherapy and Hypnosis*, 40(1), 3–39.

Yeates, L. B. (2018b). James Braid (II): Mesmerism, Braid's crucial experiment, and Braid's discovery of neuro-hypnotism. *Australian Journal of Clinical Hypnotherapy and Hypnosis*, 40(1), 40–93.

Yonelinas, A. P., Aly, M., Wang, W.-C., & Koen, J. D. (2010). Recollection and familiarity: Examining controversial assumptions and new directions. *Hippocampus*, 20, 1178–1194. doi: http://dx.doi.org/10.1002/hipo.20864

Young, P. C. (1926). An experimental study of mental and physical functions in the normal and hypnotic states: Additional results. *American Journal of Psychology*, 37, 345–356. doi: http://dx.doi.org/10.2307/1413621

Young, P. C. (1927). A general review of the literature of hypnotism. *Psychological Bulletin*, 24(9), 540–560. doi: http://dx.doi.org/10.1037/h0071891

Young, P. C. (1928). The nature of hypnosis: As indicated by the presence or absence of post-hypnotic amnesia and rapport. *Journal of Abnormal & Social Psychology*, 22(4), 372–382. doi: http://dx.doi.org/10.1037/h0075135

Young, P. C. (1931). A general review of the literature on hypnotism and suggestion. *Psychological Bulletin*, 28(5), 367–391. doi: http://dx.doi.org/10.1037/h0070084

Zajac, R., & Henderson, N. (2009). Don't it make my brown eyes blue: Co-witness misinformation about a target's appearance can impair target-absent line-up performance. *Memory*, 17(3), 266–278. doi: https://doi.org/10.1080/09658210802623950

Zaragoza, M. S., Belli, R. F., & Payment, K. E. (2007). Misinformation effects and the suggestibility of eyewitness memory. In M. Garry and H. Hayne (eds), *Do Justice and Let the Sky Fall: Elizabeth Loftus and her contributions to science, law, and academic freedom* (pp. 35–63). New York: Psychology Press.

Zaragoza, M. S., & Lane, S. M. (1994). Source misattributions and the suggestibility of eyewitness memory. *Journal of Experimental Psychology: Learning, Memory, and Cognition*, 20(4), 934.

Zaragoza, M. S., & Mitchell, K. J. (1996). Repeated exposure to suggestion and the creation of false memories. *Psychological Science*, 7(5), 294–300.

Zawadzka, K., Krogulska, A., Button, R., Higham, P. A., & Hanczakowski, M. (2016). Memory, metamemory, and social cues: Between conformity and resistance. *Journal of Experimental Psychology: General*, 145(2), 181.

Zeithamova, D., Schlichting, M., & Preston, A. (2012). The hippocampus and inferential reasoning: Building memories to navigate future decisions. *Frontiers in Human Neuroscience*. doi: https://doi.org/10.3389/fnhum.2012.00070

Zellner, M., & Bäuml, K.-H. (2006). Inhibitory deficits in older adults: List-method directed forgetting revisited. *Journal of Experimental Psychology: Learning, Memory, and Cognition*, 32, 290–300.

Zhang, Y., Pan, Z., & Guo, Y. (2018). Selectively forgetting the connection between negative information and the self. *Experimental Psychology*, 65, 236–244.

Zhao, X., Fu, J., & Maes, J. H. R. (2019). Prospective memory training in young adults enhances trained-task but not transfer-task performance. *Memory*, 27(7), 1018–1023. doi: https://doi.org/10.1080/09658211.2019.1613435

Zhu, B., Chen, C., Loftus, E. F., He, Q., Chen, C., Lei, X., & Dong, Q. (2012). Brief exposure to misinformation can lead to long-term false memories. *Applied Cognitive Psychology*, 26(2), 301–307. doi: https://doi.org/10.1002/acp.1825

INDEX